Introduction to
Word Processing

Introduction to
Word Processing

Zane K. Quible, *Michigan State University*
Margaret H. Johnson, *University of Nebraska*

Winthrop Publishers, Inc.   Cambridge, Massachusetts

Library of Congress Cataloging in Publication Data

Quible, Zane K
 Introduction to word processing.

 Includes index.
 1. Word processing (Office practice)
I. Johnson, Margaret H., joint author.
II. Title.
HF5547.5.Q52   651.7   79-27935
ISBN 0-87626-446-1

For Clare and Kenneth Quible and Mary Ruth and George Higgins

Cover and interior design by Dianne Smith Schaefer

© 1980 by Winthrop Publishers, Inc.
 17 Dunster Street, Cambridge, Massachusetts 02138

Printed in the United States of America

10 9 8 7 6 5 4 3 2

Contents

Preface

Word processing is here to stay. At the time the concept was first introduced in this country, many people were skeptical, claiming that word processing was nothing more than a fad that would vanish about as rapidly as it emerged. As a system for expediting paperwork, its use continues to expand and will become even more prominent in the office of the future. In time, the word processing concept will likely emerge into information processing.

The short history of word processing has taught us many things, including the following:

> The use of microprocessors in the design of equipment is enabling word processing technology to develop very rapidly.
>
> The unique characteristics of each organization prevent the design of one common word processing system suitable for all organizations.
>
> One large centralized word processing center in an organization may not be as satisfactory as several small decentralized centers.
>
> Most problems associated with word processing originate with people, not with the equipment or procedures that comprise the systems.
>
> Not every organization has a need for the installation of a word processing system.
>
> Word processing does not eliminate the need for secretaries who possess shorthand skills.

The authors of this text recognize that the rapidly developing technology may result in certain portions of this text being obsolete by the time it is printed. We have made every effort to include, as reasonably as possible, the most up-to-date material available at the time the text went into production.

An increasing number of colleges and universities are developing word processing courses and curricula. The primary use of this text will be in such programs. It can also be used effectively as a reference for those wishing to learn more about the word processing concept. Employees of organizations investigating the feasibility of installing a word processing system will find the text extremely helpful, as will employees of organizations involved in the installation of a word processing system.

In preparing this text, the authors have kept in mind the need to present the material in a straightforward manner, as simply and as clearly as possible. Technical material has been kept to a minimum.

The chapter sequencing is chronological in nature. That is, the text begins with a discussion of the first phase of installing a word processing system and continues through the several other phases. Chapter 10 is designed to provide the reader with a preview of the word processing concept in the office of the future.

Several aids have been incorporated into this text to help the learner master the material easily and quickly. Each chapter begins with a chapter outline and ends with a series of review questions. Each chapter also contains two cases, which are designed to give learners an opportunity to apply chapter concepts in solving realistic situations.

No text of this nature could be prepared without the assistance of others. For their part in this undertaking, the authors wish to acknowledge the following individuals: Kathy Cavill, Sherri Toohey, Marlene Riggs, Dianne Koch, and Beverlee Bornemeier.

Introduction to
Word Processing

CHAPTER 1

Word processing: An overview

In many of today's offices, word processing systems are emerging as the primary tool for expediting written communication. No office system has had as great an impact on the techniques used for preparing written communication as word processing. Although the word processing concept is very new, it has made phenomenal inroads in the modern office.

Word processing defined

Because of its rather recent origin, no definition of word processing has yet emerged as the universal definition. The fact that the structure of the concept changes from time to time has undoubtedly slowed the emergence of a universal definition.

The most common definition was developed by the American National Standards Institute. According to ANSI, word processing is the "transformation of ideas and information into a readable form of communication through the management of procedures, equipment, and personnel." The use of the term word processing in this text is consistent with the ANSI definition.

Word processing has also been defined as "automated office work," but the concept is much more broad than this definition implies. Personnel is an integral part of word processing, yet the second definition fails to mention, either implicitly or explicitly, the involvement of personnel.

Components of word processing systems

Word processing systems are comprised of three basic components: personnel, equipment, and procedures. The most effective means of providing a description of the word processing concept is to examine each of these components.

PERSONNEL

A crucial component of word processing is the personnel who perform the office functions. Division of labor is extensively used in word processing. One group of office employees, who are typically located in the word processing center, are responsible only for keyboarding and other related activities, such as proofreading. Although the titles of these individuals vary, the following are among the more common: word processing specialist, correspondence secretary, and word processing operator. Hereafter, in this text, the individual whose job is comprised mainly of typing activities is referred to as a word processing specialist.

Another position commonly found in word processing operations is the messenger, whose job tasks include transporting the rough drafts and finished work back and forth between the word processing center and the word originators' offices (hereafter called principals). A principal is anyone who originates documents, generally at the first level of management or higher.

A supply clerk is also found in an increasing number of word processing installations. This individual is responsible for maintaining adequate reserves or supplies.

In some instances, proofreaders are used in word processing installations; they are responsible for verifying the accuracy of the material prepared in the word processing center. In large word processing operations, an expeditor or scheduler is also sometimes used. The primary function of this individual is to schedule work in order to meet deadlines and to facilitate smooth-flowing operations.

Other generally routine office tasks of a nontyping nature are performed by another group of employees, known as administrative secretaries. Examples of tasks these employees perform are filing, serving as receptionists, preparing mail, telephoning, preparing and dictating drafts of material, and completing projects assigned by the principals. While the word processing specialists are typically located in the word processing center, the administrative secretaries are housed in the same areas as the principals for whom they work.

Within each of the typing and nontyping divisions, several levels of positions are often found, depending on the size of the word processing operation and the number of employees. For example, the word processing specialist classification might include two or more levels of word processing specialists and word processing operators. The administrative category is likely to consist of file clerks, receptionists, administrative secretaries, and senior administrative secretaries. Each of these two divisions is also likely to have a manager or supervisor who is responsible for day-by-day operations. In addition, there is likely to be a manager of word processing/administrative support who is ultimately responsible for both areas. In some instances, this individual will be known as an office systems analyst.

EQUIPMENT

As an office system, word processing evolved primarily as a result of the development of several new kinds of office equipment. Before most of this equipment was functional, the use of word processing for expediting written communication was not possible. The primary equipment used in word processing consists of text-editing typewriters (also called word processors), dictation/recording equipment, and copier equipment. Information processors, which generally incorporate computer technology, are also emerging as a newer type of equipment used in word processing systems.

While Chapter 4 contains a detailed description of the various kinds of equipment used in word processing, the following provides an overview of the equipment.

Text-editing typewriters. The primary function of text-editing type-writers is to facilitate the transformation of thoughts and ideas into a typewritten format. These typewriters are used in the typing/transcription process.

Several different types and many different brands of text-editing typewriters are now on the market. While some of this equipment closely resembles conventional electric office typewriters, other types more closely resemble a television screen with an attached keyboard. A distinguishing feature of the text-editing typewriter is its capability of capturing keystrokes in coded form. The keystrokes are generally stored on a magnetic medium—magnetic tapes, magnetic cards, or magnetic disks—although other formats, such as perforated paper tape, have been used.

By storing the keyboarded material on a magnetic medium, editing and revising are easily accomplished. The magnetic medium on which the material is stored is simply inserted into the text editor, and the unchanged material is automatically typed at rates of around seven hundred words a minute, depending on the brand of equipment.

Another distinguishing feature of text-editing typewriters is the ease with which they correct errors. Errors are corrected by backspacing, which erases the incorrect character stored in the typewriter's memory. The correction is made by typing the correct character, which is automatically recorded.

Information processors are becoming important equipment components in many word processing installations, especially larger ones. These processors utilize computer technology, which adds a new dimension to word processing. The use of computer technology facilitates the manipulation of information, a capability not possible when certain types of text-editing typewriters are used.

Dictation/recording equipment. An integral aspect of word processing systems is the recording of dictation for subsequent transcription. This equipment is known as dictation/recording equipment. The word processing center and the principals' offices are likely to be physically separated. The distance makes it impractical for word processing specialists who do the transcribing to be physically present in the principals' offices whenever the principals wish to dictate material. In addition, it is inefficient for the principals to handwrite material that could be easily dictated.

The dictation devices in the principals' offices and the recording units in the word processing center are often connected by telephone lines or direct wires. Some brands of dictation equipment use the telephones in the principals' offices, while other brands utilize special dictation microphones. The dictation is recorded on the magnetic medium (tape, disk, belt) in the recording unit located in the word processing center. This material is later transcribed by a word processing specialist who uses a text-editing typewriter.

Copier equipment. A third type of equipment extensively used in word processing systems is the copier. Because of word processing procedures, the use of carbon paper to make copies of the original documents is no longer efficient. When word processing is used, documents may go through several revisions before the principal releases the final draft for distribution. It is not practical to make a carbon of each draft, nor is it possible to predetermine which draft of a document will be the final draft. The alternative is to use a copier to make a copy of the final draft once it has been approved for distribution.

Reprographics, the reproduction of documents, is becoming increasingly involved in word processing as advanced copy and duplication technology emerges.

PROCEDURES

The procedures that comprise word processing systems are classified as input procedures, output procedures, and distribution procedures. While the characteristics of each category are fully discussed in Chapter 5, the following provides a brief discussion.

The input procedures involve putting into the system the material that is to be typed. Two commonly used types of input are dictation and handwritten material. Dictation input requires the use of dictation/recording units. The principal, using either a standard telephone or a special dictation microphone, dictates the material, which is simultaneously recorded on the recording unit. On the average, the use of dictation equipment rather than shorthand or handwritten material for input reduces the cost of a typical business letter as much as $2.

When the telephone is used as a dictation device, the buttons on the touchtone phone are used to activate the recording unit located in the word processing center. The buttons start and stop the recording unit, playback the dictation to verify its content, erase and rerecord material, or signal an employee in the word processing center. The functional controls on the various brands of dictation equipment that use special dictation microphones operate in much the same way as the systems that utilize telephones. When dial phones are used in the dictation process, a key-pad device may have to be installed on the phone, which activates the various functional controls on the recording unit. Certain other types of material, such as handwritten material, are typically taken by a messenger from the principals' offices to the word processing center.

Two other types of input sometimes used in word processing systems are dictation at the typewriter and form letters. When dictation at the typewriter is used for input, the typist keyboards the material as the principal dictates either in person or over the telephone. Form letters typically have constant material and variable material. The constant material is the same in each letter, while the variable material, such as names and addresses, is different in each.

Once the dictated or handwritten material arrives in the word processing center, it is logged into a schedule book. According to the time of its receipt and priority, the material is assigned to a word processing specialist.

The material is keyboarded on a text-editing typewriter and the keystrokes are simultaneously recorded on a magnetic medium. In some instances, the principal will specify that the first draft is to be a rough draft. In other instances, the principal will specify that the first draft is to be a final draft. The typed document is then returned to the principal either for revision or for authorization for distribution.

If the principal makes revisions on the rough draft, it is returned to the word processing center where a new draft is prepared. The machine automatically types the unchanged material that is stored on the magnetic medium. The word processing specialist stops the machine at the points where the changes are to be made. The desired changes are made manually through keyboarding, which eliminates unwanted keystrokes and captures the new ones in memory.

Once prepared, the new draft is returned to the principal for additional revision or for authorization for distribution. If additional revisions are made, the same steps are repeated. Before the document is distributed, a copy of the document is made on a copier. Depending on the content of the document, the magnetic medium on which the material is recorded is stored (filed) according to a predetermined retention schedule or is reused by recording other material on it.

The third phase of procedures utilized in word processing is the distribution of the document. Distribution can be accomplished in several ways, including hand delivery, mailing, transmission by facsimile, or electronic document distribution. The latter two distribution methods merit further discussion.

Facsimile transmission involves the use of facsimile sending/ receiving devices. The document to be transmitted is placed in the facsimile sending unit. The recipient's telephone number is dialed, and when the call is connected, the sender's telephone handset is attached to the phone cradle on the facsimile sending unit. The recipient's telephone handset is also attached to the cradle on the receiving facsimile unit. When the units are activated, a duplicate of the document is transmitted electrically over the telephone line in a few seconds. Some facsimile units are automatic and operate without human assistance.

Electronic document distribution (EDD) is another means of transmitting information from one location to another. This technique requires the use of compatible text-editing typewriters. The keyboarded material is recorded and stored on a magnetic medium. Once the material has been released for distribution, the information is electronically transmitted in coded form over ordinary telephone lines. The electronic codes are recorded on a magnetic medium at the destination, which is used to produce automatically the printed document.

Figure 1–1 illustrates the basic flow of work in a word processing system. An examination of Figure 1–1 reveals that after the word

Figure 1–1 WORK FLOW OF WORD PROCESSING SYSTEM

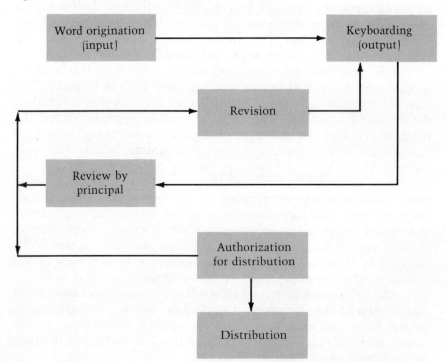

origination (input) takes place, the next step is keyboarding (output) on text-editing typewriters. Once the material has been keyboarded, it is returned to the principal for review. At this point, two alternatives are available: (1) revision of the material or (2) authorization for distribution. The review, revision, and keyboarding steps may take place several times before the material is released for distribution.

The administrative support concept

The administrative support concept, although not formally mentioned in the definition of word processing, is very closely related. Because of the division of labor characteristic of word processing, administrative support is crucial.

As the administrative support concept is evolving, some rather significant trends are emerging in the design of administrative support positions. When the administrative support personnel assume tasks formerly performed by principals, they become assistants to the principals. Consequently, the administrative support personnel perform clerical/secretarial duties of a nontyping nature as well as other tasks assigned them by principals. The abilities of the administrative support personnel are critical to determining which tasks are assigned to them.

The structure of the administrative support concept gives administrative support employees an opportunity to perform at higher levels of job responsibility than their predecessors. If the administrative support personnel are able to relieve the principals of some of their duties, the principals then will be able to devote more time and effort to their managerial tasks.

The fact that the potential abilities of the administrative support personnel are more visible to management may increase for these employees the number of promotional opportunities into middle management positions. In other words, the administrative support positions may be used effectively as a steppingstone to positions of greater responsibility.

Structure of word processing/administrative support systems

Word processing/administrative support systems are designed around the specific needs of particular organizations. Because the needs of organizations vary considerably, so do the structures of word processing/administrative support systems. Nevertheless, some common characteristics can be found.

Figure 1-2 WORD PROCESSING/ADMINISTRATIVE SUPPORT STRUCTURE

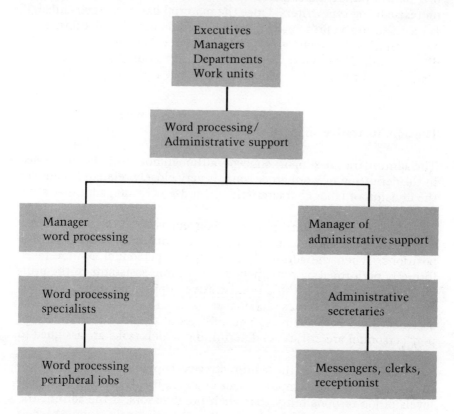

Figure 1-2 illustrates a common word processing/administrative support structure. According to the illustration, executives, managers, departments, and work units utilize the services of the word processing/administrative support structure. The word processing and administrative support units are two separate entities, each having a manager. While the word processing component utilizes word processing specialists, the administrative support component utilizes administrative secretaries.

Common word processing/administrative support structures include the following:

Centralized structure. All typing/transcription functions are performed in a large centralized word processing center, except perhaps those typing/transcription functions of top-level executives whose secretaries do most or all of their typing. Nontyping secretarial/clerical functions are handled by administrative secretaries. The typing and nontyping areas have separate supervisors, both of whom are responsible to the manager of word processing/administrative support.

Decentralized structure. A number of smaller, decentralized word processing centers are located throughout the organization. Each of the centers has a supervisor. The administrative secretaries, who are responsible for the nontyping secretarial/clerical functions, may or may not be formally supervised.

An increasing number of companies are finding that several smaller decentralized centers meet their needs better than one large centralized center. Because the word processing specialists and principals are able to work together more closely than in the centralized structure, the decentralized approach is preferred by many organizations.

Special-purpose structure. Traditional secretaries perform nontyping secretarial/clerical functions as well as light typing jobs. The traditional secretaries use standard electric typewriters rather than text-editing typewriters. Extensive typing jobs or those jobs requiring extensive amounts of editing/revising are performed in a centralized word processing center. This structure does not use administrative support.

The special-purpose structure, which uses a centralized word processing center for certain typing jobs but also makes use of traditional secretarial/clerical procedures, is favored by some organizations. The specialization of labor characteristic of the word processing/administrative support concept is not present in the special-purpose structure. This structure does not offer advantages provided by the centralized or decentralized structures, but does provide other important trade-offs that help make it a desirable approach for those who use it.

Integrated structure. All secretarial/clerical functions are performed in traditional ways, except that some departments or work units use text-editing equipment for certain jobs. Neither word processing centers nor administrative support are found in organizations that use the integrated structure.

The integrated structure is likely to be found in small organizations. The increased productivity that results from the use of text-editing equipment makes the integrated structure suitable for certain organizations.

This text is primarily geared toward developing a large centralized word processing center or a smaller, decentralized center. The fundamental differences between a large centralized center or a smaller decentralized center are the number of work stations found in the center and the formality of organization. Whereas large centers might have eight or more work stations and a high degree of formality, the small centers have two or three work stations operating on a more informal basis.

Advantages of word processing

As an office system designed to expedite written communication, word processing has several distinct advantages compared to traditional office procedures.

COST REDUCTION

The use of word processing results in some fairly significant cost reduction possibilities. Cost savings often result from a reduction in the number of typewriters needed, since only a minimum number of standard office typewriters are found in word processing/administrative support installations. Since the vast majority of typing is done in the word processing center, only those office employees who work for the top-level executives are likely to have standard office typewriters. Replacing most of the standard typewriters with considerably fewer text-editing typewriters can provide significant savings.

Personnel costs are decreased in many organizations when a word processing system is utilized. Because the office employees are more efficiently used, fewer employees can complete a greater amount of work. In time, word processing often results in yearly savings of 15 to 30 percent in clerical salaries and overhead.

Savings are also reflected in the per-unit cost of producing written correspondence. One company found that the cost of producing a letter averaged nearly $6.50 under a traditional secretarial structure. After installation of a word processing system, the cost of producing comparable letters ranged from approximately $1.60 to $4.25.

INCREASED EFFICIENCY

Compared to traditional procedures for expediting written communication, word processing often results in the use of more efficient procedures because of the specialization inherent in the division of labor involved in word processing. In a word processing/administrative support system, employees in each area become very skilled in the tasks they perform. No longer do office employees perform a wide variety of unrelated tasks; instead they perform a smaller number of related tasks.

Greater efficiency also results from the utilization of well-designed procedures for expediting written communication. Word processing/administrative support systems are often developed by professionals who have considerable expertise in the design of efficient work processes and procedures.

GREATER PRODUCTIVITY

One of the most significant advantages of word processing/administrative support systems is the increase in employee productivity. This is brought about by several factors.

Word processing makes extensive use of dictated materials as a primary form of input. Using dictating equipment rather than dictating to a secretary increases the productivity of office employees. The time formerly spent taking dictation can now be used by office employees to perform other tasks. No longer do secretaries idly sit waiting for principals to locate materials, to generate ideas, to think about proper wording, and so forth. Nor do principals have to wait until secretaries are available to take dictation.

Although handwritten materials are an acceptable input method in word processing systems, this method is much slower. Once dictation skills are developed, dictation rates are generally at least four times faster than handwriting speeds.

The use of text-editing typewriters to produce original copies of identical messages also greatly increases productivity. Keystrokes, which are captured in the first keyboarding process, can be permanently stored on the magnetic medium used by the text editor. To obtain an original copy or to revise or edit the material, the magnetic medium is inserted in the text editor and the unchanged material is automatically typed without having to be rekeyboarded. In many organizations, text-editing typewriters have increased secretarial productivity by more than 100 percent.

The productivity of word processing specialists is enhanced because typing errors are easily corrected. Errors are easily corrected by backspacing and typing the correct character. This feature permits the typists to keyboard at rough-draft speeds and also eliminates the time-consuming task of making corrections by a more awkward method such as erasing.

The productivity of word processing specialists is also aided by the elimination of the frequent interruptions (answering phones, assisting office callers, and answering questions) encountered by their counterparts in traditional offices. Their productivity is also increased as much as 20 percent when they transcribe from machine dictation rather than from shorthand or longhand.

In many word processing installations, the dictation system is functional twenty-four hours a day. Principals can dictate material anytime and anywhere they have access to a telephone. All they have to do is call the word processing center, where they are automatically connected without human intervention to the recording unit. The unrestricted flexibility is very beneficial for increasing the productivity of principals.

FASTER TURNAROUND

Another of the advantages of the word processing concept is the fast turnaround time it provides. Organizations often find that word processing reduces turnaround to only three or four hours. In a traditional situation, the secretary typically completes work according to the time of the receipt of the material and the priority assigned to the job. Thus, several hours may lapse between the time that work is given a secretary and the time it is actually completed.

As word processing systems are ordinarily designed to accommodate rush assignments, a maximum turnaround time of an hour or two on top-priority material is often possible. The error-correction feature on text-editing typewriters also shortens turnaround time.

BETTER QUALITY WORK

Many principals have found an improvement in the quality of their work when word processing is used. In a traditional situation, many principals are hesitant to make changes in the wording of documents, especially if the changes will necessitate the retyping of the document. With word processing, revising and editing changes are encouraged because they are so easily made. In the event that the principal desires an opportunity to revise the material a second time (or several other times), the revisions can be easily accommodated. Generally, the quality of the work will improve each time the document goes through revision.

Historical development of word processing

The history of the word processing concept is closely linked to the emergence of text-editing typewriters, the invention of which made word processing possible. The word processing concept, which originated in Germany, was known as *Textverarbeitung*, which means text processing. When the concept was first utilized in the United States, it was called power typing. Soon afterwards, it became known as word processing, which more accurately reflects the nature of the process.

The first automatic typewriters, developed in the 1930s, utilized pneumatic paper rolls similar to those used on player pianos. More recent automatic typewriters did not have the text-editing capability that today's text-editing typewriters have.

Since the advent of the first text-editing typewriters in 1964, approximately fifty companies have developed text-editing equipment. Two basic types of equipment have emerged: Stand-alone equipment and interactive equipment. The stand-alone text editors are self-contained. They are not electronically connected to other equipment components. The interactive equipment, on the other hand, is capable of communicating with computers or with other word processing typewriters.

PHASES OF DEVELOPMENT

The development of word processing has gone through four distinct phases, each corresponding to the development of the various types of text-editing equipment. The equipment developed during phases 1 and 2 is stand-alone equipment, while phase 3 and 4 equipment is interactive.

Phase 1: Mechanical text-editing typewriters. IBM is credited with introducing in 1964 the first mechanical text-editing typewriter, the MT/ST (Magnetic Tape/Selectric Typewriter). In 1969, IBM introduced a new text-editing typewriter, the MC/ST (Magnetic Card/Selectric Typewriter), which was found to be more functional, less costly, and easier to operate than its predecessor. The Mag Card II, a newer version of the original MC/ST, is presently used in many word processing installations.

Phase 2: Display text editors. Utilizing a cathode ray tube (CRT) or a gas plasma screen, display text editors resemble TV screens with attached keyboards and printing devices. As the keyboarding takes place, up to a page of material is held on the screen. After the screen is filled, the word processing specialist proofreads the material and makes any corrections or changes. At this point, the material that appears on the screen is transferred almost instantly to a magnetic medium, such as a disk or a card. The magnetic medium is then inserted into the printer device to obtain a paper (or hard) copy, which is transmitted to the principal for revision or for authorization for distribution.

Phase 3: Communicating stand-alone text editors. The equipment in the third phase is hybrid; it is stand-alone but also has communicating capabilities. These typewriters may be identical to those developed in phases 1 and 2 but include communicating units. The material is keyboarded and revised in one location but can be electronically transmitted to another location thousands of miles away. The communicating capability of these typewriters made "electronic mail" a reality, with documents transmitted electronically between two locations, eliminating distribution by the U.S. Postal Service.

Phase 4: Integration of data processing/word processing technology. The most recent phase in the development of the word processing concept integrates data processing and word processing technology. Several alternatives are available with the technology developed during this phase. One alternative is to use shared-logic text editors, which provide storage, retrieval, and manipulation of information capabilities. Shared-logic systems often utilize minicomputers or microprocessors.

Another alternative is to use time-shared text editors. Like the shared-logic alternative, the time-shared option also permits the storage, retrieval, and manipulation of information. The computer used in the time-shared operation does not belong to the organizations using it. Rather, the computer belongs to a service bureau, which leases computer time on a time-sharing arrangement to its subscribers. Each organization involved in the time-sharing arrangement has one or more text editors that are electronically connected to the computer. Whereas the shared-logic alternative uses minicomputers, the time-shared alternative typically involves the use of larger equipment. Because of the vast developments in minicomputer technology, the shared-logic system is used more often than is the time-sharing system.

While the four phases closely correspond with the various technological features of the equipment, each new phase of equipment does not make obsolete the equipment developed during the preceding phase. In terms of the present use of the equipment, more phase 1 and 2 equipment is used than phase 3 or 4 equipment.

PRESENT STATE OF THE ART

The nature of word processing has never been and is not likely to become static, as long as the technology on which word processing is so heavily dependent continues to develop so rapidly. At this time, several trends are emerging to shape the design of the word processing concept.

   1. More and more, organizations, even medium and small ones, are abandoning the centralized word processing structure in favor

of several smaller decentralized centers. This trend has several advantages. The word processing specialists are familiar with the style, vocabulary, and priority of the documents. The principals are geographically closer to the employees who do their work. The principals and word processing specialists are likely to know one another, which eliminates the inherent impersonality in a large centralized operation. This has had a positive impact on the attitudes and morale of the word processing specialists.

2. Because of microprocessor technology, text-editing equipment with more features and greater capabilities is being developed. The cost of this equipment is steadily decreasing, which makes the equipment more cost-justifiable. An increasing number of text-editing systems are being developed in which each component has its own microprocessor, which greatly expands the operating flexibility of the equipment.

3. Technological advances are being made in the copier, facsimile, and the electronic document distribution fields. The impact of these advances results in greater flexibility in the design and structure of word processing/administrative support systems.

4. Word processing is moving toward combining traditionally discrete office functions. The result is the integration of word processing into a total information system. Word processing is now being interfaced with such technologies as optical character recognition readers, data processing, phototypesetting, high-speed printing, communications, and reprographics.

5. The merging of data processing and word processing functions is increasingly apparent. The applications of both functions make their merging very logical.

6. The various brands of equipment are becoming more compatible with one another. This makes it possible to use several brands of components in one system, which enables an organization to obtain a greater number of appropriate equipment components for the applications being performed.

A word processing system illustrated: A narrative

The word processing/administrative support systems were installed in Arcco Corporation in Lansing, Michigan, four years ago. Arcco manufactures several components used in the assembly of heavy road construction and mining equipment.

Before the word processing center was installed, managers frequently complained about the length of time it took secretaries to complete typing jobs, the poor quality of typing, and the increasing number of secretaries needed to handle the increasing amount of paperwork.

The executives of the corporation decided the most effective means of determining the feasibility of utilizing word processing/administrative support was to hire a consultant to conduct the study. Accordingly, a consultant from the Detroit area was hired to undertake the feasibility study. To collect the data, the consultant used both questionnaires and interviews.

After the data were compiled and analyzed, the consultant prepared a report in which several conclusions were presented. Included were the following:

1. Arcco would benefit from the utilization of word processing/administrative support.
2. Over a period of three years, the corporation could expect to reduce its operating costs by an average of 10 percent per year.
3. A centralized word processing center would best meet the needs of the organization.
4. A fairly aggressive effort would have to be expended to reduce employee resistance to the concept.

The consultant recommended, on the basis of data gathered during the feasibility study, that six word processing work stations would be adequate at the beginning. The employees who worked in the word processing center at the time it began functioning included three word processing operators, two senior word processing operators, and one word processing specialist. In addition, the center had a supervisor and two part-time messengers. Originally, twenty-three persons worked as administrative secretaries. The administrative secretaries were supervised by an administrative support supervisor. Both the word processing and administrative support areas were overseen by a manager of word processing/administrative support. At the present time, eight word processing operators and specialists and twenty-six administrative secretaries are employed.

The original typing equipment consisted of magnetic card text editors, which are still being used. Display text editors were purchased for the two work stations that have been added to the center since it originally opened. Although a decision is perhaps six months away, the organization is investigating the possibility of installing a shared-logic system.

In addition, a copier is used in the word processing center. The dictation equipment is interfaced with the phone system. The three dictation/recording units are functional twenty-four hours a day.

A special attempt was made to provide the word processing specialists a pleasant office environment. The colors (red, orange, yellow, and green) are cheerful and lively. Each work station is surrounded with seventy-two-inch movable partitions onto which a work platform, filing drawer, shelves, and drawers are attached. The partitions and floor are covered with carpet. An acoustical ceiling also has a high sound-absorbent value.

The organization pays its word processing specialists an average of 10 percent more than the average secretarial salary in the community. The organization has had excellent experience recruiting and retaining quality employees. The salaries for the administrative secretaries are fairly typical of the salaries paid by other organizations in the community.

Nearly 60 percent of the material typed in the word processing center is dictated. Approximately 30 percent is handwritten—mainly fairly extensive reports written in longhand. Most of the remaining material consists of form letters, some with several variable information items.

The supervisor of the word processing center is responsible for assigning jobs to the word processing specialist. The fairly detailed production records, which are kept in order to closely monitor the center's output, have several uses, one of which is to assess the need for additional word processing operators or specialists.

Before the center opened, marketing support representatives from the vendor firms oriented the principals about the uses of word processing. They also trained the principals on the effective use of the dictation equipment. Almost from the beginning, the word processing center was supported by the principals who used it.

Every six months, the manager of the word processing/administrative support areas gathers information from the principals by means of a questionnaire. The purpose of the questionnaire is to assess attitudes toward word processing/administrative support. The information from these questionnaires has provided a base for modifying both the word processing and the administrative support systems.

Review questions

   1. Define word processing in your own terms.

   2. What are the three basic components of word processing systems?

   3. What are the major functions of the various positions found in word processing systems?

4. What are the common types of equipment used in word processing systems?

5. Why is the making of carbon copies of documents obsolete in word processing systems?

6. What types of material input are used in word processing?

7. What methods of document distribution are commonly used in word processing?

8. What is electronic document distribution (EDD)?

9. What are the characteristics of the common word processing structures?

10. What are the advantages of using word processing?

11. What trends appear to be emerging in the word processing concept?

Cases

You are a marketing representative for a manufacturer of text-editing equipment. Your accounts are primarily smaller employers in the community in which you work. As a marketing representative, your responsibilities include selling/leasing the equipment as well as helping your clients utilize the equipment in the most efficient manner. This sometimes involves revising procedures of organizations already using word processing. Client follow-up is not only a crucial aspect of your job but also provides a vital function to the clients.

You recently called on a client for the first time. When you explained that the equipment your company sells is used in word processing systems, the client's comment was, "Word processing—what's that? I've never heard of it."

Your initial analysis is that the client could effectively use word processing on a limited scale. Many of the procedures performed in the organization would lend themselves to word processing.

You realize that your explanation of the word processing concept will probably determine your success in selling text-editing equipment to this client.

1. What are you going to tell the client about the word processing concept?

2. What information should be made available to the client as a means of convincing him of the merits of the concept?

• • •

The GS Corporation, which manufactures automobile parts, is one of the largest employers in the Tucson, Arizona, area. The organization presently has nearly four hundred employees in the headquarters building. The manufacturing plant, which is adjacent to the office building, employs over seven hundred individuals.

The operating philosophy of the organization has been rather traditional. At the present time, the secretarial/clerical procedures are performed in a traditional manner. Recently, one of the vice presidents read an article about word processing that explained how one company is saving thousands of dollars each year because of utilizing word processing. After the vice president read the article, you, an independent word processing consultant, were contacted. Even though you have not yet had time to do a thorough analysis of the situation, you have arrived at some fairly definitive conclusions about the situation at GS Corporation. You have observed that

- most of the departments are quite different from the others in terms of work procedures, typical vocabulary used, and so forth.
- the management of the organization is steeped in traditionalism. Most managers are presently opposed to any changes that have a far-reaching impact on them.
- many of the secretaries are very career-conscious.
- some of the departments in the office building are geographically remote from one another.

1. On the basis of your observations, which word processing structure do you feel will be most satisfactory for the organization? Why?

2. Is there an alternative structure that might also work?

3. In comparison to the other alternative structures, what advantages should result from the structure that you feel is most satisfactory?

CHAPTER 2

Determining the feasibility of word processing

Steps in determining feasibility
APPOINT A PLANNING COMMITTEE
INFORM EMPLOYEES OF PENDING STUDY
    Communicate benefits to employees
    Overcome employee resistance to change
DETERMINE APPROPRIATE METHOD FOR UNDERTAKING STUDY
    Use of organization employees
    Use of a consulting firm
    Use of equipment vendor representatives
DEVELOP A TIME SCHEDULE FOR VARIOUS STAGES OF THE STUDY
COLLECT DATA
    Suggestions for data collection
    Data-collection techniques
        Interviews
        Questionnaires
        Analysis of office tasks
        Inventory of filed materials
COMPILE AND ANALYZE DATA
    Procedures
    Determining the nature of tasks performed by employees
        Typing activities
        Nontyping activities
MAKE THE DECISION
COMMUNICATE THE DECISION TO EMPLOYEES
SET UP MOCK WORD PROCESSING CENTER

Accurate determination of the feasibility of a word processing system is crucial to its successful implementation. Utmost care must be exercised during the study procedures to assure the accuracy of the data, which are used to determine whether or not word processing is feasible. To make a decision on the basis of inaccurate or unrepresentative data will most likely distort the perceived need for word processing. Besides determining the feasibility of word processing the assessment will also help indicate the amount of equipment needed and the appropriate word processing/administrative support structure for the organization.

One of the important factors to consider in the assessment is the nature of the various kinds of office work in the organization. The nature of the specific tasks performed by the office employees also needs to be assessed. These tasks are typically categorized as either typing tasks or nontyping tasks.

Another factor is the nature of the environment in which the office work is carried out. Two of the most common environmental situations are production-oriented situations and custom-oriented situations. In a production-oriented situation, quantity of output and quick turnaround time are important. Each secretary is typically responsible to a group of executives. In a custom-oriented situation, on the other hand, quality of output rather than quantity, is more important, and work of a specialized nature is typical. The custom-oriented situation is also characterized by having one secretary for each executive.

Steps in determining feasibility

The efficiency of the feasibility study is greatly affected by the care and skill exerted in each step of the study. The feasibility study may take eight months or longer to complete. Because of the study's multiphased nature, it requires a considerable amount of thought and planning before it actually begins. Failure to have a master plan that outlines each step will affect the validity of the study.

APPOINT A PLANNING COMMITTEE

One of the first steps, after the decision has been made to conduct the study, is to appoint a planning committee. Such a committee can be invaluable as the study progresses. The composition of the planning committee varies from organization to organization. The organization's top management is usually represented by an executive at the vice-president level. The vice president responsible for the internal affairs of the organization is a most logical choice. Having a representative from the top executive level provides evidence of top management support for the project. Other representatives to the committee are typically from the middle management, supervisory, and worker levels. Examples include administrative office managers, office supervisors, and secretarial/clerical supervisors. The secretarial/clerical ranks can be represented by high-level secretarial/clerical employees.

The committee members should have certain qualifications, including a thorough understanding of the word processing/administrative support concept. The members should also have a thorough understanding of the present procedures utilized in carrying out office work as well as be familiar with various organizational functions and policies.

The variety of functions of the planning committee include a considerable number of technical activities. The committee is likely to be involved in helping to determine which alternative or combination of alternatives—organization employees, vendor representatives, or consultants—is most appropriate for collecting the data. Depending on the alternative selected, the committee might be involved in analyzing the collected data. The committee may also provide technical assistance as the need arises during the data-collection phases of the study. In some instances, the technical assistance is quite simple, such as answering a question. In other instances, the assistance is much more complex, like documenting work flow.

In addition to the technical functions, the committee also performs a number of public relations functions. Most organizations have found greater acceptance of the feasibility study activities when employees are kept informed about the status of the project.

In some organizations, the possibility of installing a word processing system is met with a good deal of resistance. Helping to overcome employee resistance to the installation is a vital function of the planning committee. In addition, the planning committee also is able to perform a valuable indoctrination/orientation function once the decision has been made to install the word processing system.

Planning committees also take on a variety of other functions as the feasibility study gets underway. Examples include such tasks as collecting data, interviewing employees, recommending location(s) for word processing center(s), recommending types of equipment to be used, and so forth.

INFORM EMPLOYEES OF PENDING STUDY

The support of all employees in the organization is crucial to the success of the feasibility study. Without their support, important data tend to be withheld, distorted, or misrepresented. A most effective means of obtaining the support of the employees is to distribute a memorandum throughout the entire organization. Since the purpose of the memo is to explain the reasons for undertaking the pending study, the outcome of the study—the possible installation of a word processing/administrative support system—should also be mentioned. The potential employee benefits should be outlined in the memo. The names of the committee members are frequently identified in the first memo distributed to the employees. Such memos are likely to have maximum impact if they originate in the president's office and carry the president's signature.

Since many employees are not likely to be familiar with a word processing/administrative support system, orientation sessions may be very beneficial. These sessions, to which all interested employees are invited, have also been successfully used to help employees overcome many of their fears about word processing. The session can be handled in a variety of ways, utilizing films, visual presentations, demonstrations of equipment, and so forth. The orientation sessions should be conducted after the first memo has been distributed.

A second memo is often distributed to the employees soon before the actual study begins. The purpose of this memo is to inform the employees who—company employees, management consultants, equipment vendors—will conduct the study; it may also present a few specifics about the study procedures, including, for example, the types of items included in the study.

Communicate benefits to employees. It is natural for employees to become apprehensive when there is a possibility of change—especially if the change directly affects them. Every possible effort should be made to diminish apprehension. It is important for the employees to understand thoroughly the benefits of word processing/administrative support. These benefits should be related as closely as possible to each specific employee group. Outlining the benefits to employees also tends to have a greater impact when the benefits of the new system are contrasted with the present system. The contrast puts the situation in a perspective to which the employees are able to relate.

Overcome employee resistance to change. The amount of initial success of a word processing/administrative support system is often determined by the degree to which the employees support the new system. Support for the system increases as the employees cease to resist its utilization.

Several techniques have been successfully used to help employees overcome their resistance to the installation of a word processing/administrative support system. One very successful technique is frequent communication with the employees. Keeping employees informed of the status of the project reassures and makes them feel a part of the project.

Another successful technique is the direct involvement of the employees in the project. The use of participative management has long been recognized as a useful device in helping employees overcome resistance. Employee suggestions, advice, and recommendations are the foundation of participative management.

As a system for expediting written communication, word processing is often resisted because the office employees are fearful that their jobs will be eliminated. Normal attrition rates are typically sufficient to handle any employee surplus once the system has been installed. Assuring employees that none will be discharged often eliminates most of the resistance to the changeover.

Managers tend to resist word processing/administrative support systems because of their unwillingness to let "just anyone" do their typing. Pointing out to managers the benefits of word processing/administrative support is often sufficient to gain their acceptance. Managers are likely to be impressed by the knowledge that the system results in greater productivity since principals don't have to wait until the secretary is ready to take dictation, it provides a dictation system that can be utilized twenty-four hours a day, it results in faster turnaround time, it facilitates better quality work, and it allows the administrative secretaries to assume some of the tasks now performed by the managers.

Another suggestion for helping employees to overcome their resistance to word processing is a gradual phase-in of the system. Rather than converting the total organization at one time, a department-by-department conversion is often preferred. The gradual conversion permits "debugging" of one stage of the conversion before beginning the next stage.

DETERMINE APPROPRIATE METHOD FOR UNDERTAKING STUDY

Once the decision has been made to undertake the feasibility study, the next step involves determining the appropriate method for conducting the study. Three primary alternatives are available. One alternative is to utilize employees to conduct the study. Another alternative is to utilize a consulting firm that specializes in such studies. A third alternative is to use an equipment vendor. Each alternative is specially suited for certain situations. With increasing frequency, organizations use a combination of organizational employees and either equipment vendors or a management consulting firm.

Use of organization employees. Studies conducted only by the employees of the organization are being used considerably less often than in the past. However, the use of employees of the organization to conduct the feasibility study or to assist vendor representatives or consultants is advantageous from the standpoint of the employees' familiarity with the organization's operating procedures. Those responsible for the survey know whom to talk with to get desired information. In many instances, the employees will also have a fairly good idea when information provided by others has been distorted. In addition, employees will often have direct access to needed information and will not have to depend on others to provide the information. They will also be in a position to monitor growth and change within the system once it is in operation.

The rapidly changing nature of the word processing/administrative support concept makes it necessary to study continually to keep abreast of new developments and technology. Each person involved in the study should keep up to date. However, to meet these responsibilities, employees must be given sufficient time and resources. One potentially serious shortcoming of this alternative is the possible lack of a technical competence in word processing by those responsible for the feasibility study.

Use of a consulting firm. Many organizations opt to hire a consulting firm to conduct the feasibility study or to work with organizational employees. Not too long ago, only a few consulting firms had employees with expertise in the word processing/administrative support concept. Now, however, many firms have consultants with expertise in this area; in fact, an increasing number of consulting firms limit their services to the word processing/administrative support area.

The use of outside consultants is advantageous for several reasons. The consultants are objective. They will not recommend the installation of a word processing/administrative support system without sufficient justification. Because the consultants are experts in work analysis, work flow, and efficient work procedures, they are often able to spot situations where changes are needed. Even though the consultants may not recommend the installation of a word processing center, the organization is usually able to get its money's worth from these other recommendations.

The following are some of the areas in which consultants become involved:

1. Surveying, measuring, and analyzing typewritten and administrative work.
2. Designing systems.

3. Preparing manuals.
4. Training personnel.
5. Evaluating and selecting equipment.
6. Measuring performance.
7. Preparing job descriptions.
8. Designing layout and environment.

Consultants are more often used in large organizations than in small ones. Large organizations generally find outside consultants more desirable because the consultants are able to work full time on the project. This is not always possible when organizational employees are used. However, the backlog of some of the consulting firms may require a fairly long wait before the study is conducted.

When assessing the qualifications of consultants, the following factors should be considered: length of time in consulting work, nature of educational and work experiences, scope of consulting work, feedback from references, and charges for services rendered.

Use of equipment vendor representatives. For many organizations, the use of equipment vendor representatives is the most desirable of the three alternatives. Although there are no direct costs involved in this alternative, the organization ultimately pays for the study in the purchase or rental costs of the equipment. The decision to authorize a vendor to perform an in-depth study generally obligates the organization to purchase from that vendor unless some valid reason for not doing so emerges.

The use of vendor representatives to conduct the feasibility study is advantageous for several reasons. The study is conducted by individuals who have considerable expertise in this area. In addition, the vendor representatives are familiar with the characteristics of their lines of equipment. This helps assure the design of a system tailor-made for the needs of the organization.

Another advantage of this alternative, in comparison to the use of consultants, is the cost of the study. The indirect cost of the study conducted by vendor representatives is likely to be considerably less than the cost of the study conducted by consultants. Because vendors sell a service as well as a product, most include follow-up to help identify areas where changes are needed as an integral part of the transaction.

Some find the lack of flexibility a serious problem when using equipment vendor representatives to conduct the feasibility study. The vendor representatives will design the system around the line of equipment they sell. Some equipment vendor representatives also have the tendency to recommend more equipment than is necessary.

Figure 2-1 FACTORS TO CONSIDER WHEN DETERMINING THE MOST DESIRABLE ALTERNATIVE FOR CONDUCTING A FEASIBILITY STUDY

1. The size and complexity of the organization.
2. The availability of employees who are competent to undertake a word processing/administrative support feasibility study.
3. The availability of consultants.
4. The availability of reliable equipment vendor representatives.
5. The amount of money the organization is willing and able to spend on the study.
6. The extent of the perceived need for a word processing/administrative support system.
7. The amount of time available for undertaking the study.

Figure 2-1 identifies several factors that should be considered when deciding which of the three alternatives is most desirable for an organization, given the nature of the circumstances.

DEVELOP A TIME SCHEDULE FOR VARIOUS STAGES OF THE STUDY

Any activity as important and involved as a feasibility study must be carefully planned. An integral part of the planning process is the development of a time schedule for the various stages of the study. Failure to use a schedule often results in the delay of certain stages. The most effective studies are often those that are completed as expeditiously as possible.

Several factors should be considered in developing the time schedule. The greater the number of employees involved in the study, the longer the study will take to complete. The method used to collect the data will also affect the amount of time needed to complete the study. Of the three alternatives used to conduct the study, the slowest is likely to be the use of organization employees. This is especially true when the employees have other duties that must be performed while the feasibility study is in progress. The time schedule can sometimes be shortened by increasing the number of individuals directly involved in the study as well as by using experienced personnel to conduct the study.

Figure 2-2 presents a sample time schedule. The amount of time allotted for each phase should not be seen as inflexible. Rather, the time allotments are tentative and should be adjusted to each individual situation.

The explanation of the survey procedures to the employees is likely to have an impact on employee attitude toward the study. If the sessions are handled in a professional manner, the employees are more

Figure 2-2 TIME SCHEDULE FOR UNDERTAKING FEASIBILITY STUDY

Activity	Week beginning									
	6/27	7/4	7/11	7/18	7/25	8/2	8/9	8/16	8/23	8/30
Explanation of survey procedures	══	══								
Collection of data		══	══							
Analysis of data			══	══	══	══				
Feasibility study report preparation								══	══	
Presentation of findings of feasibility study										══

likely to look forward to the upcoming study than if the sessions are poorly handled. Separate sessions should be conducted for principals and for the secretarial/clerical employees since their jobs differ considerably. Individuals responsible for collecting the data should preside at these sessions.

Data collection and data analysis are discussed thoroughly in an upcoming section. The feasibility study report, a very important document, should be prepared in a formal format. Liberal use of graphic aids help make these reports easier to understand. Characteristics of, and suggestions for preparing, formal reports can be found in business report writing textbooks, of which there are several in print.

Once the feasibility study report is prepared, the next step is to present the findings to the individuals who are responsible for deciding whether or not to install a word processing/administrative support system. The findings and recommendations presented in the study report are very important since they will provide the basis for whatever decision is made. The ultimate decision should be communicated to all organization employees as soon as it is made. The decision and accompanying rationale are often communicated to the employees in a memo from the president.

COLLECT DATA

Data are an integral part of the feasibility study designed to determine the need for a word processing/administrative support system. The data can be collected by a variety of techniques. The method of data collection typically determines which techniques will be used; for example, consultants prefer to use certain data-collection methods while equipment vendor representatives tend to use others. If organization employees are used to conduct the feasibility study, materials may have to be developed to facilitate the data-collection process.

Suggestions for data collection. Several suggestions can be offered to improve the data-collection efforts.

1. Select a representative data-collection period. Collecting data during a time that is not typical of the whole has a negative impact on the validity of the data.
2. Select a data-collection period that is long enough to adjust for any unusual daily fluctuations. Normally a two-week period is sufficiently long.
3. Field test any self-developed materials. Although wording may be clear to the individuals responsible for the data-collection efforts, others may have difficulty understanding the meaning of certain parts of the materials.
4. Train the individuals who will be involved in the data-collection activities on the specifics of the research procedures. In some instances, consultants and equipment vendor representatives turn over to employees certain data-collection activities. To assure the success of the study, employees must be familiar with activities for which they are responsible.
5. Preplan the data coding and compiling activities of the study. It is often possible to simplify the data coding and compiling efforts by planning ahead, especially when designing the data-collection materials.
6. Build into the data-collection activities some means of verifying the accuracy of the collected data. Some employees distort data, which should not be used. A fairly common means of verifying the accuracy of data is to have the employees' supervisors scan the responses to check their accuracy.

Data-collection techniques. Several different data-collection techniques are used to determine the need for a word processing/administrative support system. Techniques include interviews, questionnaires, task analyses, and inventory of stored materials.

Interviews. Interviews of both principals and secretaries can be conducted for two purposes: to collect data and to verify the accuracy of data already collected. The types of questions asked during the interview will vary according to the job title of the individual being interviewed and the nature of the data being discussed.

When the principals are interviewed, the following are discussed:

1. The position of the principal in the organizational hierarchy.
2. The specific job functions of the principal.
3. The nature and amount of written communication originated by the principal.
4. The types of tasks now being performed by principals that capable assistants could perform.
5. The aspects of the principal's job in which additional support would enable him/her to perform more effectively.

When the principals are department or unit managers, additional questions should be asked about the following: the departmental or unit functions, goals and objectives of the department/unit, and an assessment of the future direction of the department/unit in terms of secretarial/administrative support.

A primary purpose of interviews with supervisors is often to clarify information or to verify the accuracy of the data collected from employees.

Some of the topics discussed pertain to:

1. Output levels of the unit for which the supervisor is responsible.
2. Types of tasks performed by employees in the work unit.
3. Production standards that are in effect.
4. Nature and number of seasonally busy and slow periods.
5. Flow of work through the department.
6. Nature and amount of written communication that the supervisors originate.
7. Job duties of the supervisors.

The types of questions asked of secretaries are quite different from those asked of other types of job holders. In some instances, the questions will be used to clarify the data already collected, while in other instances the questions will be asked primarily to collect data. Some questions frequently asked of secretaries include the following:

1. For which principals do you work?
2. What is the nature of the typing tasks you perform and in what quantity are they performed?
3. What kinds of written communication do you work with and in what quantities?
4. What percent of the material you work with is (1) machine dictation, (2) handwritten, (3) shorthand, (4) repetitive?

5. What percent of the material you work with is revised, and how extensive are the revisions?
6. What percent of the material has to be keyboarded several times because of an inability to electronically store the material?
7. What is the nature of the nontyping tasks you perform and in what quantities?

Most interviewers find an interview record sheet a convenient device to use during the interview. The sheet lists the questions to be asked and provides space for the recording of answers. An example of such a sheet is presented in Figure 2–3.

Questionnaires. As a data-collection device, questionnaires serve a useful function in the undertaking of feasibility studies. In comparison to the interview technique, the use of questionnaires for data collection is much faster. Whereas interviews are conducted on a one-to-one basis, many individuals can simultaneously complete questionnaires.

Figure 2–3 INTERVIEW RECORD SHEET

Name	Title
Department	Date

1. What is (are) the name(s) of the individuals for whom you do secretarial work?

2. What percent of your time is spent in a typing or a related typing activity?

3. What are the specific kinds of documents you type and in what quantities?
    Kind of document   *Quantity*

4. What percent of the material is machine dictation? _____
                                    • handwritten copy? _____
                                    • shorthand? _____
                                    • copy material? _____
5. What percent of the material you type is revised later? _____
6. What percent of the material you type is repetitive material? _____
7. What nontyping activities do you perform and what percentage of time does each consume?
    Kinds of activities   *Percent of time*

A variety of questionnaires have been developed for use in determining the need for a word processing/administrative support system. The questionnaires used by consultants and equipment vendor representatives are thoroughly tested before they are approved for official use. Those designed for exclusive use in one organization must also be thoroughly tested before they are used.

One of the difficult problems in designing questionnaires is the wording. Because of differing perceptions, words have different meanings for people. Unclear or ambiguous wording tends to distort the responses provided by employees, which results in the collection of data that have a questionable value.

Questionnaires are appropriate for the same categories of employees for which interviews are appropriate. Questionnaires can be custom designed for any group for which their use is appropriate. Their content is basically determined by the employee group for whom they are designed.

Questionnaires designed for use by principals cover the same basic items discussed during the interview. To be more specific, the following are typical of some of the items covered on questionnaires:

1. The nature of the written communication originated by the principals.
2. The types and amount of material input (handwritten, shorthand, machine dictation, copy).
3. The frequency with which principals revise material.
4. The frequency with which principals request the first draft to be a rough draft.
5. The amount of repetitive material.
6. The nature and number of tasks for which the principals are responsible that could be assigned to assistants.

Figure 2–4 illustrates a questionnaire for use by principals.

Questionnaires for use by secretaries contain items designed to assess the nature of their typing and nontyping duties. Figure 2–5 illustrates a questionnaire designed specifically for use by secretaries.

Analysis of office tasks. Another technique used to collect data is the analysis of office tasks. Several methods are used to analyze the tasks performed by office employees. Some of the methods tend to duplicate the material collected in the interview or questionnaire techniques. While the interview and questionnaire techniques are used for both office employees and principals, the various methods used to analyze office tasks primarily involve office employees.

Task lists summarize both typing and nontyping activities. The summarized data on the task list identify how each employee accounts

Figure 2-4 QUESTIONNAIRE FOR USE BY PRINCIPALS

Name	Title
Department	Date

1. What kinds of written communication do you create?

   a.   d.   g.

   b.   e.   h.

   c.   f.   i.

2. When you create material to be typed, which method(s) do you use and what percent does each consume?

   _____% Longhand   _____% Shorthand

   _____% Machine dictation

3. On the average, how many typed pages do you create each day by the following methods?

   _____ Longhand   _____ Shorthand

   _____ Machine dictation

4. How many hours do you spend each day creating material that is later typed?

   _____

5. Do you expect the amount of material you create to increase in the future?

   ____ No   ____ Yes—by the following amount _____.

6. When you are out of the office, how often do you create material that has to be typed?

   ____ Very often   ____ Often   ____ Not very often   ____ Never

7. Which methods do you use to create the material identified in number 6?

   _____% Longhand   _____% Shorthand

   _____% Machine dictation

8. What percent of the material you create is revised after it has been typed?

   _____

9. What percent of the material you create would you revise after it has been typed if the retyping did not create a hardship for the typist?

   _____%

10. What percent of the material you create do you have typed in rough-draft form the first typing?

Figure 2-4 CONTINUED

_____%
11. What percent of the material you create is repetitive material (is typed again at a later date)?

_____%
12. What percent of the material you create is form material with fill-ins?

_____%
13. Do you maintain a file of standard letters or paragraphs that you use during the material creation process?

_____ No   _____ Yes
14. How extensively are the standard letters or paragraphs used?

_____ Very often _____ Quite often _____ Seldom

_____ Almost never
15. On the average, what is the time lapse between the time you give your secretary material to be typed and the time it is returned?

_____ hours
16. Do you now perform tasks that could be delegated to a secretary if the secretary had time to complete them?

_____ No   _____ Yes
If you answered yes, please identify those tasks.
17. Are you generally satisfied with the quality of secretarial service you are provided?

_____ No   _____ Yes
If you answered no, please state why you are dissatisfied.

---

for each minute (or some other unit, such as ten-minute intervals) of the work period. The task lists are prepared from time logs kept by each employee. The period of time covered by the task lists should be representative and should not be affected by seasonally busy or slow periods.

Figure 2-6 illustrates a sample task list. An examination of the form reveals that tasks are categorized as typing or nontyping. Although the time span of the sample task list is one week, some other time span can be used as well.

The nature of the typing tasks of office employees can also be analyzed by means of line counts. Using a log sheet, each typist records a description of each document typed, the origin of each document, the number of lines in the document, the method of input, and whether or not the document is revised material or repetitive material. A partial line-count log sheet is illustrated in Figure 2-7.

Figure 2-5 QUESTIONNAIRE FOR USE BY SECRETARIES

Name	Title
Department	Date

1. What percent of your job consists of typing and related activities?

   _____%

2. How many principals do you presently type for? _____
3. What percent of the material you type is in the following formats?

   _____% Longhand   _____% Machine dictation

   _____% Shorthand   _____% Self-composed

   _____% Copy

4. What percent of the material you type is revised by the principal after it has been typed the first time?

   _____%

5. Of the material that is revised, what percent is revised according to the following number of times?

   ____% revised 1 time   ____% revised 2 times

   ____% revised 3 times   ____% revised 4 or more times

6. What percent of your typing is rough-draft work? _____%
7. What percent of the material you type has the following deadlines?

   _____% same day _____% one day _____% two days

   _____% more than two days

8. How many times per month are you unable to meet deadlines because of peak word periods?

   _____ number of times

9. Are erasures (or some other means of making corrections) permitted on the work you type?

   ____ No ____ Yes ____ Depends on job

10. On the average, what percent of the work you type requires copies?

    _____% requiring no copies _____% requiring 1 copy

    _____% requiring 2 copies   _____% requiring 3 or more copies

11. What percent of these copies are made by a carbon process and by a copy process?

    _____% carbon

    _____% copier

Figure 2-5 CONTINUED

---

12. What nontyping duties do you perform in your job and in what frequency?

    Duties   *Percent of nontyping time*

13. If you had more time, would the principals for whom you work delegate to you some of the tasks they perform at the present time?

    ____ No   ____ Yes   ____ Don't know

    If your answer is yes, what kinds of tasks would probably be delegated?

14. Do you prefer the typing or nontyping aspects of your job?

    ____ typing activities

    ____ nontyping activities

As an alternative to using line counts, some experts who specialize in the design of word processing/administrative support systems now recommend the use of quarter-page counts. The results are just as accurate and it takes less time to determine the number of typed quarter pages in a document than to determine the number of typed lines.

Inventory of filed materials. A fairly new technique for helping determine the need for a word processing/administrative support system is to undertake an inventory of filed materials. The inventory will identify the nature of the documents that have originated in the organization, the quantities of the documents, and who or what department was responsible for the creation of the various documents. This information will be of value in designing a word processing/administrative support system should the need for such a system exist.

COMPILE AND ANALYZE DATA

Once the data have been gathered, the next step is to compile the data. The compilation provides a variety of summary data necessary to determine the need for a word processing/administrative support system and the structural design of the system. Compilation is a fairly easy task when preplanning takes place before the data are collected.

While a considerable amount of the data are quantitative, much is of a nonquantitative nature. The quantitative data are generally easier to compile than the nonquantitative data.

Procedures. Specific procedures should be followed in compiling the data to assure accurate results. Perhaps the easiest method for compiling the data is to use summary sheets onto which data/information are transferred. Once all the data/information have been compiled, percentages are often calculated to help put the summary totals into a meaningful perspective.

Figure 2-6 TASK LIST

Name		Title	
Department		Time span of study	
Tasks		Quantity	Amount of Time
Typing:			
Keyboarding:			
Letters			
Memos			
Reports			
Forms			
Miscellaneous			
Other (specify)			
Taking dictation			
Miscellaneous			
Nontyping:			
Answering phone			
Placing phone calls			
Copying/duplicating			
Filing			
Bookkeeping			
Preparing mail for distribution			
Receiving office callers			
Arranging meetings/conferences			
Other (specify)			

Figure 2-7 LINE-COUNT LOG SHEET

Typist's name _____ Department _____ Time span _____

Description	Originator	Input method					Revision[1] # lines	Repetitive[2] # lines
		Longhand # lines	Shorthand # lines	Machine dictation # lines	Copy typing # lines	Other # lines		

[1]Number of lines rekeyboarded

[2]Number of lines manually typed on repetitive work

It is generally recommended that a few spot checks be run on the data to assure the accuracy of the summary totals. This is easily accomplished by recalculating certain portions of the data.

Once the data have been compiled, the next phase is data analysis, which is important to the decision-making process. Analysis helps to give meaning to the data/information and to identify any situations or circumstances that are out of the ordinary.

Determining the nature of tasks performed by employees. The main purpose for collecting the data is to determine the nature of tasks performed by both principals and office employees. Before the need and/or feasibility of a word processing/administrative support system can be determined, the nature of the tasks performed by employees has to be assessed. To make an accurate assessment, the data have to be carefully analyzed.

The tasks performed by employees can be put into two categories: typing and nontyping tasks. Both principals and secretaries are involved in each category. In addition, the amount of time consumed by each task is an important determinant of a word processing/administrative support system.

Typing activities. When determining the nature of the typing activities, the following are considered:

1. Methods of input (handwritten, shorthand, machine dictation, copy).
2. Extent of revision.
3. Amount of repetitive material.
4. Categories of work (letters, memos, reports, forms, and so forth).
5. Turnaround time.
6. Error-correction requirements.

Nontyping activities. The nature of the various nontyping activities also has to be assessed in order to determine whether or not word processing/administrative support is feasible. The time consumed by each of the activities must also be assessed. Among the factors considered are

1. Nontyping activities performed by office employees (telephoning, filing, copying, and so forth).
2. Tasks performed by principals that are assignable to office employees.
3. Amount of administrative support needed by principals to enable them to perform more effectively.

MAKE THE DECISION

Several factors enter into the decision as to whether or not a word processing/administrative support system is supportable. Each of these factors has to be considered separately and then jointly in making the decision.

1. Consider the available alternatives. The fact that the present system for expediting written communication is not as efficient as it might be does not necessarily warrant the installation of a word processing/administrative support system. Perhaps there are other alternatives available that are preferable to a word processing/administrative support system.

2. Consider the data that were collected during the feasibility study. In the final analysis, two overall factors emerge as being very important: the nature of the work and the amount of work. If both the nature and amount of work justify the installation of a word processing/administrative support system, then other factors should be considered.

3. Consider the financial feasibility of the system. It is doubtful that a word processing/administrative support system would cost significantly more than the present system. In many cases, the cost is less. Before a system is justifiable, it has to be cost effective or show evidence of being cost effective. In other words, the value gained must exceed the cost. In a traditional office, a secretary averages one hundred typewritten lines per day. When text editors are used, an output rate of approximately six hundred fifty final-draft lines must be typed each day by each secretary in order to achieve a lower per-line cost than when using standard typewriters in a traditional office.

4. Consider the users of the system. The installation of a word processing/administrative support system would be difficult to justify—no matter how great the need—if either management or office employees are adamantly opposed to the system. Of the three components of word processing, problems dealing with the personnel component are most prevalent. In many instances, the impact of people on the system is sufficiently strong to cause its success or failure.

Once the decision has been made to investigate further the installation of a word processing/administrative support system, the proposed system should be designed. At this point, a definitive comparison of the present and proposed systems can be made. The comparison is likely to be made in terms of cost and potential advantages and disadvantages.

The decision is now finalized and the recommendations are put into the feasibility study report. Once the report has been prepared, the findings are presented to those who will make the final decision. The executives who make the decision may leave the proposed system intact, or they may decide that certain modifications are necessary.

COMMUNICATE THE DECISION TO EMPLOYEES

Once the final decision has been made, it should be communicated as quickly as possible to all employees. To withhold information of this nature from the employees is often damaging. The decision can be communicated in several ways, including a memo to all employees, announcements to department heads who in turn disseminate the information, or announcement by a top executive to groups of employees. The expected benefits should be emphasized in the announcement.

SET UP MOCK WORD PROCESSING CENTER

Many organizations have developed small-scale mock word processing centers to help employees better understand the concept. If employees have a thorough understanding of the system, they are likely to accept it more readily.

Most equipment vendors are willing to provide the equipment for the mock center, especially if the organization is likely to use the vendor's equipment in the permanent installation. An alternative is to make arrangements to view the word processing facilities in other organizations.

Review questions

1. How do production-oriented and custom-oriented environmental situations differ from one another?

2. What are the customary functions of a planning committee with regard to determining the feasibility of a word processing system?

3. Why should employees be informed of a pending feasibility study?

4. What suggestions can you offer to help employees overcome their resistance to the installation of a word processing/ administrative support system?

5. What alternatives are available for undertaking the feasibility study?

6. When consultants are used to undertake the feasibility study, what are the typical areas with which they are concerned?

7. What suggestions can you offer to help improve the data-collection efforts?

8. What techniques are used to collect data for the feasibility study?

9. What factors should be considered when making a decision about the supportability of a word processing/administrative support system?

Cases

The Allied Insurance Company, located in Fargo, North Dakota, is growing rapidly in terms of the number of new policies that are being sold. To help overcome some of the problems resulting from the increased number of policyholders, the executive committee of the company has decided that word processing may be desirable and that its feasibility should be investigated. Recently, a planning committee of eight individuals was appointed. At their first meeting, you, the administrative office manager at Allied, were elected chairperson of the committee.

The planning committee has met several times and has made fairly substantial progress in several areas. It is now time to begin thinking about undertaking the actual feasibility study. Each time this topic is brought up, the committee becomes divided on the issue of whether to use consultants or equipment vendor representatives. Both appear to be equally suited.

1. What factors do you think should be considered in making the decision about which method to use?

2. Under what circumstances would the use of consultants be preferable to the use of vendor representatives and vice versa?

3. What advantages would result from the use of consultants? Vendor representatives?

• • •

Several executives in the Marcos Food Supplies Corporation, which is located in Cheyenne, Wyoming, have decided that conditions appear to be suitable for installing a word processing system. Although the corporation is not feeling a pressing need for conversion to word processing, the executives feel it is to the organization's advantage to be thinking about the possibility.

Rather than move rapidly in investigating the feasibility of word processing, the executives feel a slower approach should be used. The executives believe the use of organizational employees to conduct the feasibility study would be more appropriate under the circumstances than the use of either consultants or equipment vendors.

At the present time, the organization uses a typing pool, and you are the supervisor of that pool. It was logical that you be selected as the employee responsible for data collection. In your judgment, interviews and task analyses appear to be the most suitable means of collecting data.

1. What types of information will you most likely collect during the interviews?
2. What kinds of information will the task analyses provide?
3. What suggestions can you provide to help assure the success of both methods?

CHAPTER 3

Installation of the word processing system

Steps in the installation

DETERMINE PERSONNEL REQUIREMENTS
   Nature of work load
   Special characteristics of work
   Use of specialized equipment
   Need for other types of word processing personnel
   Projected rate of expansion
DETERMINE SPACE REQUIREMENTS OF THE WORD PROCESSING CENTER
   Number of employees
   Amount of equipment
   Amount of furniture
   Projected rate of expansion
   Other space requirements
DETERMINE THE PHYSICAL LOCATION OF THE WORD PROCESSING CENTER
   Proximity
   Convenience
   Expansion possibilities
   Structural features of the facility
DETERMINE EQUIPMENT REQUIREMENTS
   Nature of work performed
   Amount of work
SELECT EQUIPMENT
   Appropriateness of equipment
   Dependability of equipment
   Specifications of equipment
   Cost of equipment
   Flexibility of equipment
   Ease of equipment operation
   Standardization of equipment
   Reputation of vendor
   Services provided by vendor
   Equipment servicing and maintenance
   Leasing versus purchasing alternatives

DETERMINE FURNITURE REQUIREMENTS
  Nature of employees' jobs
  Equipment design
  Environment of the word processing center
SELECT FURNITURE
  Flexibility of furniture
  Durability of furniture
  Cost of furniture
PLAN THE LAYOUT OF THE WORD PROCESSING CENTER
  Work flow
  Safety considerations
  Communication needs
PLAN THE PHYSICAL ENVIRONMENT OF THE WORD PROCESSING CENTER
  Acoustical control
  Lighting
  Air conditioning
  Humidity level
  Circulation of air
  Cleanliness of air
  Color coordination
CONVERT TO THE NEW WORD PROCESSING SYSTEM
  Develop efficient procedures
  Develop user manual
  Training for word processing utilization
FOLLOW-UP AND EVALUATION OF THE WORD PROCESSING SYSTEM

The installation of a word processing system involves many different activities. It is not uncommon for the installation period to exceed by six or seven months the length of the feasibility study period. Once the decision has been made to install a word processing/administrative support system, thorough, detailed planning should take place. This planning should result in the development of an implementation schedule that identifies the completion times of the various activities involved in the installation.

Although the implementation schedule should be tailor-made for each organization, a sample schedule is presented in Figure 3-1. The schedule provides a list of the major activities involved in the project as well as completion times, depicted in the chart by horizontal lines.

Figure 3-1 IMPLEMENTATION SCHEDULE

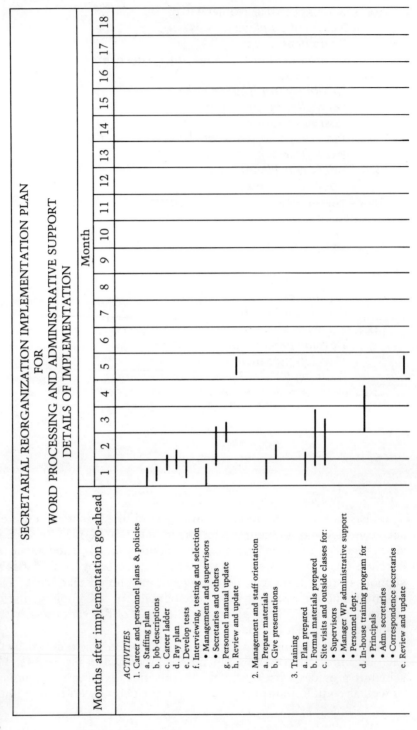

SECRETARIAL REORGANIZATION IMPLEMENTATION PLAN
FOR
WORD PROCESSING AND ADMINISTRATIVE SUPPORT
DETAILS OF IMPLEMENTATION

Month

Months after implementation go-ahead

| | 1 | 2 | 3 | 4 | 5 | 6 | 7 | 8 | 9 | 10 | 11 | 12 | 13 | 14 | 15 | 16 | 17 | 18 |

ACTIVITIES

1. Career and personnel plans & policies
   a. Staffing plan
   b. Job descriptions
   c. Career ladder
   d. Pay plan
   e. Develop tests
   f. Interviewing, testing and selection
      • Management and supervisors
      • Secretaries and others
   g. Personnel manual update
   h. Review and update

2. Management and staff orientation
   a. Prepare materials
   b. Give presentations

3. Training
   a. Plan prepared
   b. Formal materials prepared
   c. Site visits and outside classes for:
      • Supervisors
      • Manager WP administrative support
      • Personnel dept.
   d. In-house training program for
      • Principals
      • Adm. secretaries
      • Correspondence secretaries
   e. Review and update

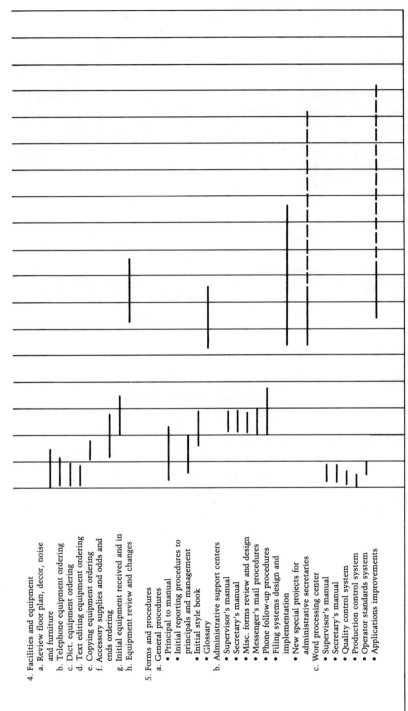

4. Facilities and equipment
   a. Review floor plan, decor, noise and furniture
   b. Telephone equipment ordering
   c. Dict. equipment ordering
   d. Text editing equipment ordering
   e. Copying equipment ordering
   f. Accessory supplies and odds and ends ordering
   g. Initial equipment received and in
   h. Equipment review and changes

5. Forms and procedures
   a. General procedures
      • Principal to manual
      • Initial reporting procedures to principals and management
      • Initial style book
      • Glossary
   b. Administrative support centers
      • Supervisor's manual
      • Secretary's manual
      • Misc. forms review and design
      • Messenger's mail procedures
      • Phone follow-up procedures
      • Filing systems design and implementation
      • New special projects for administrative secretaries
   c. Word processing center
      • Supervisor's manual
      • Secretary's manual
      • Quality control system
      • Production control system
      • Operator standards system
      • Applications improvements

Source: Walter A. Kleinschrod, *Management's Guide to Word Processing*, Chicago: The Dartnell Corporation, 1977, p. 64.

Steps in the installation

A variety of steps are involved in the installation of a word processing/administrative support system. For example, the personnel requirements and the space requirements for the center need to be determined. Other important steps are choosing the physical location of the word processing center, determining the equipment requirements, and selecting the equipment to meet the requirements. In addition, the furniture requirements have to be determined and the layout and physical environment of the center have to be planned. While several of the steps can be carried out simultaneously, others require the prior completion of certain steps.

Once all the steps have been carried out, the conversion to the new system begins. A conversion schedule should be devised to help assure an orderly transition. This discussion pertains to the installation of a centralized word processing center. In instances where several smaller decentralized or distributed centers are preferred, the installation steps can be easily modified for use in installing the small centers.

DETERMINE PERSONNEL REQUIREMENTS

An important step in the planning of a word processing/administrative support system is the determination of the personnel requirements for both the word processing specialists and administrative secretaries. The feasibility study is helpful here since it provides data on the nature and amount of office work performed.

Personnel requirements have two dimensions, the number and the qualifications of personnel. Depending on the design of the word processing/administrative support system, certain specialized qualifications other than those necessary in a traditional office might be required. The various factors to be considered in determining personnel requirements are discussed in the following sections.

Nature of work load. An important factor to consider in the determination of personnel requirements is the nature and amount of typing and nontyping activities. The activities that involve typing help determine the word processing specialist requirements, while those activities of a nontyping nature help determine the administrative secretarial requirements. The quantity of the two types of activities has an impact on the number of personnel needed. The qualifications of the two categories of employees are based on the types of the activities they perform.

Special characteristics of work. Another factor to consider when determining the personnel requirements is the nature of any special characteristics of work. For word processing specialists, these might include considerable amounts of statistical typing, large numbers of reports, and the frequent preparation of a large number of original copies of documents. Examples of special characteristics with an impact on administrative secretaries are financial data, research projects, and materials of a technical nature, such as advertising. A large amount of unusual work, either of a typing or a nontyping nature, often results in the need for personnel with special qualifications.

Use of specialized equipment. The nature and amount of work performed in an organization may call for the use of specialized equipment. This may result in a need for personnel with special qualifications. For example, photocomposition equipment for typesetting is being utilized in an increasing number of word processing operations. Specially trained personnel are often needed to operate such devices. Equipment that integrates word processing and data processing functions might also require specially trained individuals.

Need for other types of word processing personnel. The nature and amount of work performed in an organization may require other types of word processing personnel, such as proofreaders, supply clerks, and schedulers or expeditors, in addition to those customarily found in word processing systems.

In some instances, word processing specialists are totally responsible for proofreading their work. In other instances, this responsibility might be shared by the word processing center supervisor and the specialists. In still other instances, especially when a considerable amount of statistical work is performed in the center, proofreaders are utilized. Proofreaders are also used in instances where the turnaround time is short. This enables the word processing specialists to spend more time keyboarding and less time proofreading.

When time permits, the word processing center supervisor is responsible for making work assignments. Since the supervisor may not have time to perform this function in a large-scale operation, schedulers or expeditors are used. They are generally responsible for making sure that work is completed on time as well as for preparing materials to be returned to the principals for their examination/ review.

Projected rate of expansion. To help determine personnel requirements, the projected rate of expansion of the word processing/ administrative support system should also be considered. If the analysis indicates a shortage of qualified employees at the time the system becomes functional or shortly thereafter, sufficient lead time will help assure the hiring of qualified personnel when needed. A shortage of qualified employees at any time tends to discredit the system. The blame is often placed on the system rather than on the short-term problem of personnel shortage.

DETERMINE SPACE REQUIREMENTS OF THE WORD PROCESSING CENTER

Another of the important steps in the installation of a word processing system is the determination of the center's space requirements. Before this can be done, the number of personnel who will work in the center has to be decided.

Number of employees. The number of employees directly involved in the word processing center is usually a basic determinant of the amount of equipment and furniture that will be required. As the number of employees increases, so does the amount of equipment and furniture that will be used in the center. In turn, the number of personnel is a function of the amount of work that has to be done. The task lists prepared as part of the feasibility study help determine the appropriate number of personnel for the center.

The amount of space allocated for each employee is based on the employee's job duties and the type of equipment used by the employee. To calculate the amount of square footage for each employee, the following scale is helpful:

Word processing specialist	40–60 square feet
Supervisor	70–90 square feet
Manager of word processing center	100–150 square feet
Proofreader/expeditor	60–80 square feet

Amount of equipment. Another factor that has a bearing on space requirements is the amount of equipment located in the center. Most of the text-editing equipment is a fairly uniform size. The equipment in the interactive category tends to consume more space than does the stand-alone variety. The amount of space allocated for each word processing specialist already includes the space allotted for text-editing equipment. Other pieces of equipment and the amount of space to be allocated include:

Copy machine area	50–100 square feet
Facsimile equipment	20 square feet
Photocomposition equipment	30 square feet
Central dictating unit	20 square feet

Other specialized pieces of equipment must also be taken into consideration when determining space requirements.

Amount of furniture. Although most of the furniture used in a word processing center has already been incorporated into the personnel space requirements, some exceptions exist. For example, space requirements for storage cabinets/shelves and for furniture used for breaks/rest periods must be established. The amount of furniture for breaks is determined by the number of personnel who work in the center. Appropriate space allocations for storage cabinets/shelves vary from twenty to sixty square feet, depending upon the size of the center. The break area should have from thirty to eighty square feet of space.

Projected rate of expansion. Just as the number of personnel needed for growth has to be estimated, space requirements for future expansion also have to be calculated. To plan a word processing center only to meet today's needs is not justifiable. The amount of space needed for the future can be closely approximated by calculating the space required for the additional employees who will be needed.

Other space requirements. Other factors having an impact on the amount of needed space are air circulation and corridor/aisle space. Sufficient air circulation can be achieved by adding an additional 10 to 15 percent to the total amount of space required. Aisles three feet wide are generally sufficient.

DETERMINE THE PHYSICAL LOCATION OF THE WORD PROCESSING CENTER

Once the size of the word processing center has been calculated, it is possible to select its physical location, an important determinant of the success of the operation. Several factors have to be considered when determining the appropriate location of the center. Included are such factors as proximity to users, convenience, possibility for expansion, and structural features of the facility.

Proximity. For greatest efficiency, the word processing center should be located as close as possible to those who will use its services, which can be determined by an analysis of the location of the offices of the principals. In addition, the flow of work through the organization might be used to help determine the appropriate location of the center.

Convenience. Another factor that helps determine the appropriate location of the word processing center is convenience. The center should be located where it is easily accessible—near an elevator or along a major corridor, for example. Most of the material coming into and going out of the center is likely to be carried by a messenger. However, some material is brought to the center or is taken from the center by administrative secretaries or principals.

Expansion possibilities. Although extra space for expansion is included in the original design of the word processing center, it is possible that the center may expand at a faster rate than was expected. For this reason, adjoining space suitable for expansion should be available. If such space is not available, the word processing center may have to be moved to an entirely new location at some point in the future.

Structural features of the facility. To select the appropriate location of the word processing center, the structural features of the facility must be considered. Included are such items as conduits for wires and locations of electrical outlets. In addition, wires may have to be installed to connect the dictating devices in the principals' offices to the recording units in the word processing center. When a building contains support pillars, the degree of difficulty with which equipment and furniture can be installed around them must also be considered.

DETERMINE EQUIPMENT REQUIREMENTS

The nature and amount of work are two basic determinants of the equipment requirements. Equipment typically used in word processing systems includes text editors, dictation/recording units, and copiers.

Nature of work performed. The equipment requirements/specifications are partially determined by the nature of the work performed. To illustrate, if a considerable number of forms are typed, a nondisplay text editor is preferable in most instances to a display text editor. If data or information have to be communicated from one location to another, equipment with a communicating capability is needed. If a considerable number of revisions are made, the display text editor may be more efficient than a nondisplay typewriter.

Because of the wide range of operating speeds of text-editing typewriters, turnaround times should also be considered when determining equipment requirements. The primary input methods may also have an impact on the selection of the type of text-editing equipment. Finally, if certain types of work require data/information manipulation, such as rearranging a mailing list into ZIP code order or adding numbers on a financial statement, equipment with a computing capability is desirable.

When determining the requirements of the dictating/recording equipment, several factors should be considered. If the principals would find twenty-four-hour dictation/recording service useful, a system interfaced with telephones should be considered. The same is true if most of the principals have immediate access to phones in their offices. A dictation system utilizing the principals' phones may be preferable to those systems using self-contained dictation devices.

Copier equipment requirements are determined by the number of originals that need to be copied and the number of copies needed. Generally, higher quality copy work is needed on documents sent outside the organization than on internal documents.

Amount of work. As a determinant of equipment requirements, the amount of work should be considered. Generally, as the amount of work increases, equipment with high operating speeds becomes more desirable. Of special importance is the fact that some types of text-editing equipment do not permit simultaneous input and output. This results in a decrease in the net operating speeds of the equipment. When considerable amounts of work need to be completed and a fast turnaround time is important, display text editors may be preferable to mechanical text editors since they do permit simultaneous input-output.

A thorough understanding of equipment capabilities and operating features is necessary when determining equipment requirements. Equipment vendor representatives and consultants are very helpful in matching equipment requirements and the nature and amount of work performed. The use of their services is strongly recommended.

SELECT EQUIPMENT

Once the equipment requirements have been determined, the appropriate equipment to meet the needs of these requirements can be selected. Equipment is quite variable in appropriateness, dependability, flexibility, and so forth. These are some of the factors that should be considered when selecting the equipment. Forms used for comparing various brands of equipment are discussed in Chapter 4.

Appropriateness of equipment. Once the nature of the work has been analyzed, the equipment requirements can be determined. On the basis of these requirements, the appropriate equipment can be selected. In some instances, the most suitable equipment costs more than the organization is willing or able to pay. In such cases, someone will have to determine whether or not the less suitable equipment can be justified in terms of lower cost. No matter how much the cost differential is, most of the needed features must be present on equipment to justify its selection.

Dependability of equipment. No word processing system is more effective than the equipment used in the system. Equipment that requires frequent repairs tends to have an adverse impact on the system's effectiveness.

Several methods can be used to assess the dependability of the equipment used in a word processing center. One means is to contact other users of the same type of equipment. Most vendors willingly provide the names of their satisfied users, but other users should be contacted as well. In some instances, nonreferred users may provide a more realistic assessment than the referred users. Equipment dependability can also be determined by examining reports prepared by such independent organizations as Buyers Laboratory, a New York-based testing firm.

Specifications of the equipment. Equipment specifications refer to such items as size, electrical requirements, installation requirements, and special structural requirements. Although specifications are not important in all types of equipment, they must be thoroughly considered when they are important.

Cost of equipment. Another frequently considered factor is its cost. While it is important for organizations to maximize the return on their equipment investment, some organizations place too much emphasis on the investment return. The result is likely to be the selection of equipment that may not be as dependable or as maintenance-free as equipment that costs a little more. In some instances, the lower priced equipment is not entirely suitable for the purposes for which it is to be used.

Flexibility of equipment. Increasingly, equipment used in word processing operations has provisions for add-on attachments. Several of the text-editing typewriters presently marketed have add-on features, such as a communicating unit that is used in communicating with other compatible text editors. Another feature available on some text-editing typewriters is a built-in calculator that is used to perform arithmetical functions so that, for example, the totals on a financial statement can be automatically calculated. Although the add-on features may not be needed at the time the equipment is obtained, the potential need for them should be considered when selecting equipment.

Another dimension of the flexibility factor is the use of equipment for more than one work process or activity. For example, some brands of dictation/recording units utilize a standard telephone as the dictation microphone.

Ease of equipment operation. Equipment used in word processing operations is not equally easy to learn to operate nor equally easy to operate. A useful way to assess the ease of equipment operation is to talk with users of comparable equipment. Because most equipment used in word processing is somewhat sophisticated, training time is important. The longer it takes for employees to develop an operating competency, the lower the initial production rates tend to be.

Standardization of equipment. The utilization of fairly standard equipment tends to have a positive impact on operating costs. Generally, most organizations select the same brand of text-editing typewriters when the word processing system is first installed. As equipment is traded in for new equipment, some organizations select a different brand of text editors. Because of the need to store permanently some of the magnetic cards, equipment compatibility should be considered. Not all brands of equipment are yet able to accommodate an interchange of the magnetic media on which information is recorded.

Standardization of equipment also tends to have a positive impact on maintenance charges since several pieces of equipment can be repaired during one service call. Standardization of brands also helps to reduce the costs of supplies, as the organization can take advantage of quantity buying.

Reputation of vendor. Another of the factors that needs to be considered in equipment selection is the reputation of the vendor. Specific items to be considered are age of the vendor firm, size of the firm, financial stability of the firm, and community attitude toward the firm. The overall reputation of the vendor is likely to be related to the ultimate satisfaction the organization has with the equipment.

Services provided by the vendor. Because of the specialized nature of most kinds of word processing equipment, training in the proper operation of the equipment is necessary. Although most equipment comes with fairly extensive training manuals, most manufacturers prefer to provide some hands-on training experience as well. In most cases, it is up to the vendor to provide these training experiences.

Once the system has been installed, many vendors provide a variety of support activities. Included are periodic follow-up sessions to determine how well the system is functioning. Most vendors realize that satisfied customers are a good source of advertising.

Organizations should be somewhat cautious about dealing with vendors who do not offer much in the way of training or support activities. The nature of the services provided by the vendor helps determine the vendor's reputation.

Equipment servicing and maintenance. When selecting equipment for a word processing system, the servicing and maintenance provisions are important. Malfunctioning or inoperable equipment creates serious problems in word processing systems. The fact that there are so few typewriters in the word processing center requires their proper functioning at all times.

No equipment is better than the quality of maintenance service the vendor is able to provide. Such factors as the time lapse between the service request and the equipment repair should be evaluated. In addition, the quality of service should be evaluated. An effective method for assessing these factors is to make inquiries of other clients of the vendor.

Most equipment manufacturers now provide service contracts on their equipment. While the client typically has to pay for the cost of the repair parts, the labor charges are included in the contract. Before service contracts are entered into, an analysis should be made to determine whether or not the contract is worthwhile in terms of its cost.

Leasing versus purchasing alternatives. A thorough analysis should be made of leasing and purchasing alternatives before deciding which alternative is most satisfactory. In many instances, one alternative has distinct advantages over the other.

Before deciding which alternative is more appropriate, the following questions should be answered.

1. How soon are new technological developments likely to make existing equipment obsolete? New technological developments are continually occurring in word processing equipment. If new developments will result in equipment obsolescence, equipment leasing is perhaps preferable since updating is easier with leased equipment than with purchased equipment.
2. How much money can the organization afford to invest in word processing equipment? Because of the cost of word processing equipment, some organizations find a leasing arrangement preferable. This way, capital that may be needed for other uses is not invested in expensive equipment.

3. To what extent is the organization concerned about the return on its equipment investment? If concern is great, purchasing equipment is preferable since leasing provides no investment return.
4. What kinds of leasing arrangements are the vendors willing to provide? In any geographical area, leasing arrangements provided by vendors tend to be quite competitive. In many instances, vendors tend to provide conditions that make leasing more advantageous than purchasing.
5. What is the per-unit cost of work when leasing equipment in comparison to the cost when purchasing equipment? The alternative that results in the greatest financial advantage should be given prime consideration.
6. What special provisions are made available when leasing equipment? Most lease agreements make the lessor responsible for equipment maintenance, which makes leasing a very desirable alternative.

Two different types of leases are found: true leases and leases with the option to purchase. With a true lease, the lessee never intends to purchase the equipment being leased. True leases are available for variable lengths of time and usually include a renewal provision.

A lease with an option to purchase gives the lessee an opportunity to purchase the equipment at some point in the future. At the end of the lease period, or at any point during the time the lease is in effect, the lessee has an option to purchase the equipment. The amount the lessee has paid on the lease is often applied to the purchase price of the equipment. This option gives the lessee an opportunity to determine how satisfactory the equipment is before making a purchase.

Leasing equipment results in several advantages:

1. The organization is able to utilize up-to-date equipment. When new equipment is put on the market, the old equipment can often be easily exchanged for the new equipment.
2. Lease payments of the true-lease type are tax deductible. The lease with an option to purchase is considered to be a conditional sales contract and is not deductible.
3. Leasing conserves capital that may be needed for other purposes. Some organizations find that it is financially impossible to invest working capital in word processing equipment.

Among the disadvantages of leasing office equipment are the following:

1. Leased equipment, over the long run, may cost more than purchased equipment.

2. Only true leases are tax deductible. This tends to limit the desirability of leases that contain options to purchase.

3. Some lessors require the lessee to keep very detailed records on the leased equipment. In some cases, the paperwork can become quite burdensome.

Purchased equipment has the distinct advantage of providing a return on the investment. Tax advantages result from the depreciable nature of the equipment, and tax investment credits on purchased equipment are also possible. In addition, if the equipment is purchased on time, the interest on the loan is also deductible. Finally, most equipment will still have value at the time it is traded in for new equipment.

Purchasing equipment results in two major disadvantages. Working capital is not available for other uses. Secondly, purchased equipment that is technologically obsolete is not as easily traded in for new equipment as is leased equipment.

DETERMINE FURNITURE REQUIREMENTS

The furniture in a word processing center is often used to complement the equipment that it accompanies. For this reason, equipment is generally selected before the furniture is chosen. Among the factors to take into consideration in determining furniture requirements are the nature of the employees' jobs, the design of the equipment, and the environment of the word processing center.

Nature of employees' jobs. The nature of the job of each employee who works in the word processing center should be considered when determining the furniture requirements. Furniture tends to have an impact on the efficiency with which employees are able to perform their jobs.

Employees who work in word processing centers often need to be free from distractions and to be able to concentrate. For this reason, movable partitions are frequently used in word processing centers. Figure 3–2 illustrates modular work stations with movable partitions. The partitions surround the occupant while also providing noise-deadening and aesthetic qualities. Movable partitions are often used to surround the work stations of word processing specialists, proofreaders, supervisors, and managers.

The nature of the employees' jobs will also determine how much storage space and working area are needed. An advantage of modular work stations is the number of features that are available. If considerable amounts of shelf space but little storage space is needed, for example, this can easily be accommodated by the design of the partitions.

Figure 3–2 MOVABLE PARTITIONS

Source: Courtesy of Steelcase, Inc., Grand Rapids, MI

Equipment design. Because of the rather bulky design of some of the text-editing typewriters, one has to make sure the furniture and equipment are compatible. Some brands of work stations accommodate the equipment much more effectively than do other brands. Whatever type of furniture is selected, it should be sufficiently flexible to accommodate most text-editing equipment because furniture tends to have a longer life than equipment. If old equipment is traded in for new equipment and the work station will not accommodate the new equipment, the furniture may also have to be replaced.

Environment of the word processing center. When the furniture requirements are determined, the environment of the word processing center should also be taken into consideration. The environment is affected by such elements as aesthetics, noise control, privacy, color coordination, and functionalism.

Furniture is available in a variety of sizes, shapes, and colors. Modular work stations and movable partitions are very useful for a number of purposes. Not only do they improve the appearance of the center, but they can also be used as a noise control device. The partitions can be covered with a variety of noise-deadening coverings, such as carpeting or cork. In addition, the modular work stations produce a feeling of privacy, of having one's own territory. The number of color schemes available on modular work stations/movable partitions is almost unlimited. To have a positive impact on the environment of the word processing center, furniture must be functional and useful for the purposes for which it is intended.

SELECT FURNITURE

Once the furniture requirements have been determined, the appropriate furniture can be selected. Several criteria should enter into the evaluation process, including flexibility, durability, and cost.

Flexibility of furniture. The changing nature of work processes makes it especially important for the furniture to be flexible. One of the unique features of the modular work station/movable partition concept is its flexibility. Furthermore, other components can be added later, thus enhancing the utility of the furniture.

Durability of furniture. When evaluating the suitability of furniture for use in a word processing center, the durability of the furniture should also be determined. Partition coverings, whether fabric, carpeting, plastic, or paint, should be cleanable. The partition coverings should also be easily changed. The furniture, especially the partitions and modular work stations, should also be constructed well enough to withstand dismantling and reassembling in other configurations.

Cost of furniture. Cost frequently determines whether or not certain types and brands of furniture are feasible. Indeed, in too many instances, cost is the primary factor in determining the feasibility of certain types of furniture. The result may be the selection of furniture that, although affordable, does not meet the needs for which it will be used or that is below standard quality.

PLAN THE LAYOUT OF THE WORD PROCESSING CENTER

Once the dimensions of the word processing center have been determined, the layout of the center can be planned. The layout is planned around the number of personnel who will be located in the center, the type and amount of equipment and furniture, and the impact of the environment. Factors to be taken into consideration when the layout of the word processing center is planned include work flow, space requirements, safety considerations, and communication needs.

Figure 3-3 WORD PROCESSING CENTER LAYOUT

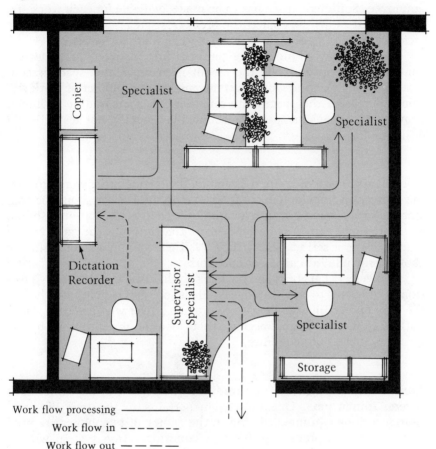

Work flow processing ——————
Work flow in – – – – – – –
Work flow out — — — —

Source: Courtesy of Herman Miller, Zeeland, MI

Work flow. To design an efficient layout of the word processing center, the flow of work through the center must be planned. Work flow refers to the movement of materials in and out of the center. The objective is to design the layout so the materials flow in as straight a line as possible, so there is no backtracking, and so the materials move a minimum distance.

Figure 3-3 illustrates the work flow in and out of a word processing center. The work flow can be determined by examining the lines that depict *work flow in, work flow out,* and *work flow processing.* Equipment items, such as the office copier and recording units, should be located near those who use the equipment. This reduces the amount of travel time to and from employees' desks to the equipment. Space requirements are also considered when planning layout, especially when determining the appropriate location of each employee. Sufficient space has to be made available for each work station as well as for the copier, the break/rest area, and for the storage area. In addition, sufficient space has to be allotted for aisles.

When the word processing center is first installed, space for expansion is provided. When the layout is planned, this space is consumed by the existing work stations and, as the number of work stations increases, the space between them is decreased accordingly. Leaving the expansion space unoccupied is generally not aesthetically desirable.

Safety considerations. When designing the layout of the word processing center, several elements that affect employee safety should be considered. For example, the location of the work stations should facilitate rapid exit. Any design feature that impedes the rapid exit of employees is a serious safety flaw. Neither equipment nor furniture should protrude into aisles or corridors.

The electrical cords and outlets should also be strategically positioned so as not to trip employees. Electrical power poles attached to the floor and ceiling can be used to provide power where needed. Floor outlets are not as flexible because their location is determined by the location of the floor conduits.

Communication needs. The communication needs in the center have several dimensions. One dimension pertains to the type of dictation/recording equipment found in the center. If telephones are used in the dictation process, a different communication system will be used from the one that would be used when the dictation units utilize self-contained dictation microphones.

Another dimension is the frequency with which the word processing specialists have to talk with principals. Perhaps the conversations will be frequent enough to warrant each specialist's having a phone. If each specialist has a phone, the telephones should not be equipped with traditional ringing devices as these tend to disturb others.

The nature and extent of face-to-face communication should also be assessed since most of the conversation will be with employees not affiliated with the word processing center. Convenience in communication is of utmost importance.

Once the proper layout has been determined, a scale model is prepared. Several devices are available for preparing the scale model, including such devices as templates, cutouts, and magnetic boards.

PLAN THE PHYSICAL ENVIRONMENT OF THE WORD PROCESSING CENTER

The physical environment of the word processing center should complement the layout of the center. Without a satisfactory physical environment, an efficient layout is meaningless.

The physical environment of the center has several important aspects, including acoustical control, lighting, air conditioning, and color coordination.

Acoustical control. The control of noise is especially important in the word processing center. When noise levels exceed a certain range, employees become fatigued, develop nervous conditions, and have high tension levels. Continuous high noise levels can cause a permanent hearing loss.

Because of the noise-producing nature of the text-editing equipment, special consideration will have to be given acoustical control. Decibels are used as the unit measure of sound. The faintest sound that can be detected by the human ear is zero decibels. The noise level for the average office is fifty decibels. Noisy offices average seventy decibels, and loud office machine rooms produce ninety decibels. The closer the sound level is to fifty decibels, the more pleasant the environment will be for the employees.

A method for controlling office noise is to use sound-absorbing materials in the center, including carpeting, draperies, and fabric on movable partitions. Carpeting can be installed on walls as well as on the floor. In addition, an acoustical ceiling is useful to control noise levels.

Sound-absorbing and sound containment devices are also used for acoustical control. The use of padding under typewriters helps absorb noise while sound-containment covers can be placed on typewriters. In addition, a noise-masking system might be installed using the public address speaker system to transmit an indistinguishable sound resembling the noise of air passing through a pipe or tunnel. The sound, which is not noticeable to humans, helps muffle voices and typewriter noise.

Lighting. Research has shown that insufficient light has a negative impact on the productivity of employees. The unit measure of light is the foot-candle, which is the amount of light produced by one candle at a distance of one foot from the candle. One watt of light per square foot produces approximately fifteen foot-candles. Between one hundred and one hundred fifty foot-candles are recommended for most types of office work.

Several types of lighting systems are utilized in offices. The most recent development is task lighting, which incorporates the light fixture into the furniture. Task lighting is commonly found in modular work stations. A light fixture, which most likely uses fluorescent bulbs, is mounted approximately three feet above the work area. Task lighting results in several advantages. Because the fixture is closer to the work surface than ceiling lighting, the light travels a shorter distance, and less wattage is needed. Because task lighting is considered to be part of the furniture, certain tax advantages are possible that are not available with ceiling light fixtures.

When a ceiling light system is used, indirect lighting is the most appropriate system for offices. With indirect lighting, 90 to 100 percent of the light is first directed upward to the ceiling and walls. The light then becomes diffused and is reflected downward to the working area. Indirect lighting eliminates most glares and shadows.

Air conditioning. Another aspect of the physical environment that must be planned is the conditioning of the air in the center. The air temperature, humidity level, circulation of the air, and cleanliness of the air are factors that must be considered.

When the humidity level of the office is within the proper range, the ideal working temperature of an office is sixty-eight degrees. In addition to the heat provided by the building's heat sources, the electrical equipment also produces heat, as do lights. A certain amount of solar heat is also found in many buildings that have numerous windows. Because of the complexity of heating-cooling systems, the services provided by professional consultants are recommended for planning this system.

Humidity level. To maximize comfort, the humidity level in an office should range somewhere between 40 and 60 percent, with the optimum level around 50 percent. An all-season air conditioning system humidifies the air in the winter and dehumidifies in the summer. Because of the impact of humidity on human comfort, proper humidity levels should be observed.

Circulation of air. If an air conditioning system is to have its maximum impact, the air in work areas must be properly circulated. Otherwise, the temperature of the air surrounding employees tends to increase, which causes a certain amount of discomfort. An air circulation exchange rate of twenty-five cubic feet per person per minute is adequate. If the circulation rate is faster than this standard, a draft is created.

Cleanliness of air. An increasing number of air conditioning systems have air-purification systems. These devices cleanse the air of germs as well as remove dust and dirt.

Color coordination. Color can impact significantly on how pleasant employees find their work areas. The psychological impact of color can affect production, fatigue, attitude, and tension. Therefore, color not only provides an aesthetic value but also a functional value.

Each color tends to have a distinct impact on the mood it creates. The cool colors—blue, green, and violet—create a calm and retiring mood. The warm colors—red, orange, and yellow—create a warm and cheerful mood. Natural colors, such as beige, buff, and off white, have a mildly stimulating effect, while deep purple and pale violet are considered to have a depressing effect. Gray tends to have a sleep-inducing impact.

CONVERT TO THE NEW WORD PROCESSING SYSTEM

When all of the previously discussed steps have been carried out, the next step is to make the conversion to the new system. The smoothness with which the conversion takes place is likely to influence employees' feelings and impressions about the system. If the conversion is marred by a series of problems, employee reaction to word processing may be somewhat less than satisfactory.

Develop efficient procedures. One factor that will have a significant impact on the success of the word processing system is the set of operating procedures. The fairly intricate nature of word processing necessitates the utilization of uniform procedures for such activities as dictation techniques, use of dictation equipment, use of handwritten materials, priority or rush jobs, editing and revising materials, duplication of documents, storage of information on magnetic media, and so forth. These are all items for which operating procedures need to be developed before the system begins functioning. Once the system is put into use, certain procedures may have to be modified. The procedures should be carefully outlined in a user's manual for the principals. The word processing specialists should also have access to a manual that outlines important procedures for them to follow.

The consultants and equipment vendor representatives who are often used in designing the word processing system are very helpful in designing operating procedures.

Develop user manual. The user manual for the principals is an extremely helpful document. Manuals have been found to be helpful in reducing training time, improving the quality of the documents, increasing productivity, and improving operating procedures. Since the quality of the manual often determines how quickly the principals learn to use the system effectively, a considerable amount of thought should go into the preparation of the manual.

The usefulness of the manual is likely to be determined by the design, wording, and format of the manual. Procedures presented in a step-by-step outline are the easiest to follow. Writing should be concise, and the content should be indexed. Specific guidelines for preparing user manuals are presented in another chapter.

Training for word processing utilization. Nearly every employee in the organization—principals and secretaries—benefits from training. The areas in which employees receive training are determined by their job titles.

Principals often receive training on the proper use of the dictation equipment, dictation techniques, and ways to improve written communication. Although this training might be provided by representatives of the vendor from whom the equipment is purchased, it might also be provided by employees who have expertise in the areas in which training experiences are provided.

Word processing specialists need training on the proper operation of the equipment, such as text editors, transcription units, facsimile devices, copiers, and so forth. This training is often provided by the equipment vendors, or employees may receive training from others who are familiar with the equipment. Also, most of the equipment is accompanied by a thorough training manual which might enable most of the employees to train themselves.

Administrative secretaries will need varying amounts of training on those tasks they perform. For example, if an administrative secretary is largely responsible for certain research activities, appropriate training should be provided.

First-time supervisors are often given training on the fundamentals of supervision, including such areas as delegating work, motivating and evaluating employees, relating to employees, and so forth.

A variety of techniques are available for training employees. The techniques range from in-house training, to training provided by a vendor, to training offered by a school. The most appropriate training technique depends on the situation for which the training is being offered. Many organizations have found the use of consultants to develop and/or teach the programs to be very advantageous.

The training of word processing specialists to use the text-editing equipment has been found to be most effective when they are able to proceed at their own rates. When training is provided by the vendor, increasingly the training takes place in the learner's organization rather than at the vendor's location. The instructor provided by the vendor helps guide the students through the training materials. These training experiences devote approximately half the training time to teaching the basic operations of the equipment and the remaining time to specific job applications.

Once training programs have been completed, their effectiveness should be evaluated. Such programs can be evaluated in several ways, including evaluating the trainee's feelings about the program. Another way is to measure how much more proficient the trainees are in the areas in which they receive training than they were before the training program was offered.

FOLLOW-UP AND EVALUATION OF THE WORD PROCESSING SYSTEM

About six months after the word processing system has been installed and is functioning, its effectiveness should be evaluated. It is difficult to justify continued use of a system that is inefficient, especially when the situation can perhaps be easily corrected.

The effectiveness of the word processing system can be evaluated in several ways. A comparative analysis of the per-unit cost of work before and after the system is installed is a possibility. The analysis should include such costs as equipment depreciation or rental charges, employee time, supplies, electricity, and space. By comparing the pre-installation costs with the post-installation costs, the system's effectiveness can be evaluated. It is normal for some new systems to cost more for a period of time than the systems they replace.

A user attitude survey can also be effectively used to determine satisfaction with the system. An attitude survey utilizes a questionnaire on which employees provide answers to several questions. A comments section should also be included to obtain suggestions for eliminating any present weaknesses.

An important part of a word processing system is the setting of production or work standards. A discussion of such standards appears in Chapter 8. The degree to which the word processing specialists are able to meet the standards is another effective means of assessing the word processing system. If the specialists continually fail to meet the standards, causes should be determined and corrections should be made.

A comprehensive efficiency analysis can also be undertaken. Answers to the following questions should be provided:

1. Has the quality of written communication improved in appearance and wording?
2. Is the turnaround time shorter than it was in the traditional system?
3. Do principals now have more time for other activities?
4. Are employees more satisfied with the procedures involved in

expediting written communication than was the case with the traditional system?

5. Is more work produced in a shorter time?

Review questions

1. What factors are considered when determining the personnel requirements of a word processing center?

2. How are the space requirements of the word processing center determined?

3. What factors are considered when determining the physical location of the word processing center?

4. When selecting equipment for the word processing center, what factors should be considered?

5. When determining whether leasing or purchasing equipment is preferable, what factors should be taken into consideration?

6. How do true leases and leases with option to purchase differ from one another?

7. When planning the layout of the word processing center, why is the flow of work through the center an important consideration?

8. What items are included in a word processing manual?

9. How can the effectiveness of a word processing system be evaluated?

Cases

The Blackburn Medical Center, located in Detroit, Michigan, is comprised of twenty-five doctors who have formed a corporation. Nearly every specialization in medicine is represented in the corporation.

The office employees have been experiencing a considerable amount of difficulty in processing the volume of paper work. Approximately half of the paper work arises from the patient-physician relationship. There is an ever-increasing amount of paper work resulting from patient referrals.

The number of records required by the federal and state governments is also rapidly increasing. Other areas responsible for generating a fairly extensive amount of paper are correspondence dealing with insurance claims, purchasing, and employee records.

About six months ago, a study was completed by a consulting firm to determine the feasibility of using text-editing typewriters in the center. The recommendation was to obtain three text editors for use in an integrated word processing structure. The doctors are trying to decide now whether the text-editing equipment should be leased or purchased.

1. Discuss the factors that should be considered in deciding whether the equipment should be leased or purchased.
2. What advantages and disadvantages result from purchasing equipment? Leasing equipment?
3. If the doctors decide to lease the equipment, what leasing alternatives are available?
4. Which alternative do you recommend? Why?

• • •

Located in Jackson, Mississippi, the ABC Corporation recently installed a word processing center. The building in which the corporation is located is about forty years old. Structurally, the building is in excellent condition.

When the word processing system was installed, the project was completed with no outside assistance. Organization employees undertook the feasibility study. When the project had progressed to the point where the equipment was selected, the planning committee met with several vendors and outlined their equipment needs. The vendor who provided the best price on the equipment was selected.

The word processing center is located at one end of the room in which the accounting department is housed. Other than the new furniture that was purchased to accommodate the word processing equipment, nothing was done to try to make the environment of the word processing center a pleasant place in which to work.

Since the time that the word processing center began functioning, the word processing specialists have been complaining about the high noise levels in the center. Because of the frequency of complaints and the dissatisfaction of the center's users with productivity levels, the firm decided to hire a consultant to make appropriate recommendations for improving the physical environment of the center. You are the consultant who is working with the organization.

1. What recommendations can you offer to help control noise levels in the center?
2. What other aspects of the physical environment do you feel should be analyzed?
3. What benefits will a more pleasant environment provide?
4. Explain how you plan to analyze and assess the environmental problems in the center.

CHAPTER 4

Equipment used in word processing

Text-editing typewriters
  STORAGE MEDIA
      Perforated paper tape
      Magnetic tape
      Cassettes
      Magnetic cards
      Magnetic paper cards
      Floppy disks
      Core memory
      Built-in storage devices
  PRINTING MECHANISMS
      Typebars
      Elements
      Daisy wheels
      Ink-jet printers
      Laser printers
  CLASSIFICATIONS OF TEXT-EDITING TYPEWRITERS
      Mechanical text editors
      Display text editors
      Communicating stand-alone text editors
      Shared-logic text editors
      Time-sharing text editors
Dictation/recording equipment
  DISCRETE MEDIA EQUIPMENT
      Portable units
      Desk-top units
      Centralized recording systems
  TRANSCRIPTION UNITS
  ENDLESS LOOP MEDIA EQUIPMENT
Copier equipment
  PLAIN-PAPER COPIERS
  SENSITIZED-PAPER COPIERS
Telecommunications in word processing
  FACSIMILE
  OPTICAL CHARACTER RECOGNITION (OCR) READERS
  TELEPHONE SYSTEMS
Photocomposition equipment
Equipment evaluation

The equipment used in word processing systems continually changes. Most of the changes are technological, which often result in changes in the applications for which the equipment is used.

Almost daily, either a new line of equipment is introduced or new models of existing equipment are announced. Like computer equipment, word processing equipment has evolved rather rapidly, most likely because of the technological advances.

A variety of equipment is used in word processing systems. Text-editing typewriters are used in the keyboarding process, dictation equipment is used for the inputting of material into the system, and copiers are used to make multiple copies of the documents prepared in the word processing center.

In addition, photocomposition equipment can be interfaced with the text editors for the typesetting of material, and facsimile devices are used to electronically transmit documents over telephone lines. Optical character recognition (OCR) equipment, which is capable of scanning or reading material typed in OCR-compatible type style and inputting the material onto a magnetic medium, is also found.

Text-editing typewriters

Of the three standard word processing equipment components—text-editing typewriters, dictation/recording units, and copiers—greater variability exists with the typewriters than with the other two types of equipment. The text editors utilize several types of storage media.

STORAGE MEDIA

An important aspect of the text-editing typewriters used in word processing is the medium on which the keyboarded material is stored. The type of storage medium used by a text editor varies according to the particular brand of equipment. When selecting text-editing equipment, the type of storage medium utilized by the equipment should be considered. These types of storage media vary in terms of cost, ease of use, durability, and amount of information that can be stored.

Perforated paper tape. A limited number of the typewriters used in word processing and some of the photocomposition units use perforated paper tape for the storage of information. As material is keyboarded, holes are punched in the tape to represent the keystrokes. As a storage medium, perforated paper tape does not lend itself to heavy editing and revising of material.

Magnetic tape. The text editor (IBM's MT/ST) that is generally credited with making word processing possible utilized magnetic tape. Resembling the tape used in tape recorders, magnetic tape is a strip of plastic coated with a chemical containing magnetized particles. Magnetic tape is either encased in cartridges or wound around reels.

Cassettes. The cassette is a strip of magnetic tape enclosed in a cassette. Although the cassette may be the same size as those used in tape recorders, some equipment uses smaller cassettes. The number of pages that can be stored in a cassette is determined by its size, but most will hold fifteen or more pages of material.

Magnetic cards. Commonly used as a storage device, magnetic cards are the same size as data processing punched cards. The cards are made by coating pieces of plastic with a magnetic particle coating. The amount of material that can be stored on the card is determined by the brand of equipment. Most cards will hold around fifty lines of information (one page singlespaced, two pages doublespaced).

Magnetic paper cards. Some brands of equipment utilize magnetic paper cards, which are generally less commonly used than other media. Paper cards—resembling punched cards in size, weight, and shape—have strips of magnetic tape affixed to one side. Cards are limited to approximately twenty lines of information.

Floppy disks. Resembling 45 rpm phonograph records, floppy disks are being used increasingly often as a storage device. The disks, which are made of plastic, hold approximately sixty pages of material per disk. Some equipment now utilizes dual floppy disks, which store material on both sides. Minidisks, which are much smaller than the standard floppy disk, are also used on some of the equipment.

Core memory. The text-editing typewriters that are interfaced with a computer are likely to utilize a core memory for information storage. Core memory, which is built into the equipment, is an internal storage medium.

Built-in storage devices. Some typewriters, such as the IBM memory typewriter, have a built-in storage device. The storage device in the memory typewriter, which can hold up to one hundred pages of material in storage, cannot be removed from the typewriter. When the storage device is filled to capacity, additional material is recorded "on top" of the earlier recorded material, erasing the earlier recorded material. Typewriters using such storage devices have limited

Figure 4–1 MAGNETIC MEDIA USED BY TEXT EDITORS

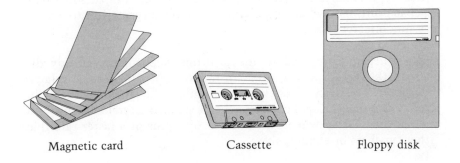

Magnetic card   Cassette   Floppy disk

usefulness in most word processing operations because of the inability to store keyboarded material permanently.

Each of the storage mediums, except for perforated paper tape, can be erased and reused. The reuse feature makes the erasable media much more useful than perforated paper tape for most of the word processing applications.

The fact that the various types of magnetic media are not compatible with one another often necessitates the need for media conversion, especially when replacing one brand of equipment with another brand. A device is available for use in converting magnetic cards to magnetic disks. For example, the 3–M Mag Card Reader/Writer transfers information from magnetic cards to disks in twenty seconds.

Figure 4–1 provides illustrations of some of the media used by various brands of text-editing typewriters.

PRINTING MECHANISMS

Just as the text-editing typewriters vary considerably in terms of the storage media they use, the typewriters also vary in terms of the printing mechanisms they use. Five printing mechanisms—typebars, elements, daisy wheels, ink-jet printers, and laser printers—are used.

Typebars. Of the five printing mechanisms, typebars are the oldest. Because of the fast typing speeds of text-editing typewriters, equipment with typebars is not as practical as some other types of equipment. Nor is equipment using typebars as competitive as other equipment because of these slow output rates.

Elements. Developed by IBM and first introduced on the IBM Selectric typewriter, elements, which are now used on several other brands of equipment, have been the mainstay of printing mechanisms.

A distinct advantage of equipment using elements is the ease with which type sizes and styles can be changed. In comparison to the typebar printing mechanism, elements enable a typewriter to operate at a much faster speed.

Daisy wheels. Compared to the printing mechanisms already discussed, the daisy wheel, first introduced in 1974, is a relative newcomer. The daisy wheel, which resembles a daisy flower, has a different letter on each spoke. Daisy wheels are also interchangeable with one another. Daisy wheels are capable of typing at a faster rate than either typebars or elements.

Ink-jet printers. Ink-jet printers, one of the newest printing mechanisms, are also among the fastest. Ink-jet printers are capable of printing speeds up to eleven hundred words per minute. The characters are formed by spraying onto paper electrostatically charged droplets of ink. Ink-jet printers were originally developed for use by computer printing equipment and were first used in word processing equipment in 1976.

Unlike the first three types of printing mechanisms, ink-jet printers are nonimpact. They are therefore noiseless since the printing device does not strike a platen.

Laser printers. First used on data processing equipment, the laser printer is being used on some of the more advanced word processing equipment. The technology of laser printers, which use laser light beams, results in a very rapid printing speed. The use of laser printers in word processing applications will undoubtedly continue to expand at a fast pace.

CLASSIFICATIONS OF TEXT-EDITING TYPEWRITERS

Text-editing typewriters are classified as either stand-alone or interactive. As the terminology implies, stand-alone text editors are basically self-contained, which means that they are not connected to other equipment components in the word processing system. Interactive text-editing typewriters, on the other hand, have a communicating capability, which enables them to interact with one another.

The two basic types of stand-alone typewriters are mechanical text editors and display text editors. The characteristics of each are discussed in the following sections.

Mechanical text editors. Comprising the largest category of text-editing typewriters, mechanical text editors are presently the backbone of most word processing installations. Mechanical text editors use a variety of storage media, including magnetic media, cassettes, and disks. They more frequently use either the element or daisy wheel as the printing mechanism, although a few use typebars.

One of the unique characteristics of typewriters utilizing a magnetic storage medium is the ease with which errors are corrected. When an error is made, the typist simply backspaces to the location of the error and types the correct character. The error is erased in memory and replaced with the correct character. Revisions in the material are easily made the same way. Once the material has been keyboarded and stored on the magnetic medium, it does not have to be retyped, except to correct errors or to change the content.

When changes are made in the material, the typist uses the automatic mode of the typewriter to output or playback the unchanged material. The typist stops the typewriter at the point of the change, keyboards the change (which automatically changes the material stored on the magnetic medium), and then puts the typewriter back on automatic mode until the location of the next change is reached.

Mechanical text editors have two components: The keyboard/ printing unit and the console. The former is used for the keyboarding and playback of material, while the console provides the typewriter with its "intelligence." The magnetic medium, when used to activate the machine during playback, is inserted in the console.

A variety of features are found on mechanical text-editing typewriters, including the following: automatic tab set; automatic margin adjust; backspace correction by letter, word, line, or sentence; automatic centering; automatic underlining; and a revision mode that allows the typist to retrieve characters, lines, sentences, paragraphs, or pages.

Some brands of standard office typewriters (IBM's Selectric in particular) are capable of being converted into mechanical text editors. A base plate, which is attached to the underside of the typewriter, is used to activate the printing mechanism. The magnetic medium is inserted in the console, which causes the typewriter to function.

The cost of and the available features on mechanical text editors vary considerably, depending on the brand of equipment. The least expensive typewriter costs approximately $4,000, while most average around $10,000. Figure 4–2 illustrates a mechanical text editor.

Display text editors. Another of the stand-alone devices is the display text editor, which utilizes a cathode ray tube (CRT), a gas plasma screen, or a matrix screen. The three components of display text editors are the keyboard unit, the screen display unit, and the printing device.

Figure 4-2 MECHANICAL TEXT EDITOR

Source: Courtesy of Adler-Royal Business Machines, Inc., Union, NJ

As material is keyboarded, it appears on the screen, not on paper, as is the case with mechanical text editors. The various brands of display text editors hold from one line to sixty-six lines of material. When all corrections have been made, the material that appears on the screen is transferred to a magnetic medium. Errors are corrected and changes are made simply by moving a cursor (or pointer) to the location of the error or change and then typing the appropriate character.

Once the material that appears on the screen has been proofread, corrected, and transferred to the magnetic medium, the magnetic device is inserted in the printer. At this point, a paper copy is prepared.

When compared with mechanical text editors, display typewriters have several distinct advantages. On most brands of equipment, the first paper draft of material prepared on mechanical text editors has strikeovers because of the error-correction process. Depending on the number of strikeovers, a second paper copy may have to be prepared for use by the principal in the review/editing process. With the display text editors, errors are corrected before the first paper copy is prepared.

Another advantage of the display editors, when compared with the mechanical editors, is the simultaneous keyboarding/playback capability. As the word processing specialist keyboards material, the

Figure 4–3 DISPLAY TEXT EDITOR

Source: Courtesy of AM Jacquard Systems, Santa Monica, CA

printing device can be simultaneously used for the output of the material. Since mechanical text editors utilize the same printing device for keyboarding and playback, simultaneous keyboarding and printing are not possible.

Finally, once the material has been transferred to the magnetic devices, changes can be made more quickly with the display text editors than with the mechanical devices. With some mechanical devices, material may have to be played out to the point where the change is to be made. If this is at the end of the material stored on the magnetic device, a time lapse occurs. The cursor on the display device can be quickly moved either vertically or horizontally to the point where the change is to be made. This eliminates having to playback all the material stored on the magnetic device up to the point of the correction.

Display devices tend to cost more ($10,000 to $20,000) than the mechanical text editors, and the material displayed on the screen tends to be somewhat difficult to read, which results in eyestrain over a period of time. Figure 4–3 provides an illustration of a display text editor.

Interactive systems, those with a communicating capability, include the following types of equipment: communicating stand-alone text editors, shared-logic text editors, and time-shared text editors. A discussion of each type follows.

Communicating stand-alone text editors. Some of the mechanical and display text editors can be equipped with a communicating component, which converts such devices to communicating stand-alone text editors. Although used primarily in a word processing capacity, communicating text editors can also be used as computer terminals. Communicating text editors are also used as terminals for Telex or TWX operations.

Communicating text editors are capable of communicating with other compatible equipment. Material is keyboarded in the same way as when a noncommunicating stand-alone text editor is used. Once the material has been approved for transmission, the telephone number of the recipient of the message is dialed. The handsets on both phones are attached to the console units and the transmission begins. A data set or modem is the apparatus that enables these devices to communicate with one another.

Communicating text editors make electronic mail or electronic document distribution possible. Rather than sending documents through the U.S. Postal Service, text editors can transmit material in a matter of seconds from one location to another. The cost of the transmission is the telephone toll charge and the electricity used to operate the equipment.

Some brands of word processing equipment are incapable of communicating with one another. Some equipment can be fitted, however, with special converters that enable two different brands of equipment to communicate with one another.

On some brands of equipment, the communicating component is an add-on device. Thus, the text editor can be obtained without the communicating package, which can be added later when the need is established. The communication component is likely to add at least $1,000 to the purchase price of the typewriter. A communicating text editor is illustrated in Figure 4–4.

Communicating text editors are often used to facilitate the communication between the home office of an organization and its various branches. The communication is fast and a written copy is provided.

Shared-logic text editors. The use of shared-logic text editors in word processing systems is increasing. Most shared-logic systems utilize a minicomputer or microprocessor as the central processing unit. Other systems use a computer that performs the organization's data processing functions.

Figure 4–4 COMMUNICATING TEXT EDITOR

Source: Photo courtesy of Wang Laboratories, Inc., One Industrial Ave., Lowell, MA 01851

In a shared-logic system, several typewriting terminals share the logic and storage component of the central processing unit. Shared-logic systems are generally in-house and are centralized throughout the organization. The sharing of the computer logic enables several office employees, each using a keyboard terminal, to work on different sections of the same document at the same time. An example is the preparation of a long report on which several employees simultaneously keyboard.

While several different types of magnetic media can be used in shared-logic systems, most use floppy disks. Many of the systems can also be equipped with visual screens. An increasing number of the systems can be interfaced with a photocomposition unit for use in typesetting, as well as equipped with communications units designed to facilitate interaction with another system. Other peripheral devices sometimes used are high-speed printers and optical character recognition readers. Both OCR readers and photocomposition equipment are discussed in another section of this chapter.

A distinct advantage of shared-logic systems is their ability to expand as the work load expands. Additional terminals can be added as the need arises.

Shared-logic systems are most useful in organizations with a large volume of reports and long documents, perhaps averaging thirty to fifty or more pages in each report. These devices range in price from $12,000 to $70,000. Figure 4–5 illustrates a shared-logic system.

Time-sharing text editors. Whereas the shared-logic systems are typically internal systems, time-sharing systems are most often external. The computer's central processing unit used in the time-sharing operation is most often owned by a service bureau. Because many organizations use the computer, or share computer time, the user cost is greatly reduced.

Typewriter terminals are located in users' offices. The terminals and the central processing unit are connected by telephone lines. Although the printed copy (output) can be received on the users' terminals, it is generally printed on a high-speed printer in the service bureau and delivered to the user.

Several large time-sharing word processing service bureaus exist. These bureaus include Browne Information Systems (New York), Pacific International Computing Corporation (San Francisco), Vitro Laboratories (Silver Springs, Maryland), and Business Information Systems (Washington, D.C.).

When investigating the practicality of using time sharing in word processing applications, special attention should be focused on the pricing structure of the arrangement. Charges are frequently broken down into the following categories: telephone connect time charges, internal processing charges, immediate access storage charges, and telephone terminal rental. Other charges may be generated by the use of high-speed printers and special processing, such as sorting information or printing in multicolumns.

One of the most significant disadvantages of using time sharing is the fact that the first paper draft is often unacceptable for revision/editing because of the numerous machine control codes that will appear on this draft. For example, if the word "stocky" were to be replaced by the word "robust" whenever the latter appeared in a certain document, the control code "r stocky; robust," would appear in the text. If these codes appear frequently, they make the first draft difficult to use in the editing/revising process.

Like shared-logic systems, time sharing is most useful for preparing long documents of thirty or more pages. If most of the material created by the principals consists of letters and memos, one of the stand-alone systems may be easier to justify.

Figure 4-5 SHARED-LOGIC SYSTEM

Source: Courtesy of IBM Office Products Division, Franklin

Some organizations utilize time sharing for work backlogs. The in-house system is continuously used and the time-sharing system is used when jobs cannot be completed internally on time. Since time sharing is a "pay when you use" system, it is likely to be financially feasible under certain circumstances.

Dictation/recording equipment

The use of dictation/recording equipment in word processing is essential. Once dictation skill is developed, the use of dictation equipment for input is much more productive than using other types of input, such as shorthand or longhand.

The dictation/recording equipment is used in the following way. The principals, using a dictation device located in their offices, dictate material, which is simultaneously recorded on a recording unit in the word processing center. The recorded material is assigned to a word processing specialist who uses a text editor to keyboard the material. The specialist uses a transcription unit to amplify the dictation.

Dictation/recording equipment is typically categorized by the type of recording media used by the equipment, either discrete media equipment or endless loop media equipment.

DISCRETE MEDIA EQUIPMENT

Dictation equipment using discrete media is very common in word processing systems. Discrete media means that the recording unit has a removable recording medium, which is placed in the transcription unit when the dictation is transcribed. The fact that the medium is removable facilitates permanent storage.

The magnetic media used in discrete media equipment consists of belts, disks, and tape cartridges or cassettes. Belts generally hold up to fifteen minutes of dictation; disks hold up to six minutes, but when stacked in a cartridge they hold up to five hours of dictation; and cassette tape holds up to two hours of dictation. In some instances, inscribed media, which provides a permanent recording that cannot be erased, is used. Instead of using a magnetic belt, inscribed media involves the use of a plastic belt.

The three types of discrete media equipment are portable units, desk-top units, and central recording systems.

Portable units. The portable units, which are battery operated, are especially desirable for those principals who travel frequently or who are out of the office a considerable amount of time. They are found in a variety of sizes, with some weighing as little as half a pound and small enough to fit into a coat pocket or a handbag. Others weigh several pounds and are somewhat larger. The portable units typically use minicassettes or belts. Whatever magnetic medium is used in the portable unit, the transcription unit will have to use the same medium unless equipment is available to convert the material from one medium to another.

Principals who are away from the office for extended periods of time find the portable units especially useful since the magnetic media can be mailed to the word processing center for transcription. The units are also extremely useful for notetaking.

Portable units have several functions, including *dictation*, *playback*, (used when the principal wishes to listen to the dictated material), *review* (used when the principal wants to listen to the last few seconds of dictation in order to determine the need to change or correct material), and *stop*.

Figure 4-6 PORTABLE DICTATION UNIT

Source: Courtesy of IBM Office Products Division, Franklin Lakes, NJ

Portable units are also equipped with an indexing system that makes a mark on a paper strip at the location of each change or correction. In some instances, changes or corrections are recorded at the end of each letter. If the word processing specialist were not aware of the corrections/changes until reaching the end of the letter, the desired corrections or changes would have to be retyped. The indexing system also makes a mark on the paper strip at the end of each letter. The specialist can thus visualize the length of the letter, which helps facilitate letter placement.

The cost of portable units varies from approximately $100 to around $400. Figure 4-6 presents an illustration of a portable unit.

Desk-top units. Many different brands of desk-top units are available. Because of their size and electrical power requirements, desk-top units are not as transportable as portable units.

Desk-top units vary according to the functions they perform. Some units can be used only to record dictation. Other units can be used only for transcribing dictation, while others have both dictation and transcription modes. In most instances, the single-mode equipment is recommended for word processing systems. The principals use equipment with the dictation mode, and the word processing specialists use equipment with the transcription mode. Rarely would either need equipment with both operating modes.

The functions found on desk-top units include those found in the portable units, in addition to a few others. A common additional feature is a warning buzzer that signals the end of the recording medium. Many of the new desk-top units also utilize electronic indexing, which replaces the "paper-strip" indexing found on the older equipment.

Although many centralized word processing systems have a centralized dictation/recording unit located in the word processing center, desk-top dictation units may also be very useful. Principals who dictate considerable amounts of material find such units useful since they don't tie up the centralized system for long periods of time. Too, with desk-top units, confidential material does not have to be stored in the central recording unit, so it is less accessible to others.

Increasing numbers of organizations are installing several smaller decentralized word processing centers rather than one large centralized center. Desk-top units are a frequently used type of dictation/recording equipment in such centers because the cost of installing a centralized dictation/recording system in each center may not be financially feasible.

The cost of desk-top dictating units varies from approximately $300 to $1100. Illustrated in Figure 4–7 is a desk-top dictation unit.

Centralized recording systems. Many large, centralized word processing centers utilize a centralized recording system. Centralized systems are of two types: private wire and telephone line.

Centralized dictation systems are most appropriate in those situations in which the principals dictate in low to medium quantities. For high-volume principals, the desk-top units are preferable to avoid making the recording equipment inaccessible to others for a long period of time. High-volume users in centralized systems have a negative impact on turnaround time.

Centralized systems function in the following way. The principal, using the dictation device (either a phone handset or a dictation microphone), is connected to the recording unit in the word processing center. When a telephone line system is used, the connection is established by dialing the telephone number of the word processing

Figure 4-7 DESK-TOP DICTATION UNIT

Source: Courtesy of IBM Office Products Division, Franklin Lakes, NJ

center. The connection in a private wire system is made by flipping a switch.

The telephone line systems use the telephone dial or keys on the touchtone phone to control the recorder functions. For example, if a principal wishes to review the last few seconds of dictation, the number 4 is dialed on a dial phone or the 4 key is depressed on the touchtone phone. Each of the vital recorder functions is controlled by the standard phone in the principal's office. Some dial phones require a key-pad device to activate the controls on the recorder unit in the word processing center.

With a private wire system, on the other hand, the buttons controlling the various recorder functions are located on the microphone or on a control box located on the principal's desk.

Depending on the brand of equipment, telephone line systems may be operable twenty-four hours a day. A dial or touchtone phone anywhere in the world can be used at any time in the dictation process.

Telephone line systems require the use of a special apparatus (either a trunk link or a recorder coupler) that interfaces the telephone equipment and the recorder equipment. Without the special device, the recorder units would not be able to accept the instructions (record, playback, review, correction, end of dictation, and so forth) controlled by the numbers on the telephone.

The number of recorders used in the central recording system is determined by the number of users and the frequency of use. Principals who frequently have to wait to use the system tend to be less satisfied than do those who have access to the system whenever desired. Central systems have the advantage of accommodating additional recorders as the need arises.

In comparison to telephone line systems, private wire systems tend to be less costly to purchase. Whereas the private wire systems cost from $600 to $1700 per recorder unit, telephone line systems cost between $1100 to $2700 per recorder unit. The telephone line systems do have the advantage of utilizing existing telephones, whereas private wire systems require the use of special dictation devices. Also, some telephone line systems can be used twenty-four hours a day anywhere in the world, provided the user has access to a dial or touchtone phone. Private wire systems, on the other hand, are functional only when the user is on the premises.

A new microprocessor-based central dictation system was recently placed on the market. The system gives users spoken instructions and warnings to enable them to dictate as properly and efficiently as possible. When a user is connected with the device, a recorded voice asks for the user's identification number, which is entered by depressing buttons on the phone, and then briefly gives all the instructions the user needs.

When using the new system, users can record in either dictation, message, or priority modes. In message mode, the mechanism automatically ejects the cassette as soon as the message is completed. The priority mode also ejects the cassette as soon as the dictation is recorded. The system provides printed information to help organize and control work flow as well as provides data for recordkeeping. For each recording, the system prints on a paper strip the following information: user's identification number, date, time, length of dictation, the status of the dictation (message, regular dictation, or priority dictation), and the time a cassette is ejected.

TRANSCRIPTION UNITS

The discrete media systems require a transcription unit for each word processing station. The units consist of the listening device (earplug or headset), a foot pedal control, and the playback unit into which the magnetic recording medium is inserted. Playback units typically have controls for volume, clarity, speed, and tone, as well as a slot into which indexing paper is inserted. The foot pedal controls the forward and reverse directions on the playback unit. Some brands also use the foot pedal control to have the machine repeat the last few words before

Figure 4-8 TRANSCRIPTION UNIT

Source: Courtesy of Lanier Business Products, Inc., Atlanta, GA

going on to the next segment of words. An illustration of a transcription unit is presented in Figure 4-8.

ENDLESS LOOP MEDIA EQUIPMENT

Unlike discrete media equipment, all endless loop media equipment uses the same type of recording medium—magnetic tape. A considerable amount of magnetic tape is enclosed in the tank component of the unit. Because each unit is equipped with both recording and transcription units, both dictation and transcription can occur simultaneously. A schematic drawing of an endless loop system is presented in Figure 4-9.

In comparison to discrete media equipment, endless loop media equipment enjoys several distinct advantages. For example, the endless loop system does not require the continual replenishment of the recording medium, as discrete media equipment does. Therefore, the recording unit attendant does not have to monitor the system as closely as required by discrete systems.

Secondly, because of the simultaneous dictation/transcription feature, the word processing specialist can begin transcribing before the principal finishes dictating, should the need arise. This is not possible with discrete media equipment since the medium has to be removed from the recorder unit and placed in the transcription unit.

Some fairly sophisticated work assignment techniques have been used in centers with endless loop media equipment. At one time, each word processing specialist was responsible for a recording unit. Depending upon the unit on which dictation was recorded, some specialists had big backlogs, while others frequently waited for material to transcribe. A new system utilizing a minicomputer assigns

Figure 4-9 SCHEMATIC DRAWING OF ENDLESS LOOP CENTRALIZED DICTATION SYSTEM

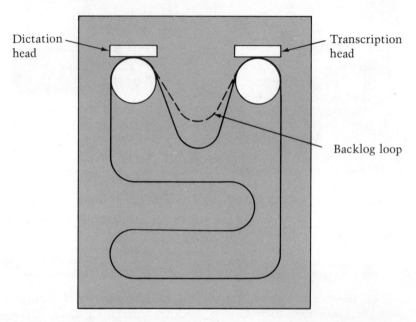

work on an equal basis, which helps make work loads more uniform.

Endless loop equipment is available for private wire and telephone line systems. The cost of a dictation/transcription endless loop unit varies from around $1,300 to more than $2,500. Unlike the centralized discrete media systems, a separate transcription unit is not needed in an endless loop media system, where the transcription unit is part of the basic tank component.

Many principals, when dictating, pause between the phrases and sentences. If the principal lets the recorder continue to run during these pauses, the word processing specialist has to "wait out" these pauses during the transcription process. The voice operated relay (VOR) device stops the recorder during the pauses and activates it again when the principal begins to dictate. The result is the elimination of periods of silence, which can increase the specialist's transcription rate by 40 to 50 percent. The relays can be used on both discrete and endless loop media equipment.

Some problems can occur with VOR devices. If they are improperly adjusted, they tend to miss the first few syllables of dictation when the recorder is activated after a period of silence. Consider, for example, the impact of clipping off the prefix "a" of "atypical," "un" of "unlikely," or "in" of "inconsistent." To make sure the recorder has been activated before again starting to dictate, some principals tap the dictation device, which produces a sound and activates the unit. Some of the newer dictation/recording units on which VOR devices are used have a buffering device, which is designed to eliminate the clipping of syllables. The buffering device stores the dictation until the recorder is fully functioning.

Copier equipment

In word processing, it is often impossible to determine which draft of a document will be the final draft until after it has already been typed. Unless a carbon copy is made of each draft of a document, which is not justifiable, the final draft emerges without a file copy. Almost without exception, file copies, or any additional copies that are needed, are made on an office copier.

The two categories of office copiers are those that use plain paper and those that require sensitized paper.

PLAIN-PAPER COPIERS

The only plain-paper copiers presently available use the xerographic copy process. Xerography is based on the physics principle that while unlike electrical charges attract each other, like charges repel one another.

The xerography process uses a camera to transmit the image of the original document to a positively charged selenium-coated drum. The nonimage areas on the original document allow light to strike the drum, which causes the positive charge in those areas to dissipate, while the image areas on the drum hold the positive charge. At this point, a negatively charged black powder is spread on the drum, and since unlike charges attract one another, the powder adheres to the areas where the images appear on the drum. This produces a reverse likeness of the original document on the drum. A piece of plain paper is passed over the drum, which causes the powder images to transfer to the paper. A heat-transfer process is used to permanently affix the powder to the paper.

Plain-paper copiers produce a quality copy without the use of chemicals or liquids, which are required by some of the sensitized paper copiers. When considering the cost per unit, plain paper copiers are most economical in high-volume operations.

SENSITIZED-PAPER COPIERS

Several different copy processes, including diffusion transfer, dye transfer, diazo, stabilization, and thermography are used by the sensitized-paper copiers. While thermography, the most popular of the processes, is a dry process, the other sensitized paper processes are wet processes.

Thermography is also known as infrared or heat-transfer process. It works on the principle that dark areas or substances absorb heat while light areas or substances do not absorb heat. The original copy is placed beneath the copy paper. As the original and copy paper are exposed to the infrared rays, the image areas on the original hold heat, which causes the sensitized paper to darken in these areas. This produces on the sensitized copy paper the images of the original document. Thermography requires the use of printing substances that hold heat long enough for the heat-transfer process to take place.

For copied documents requiring longterm storage, the thermography process is not as satisfactory as the xerographic process since the sensitized paper tends to become brittle and will darken with age.

Telecommunications in word processing

The use of telecommunications in word processing is rapidly growing. Telecommunications, the transmitting of voice and written communications from one machine to another at different locations, has significant implications for word processing.

FACSIMILE

A device becoming more frequently used in word processing is facsimile. Telecommunications is involved since facsimile devices use telephones in the transmission process. Facsimile is increasing in popularity because of the ever-increasing cost and longer delivery times of mail service.

Facsimile transmission requires two units—one at the sending location and another at the receiving end. The units are capable of both sending and receiving functions. When transmitting, the original document is placed on the sending unit and the recipient's telephone number is dialed. Once the connection is made, the telephone handsets are attached to their respective units. When both units are activated, the transmission process begins. Some devices are capable of transmitting a full page in fifteen seconds. Virtually anything, including handwritten or typed material and photographs, can be transmitted.

Facsimile processes are either analog or digital. The analog process involves scanning everything on a page, line by line. This process is also capable of reading white, black, and gray. When a high-quality reproduction is required on specialized work, such as blueprints or x-rays, the analog process is frequently used. The digital process, which also reads line by line, reads only black and white. Of the two, the digital process is capable of a much faster transmission rate.

The flexibility of facsimile makes its use very practical. Portable units are available that can be used by traveling executives to transmit materials back to the word processing center.

A distinct advantage of some facsimile units is their ability to operate unattended. Some equipment is capable of automatic dialing and transmission at preset times. When long distance phone rates are at the lowest level, the transmission can take place in the absence of an operator at either or both the sending and receiving locations. Some facsimile devices have automatic document feed apparatuses that facilitate the transmission of documents without human intervention. Another feature found on some equipment is polling, which enables one unit to call another attended or unattended unit to receive messages.

A fairly new development in facsimile technology interfaces fac-simile units with computers. This makes it possible to enter the transmitted material into computer memory. Other systems interface facsimile and copiers.

Before installing a facsimile system, a thorough communications network analysis should be made. Answers to the following questions should be obtained:

What information is sent where?
What transmission methods are used?
How much information has a high-priority value?

An illustration of a facsimile unit is presented in Figure 4–10.

OPTICAL CHARACTER RECOGNITION (OCR) READERS

Another device in word processing that utilizes telecommunications technology is the OCR reader. This device contains a scanner that reads typewritten pages. Using a standard office typewriter fitted with OCR-compatible type style, the material is keyboarded. At this point, the document might be returned to the principal for review. Upon the return of the document, which contains the revisions, the document is placed in an OCR reader which scans the characters and records them on a magnetic medium. The revisions are keyboarded on a text editor using the same type of magnetic medium. The text editor makes the corresponding changes on the magnetic medium, which is then in-serted in a printer device to obtain a final draft. Figure 4–11 illustrates this process.

Figure 4-10 FACSIMILE UNIT

Source: Credit, Xerox Corporation

Not only is OCR used in the output of material, but it is also extensively used for the input of external materials into a system. Suppose, for example, a long report is received from someone outside the organization. Perhaps there are certain sections of the report the recipient organization would like to store on a magnetic medium. If the report is typed in the OCR-compatible type style, the pages can be inserted in an OCR reader, which records the material on the magnetic medium. Then, when the various sections of the report are used, the material is already stored on a magnetic medium that eliminates the need for keyboarding.

Organizations that have branches or divisions located across the country find OCR equipment very convenient for the inputting of each division's materials into the system. Once the material is stored on the

Figure 4–11 OCR WORKFLOW CHART

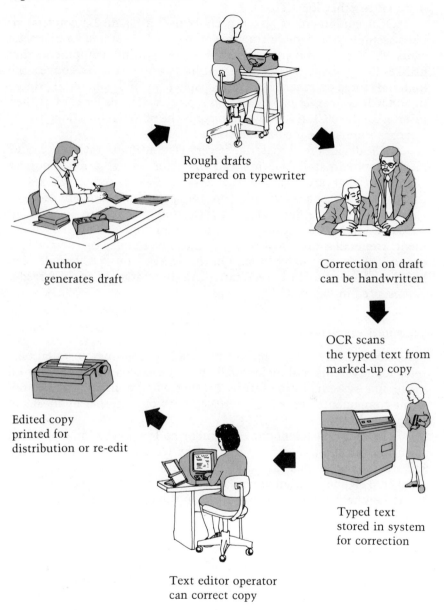

Rough drafts
prepared on typewriter

Author
generates draft

Correction on draft
can be handwritten

OCR scans
the typed text from
marked-up copy

Edited copy
printed for
distribution or re-edit

Typed text
stored in system
for correction

Text editor operator
can correct copy

A word processing system using optical character recognition

Source: Courtesy of Hendrix Electronics, Manchester, NH

medium, communicating text editors can be used to transmit the material to other locations.

OCR equipment is also especially useful for media conversion. Let's assume considerable amounts of material are stored on magnetic cards. If the organization purchases text-editing equipment that utilizes floppy disks, media incompatibility will result. To convert the material stored on magnetic cards, a paper copy of the material printed in an OCR type style is prepared on a printer. The paper copy is then inserted in the OCR reader which records the material on a floppy disk, thus accomplishing media conversion.

OCR devices read material at very fast, accurate rates. The error rate is approximately one misread character for every ten thousand characters that are read by the device. Two common causes of misreading are specks of dirt on the paper and broken or light characters. OCR readers range in price from $14,000 to $50,000. In large operations, the use of OCR readers helps reduce the cost of equipment. Generally, one OCR reader is capable of replacing the need for approximately ten text editors. On the average, one OCR reader can handle the output of forty secretaries. An illustration of an OCR reader is presented in Figure 4–12.

TELEPHONE SYSTEMS

Now extensively used in many word processing installations, telephone systems will undoubtedly be more extensively used in word processing systems in the future. An increasing number of the equipment components are being interfaced with one another by means of telephone lines.

The fact that telephone equipment no longer has to be obtained from the telephone company but can be leased or purchased from a private telephone manufacturer has resulted in a very competitive market. Telephone interconnect is responsible for the development of many new telephone features—much to the customer's benefit.

Photocomposition equipment

Increasingly, word processing equipment is interfaced with photo-typesetting or photocomposition equipment that is used in printing operations. In comparison to the old methods of typesetting, photo-typesetting is relatively simple.

Three categories of typesetting are presently available: direct-input, tape-operation, and computer systems. The first two categories have a closer relationship to word processing than do computer

Figure 4-12  OCR READER

Source: Courtesy of Hendrix Electronics, Manchester, NH

systems. Direct-input interfaces a text editor (input unit) and a type-setter (output unit). The prices of direct-input systems range from $10,000 to $17,000. Figure 4-13 provides an illustration of a direct-input photocomposition unit.

Tape-operation systems are more sophisticated than are direct-input systems, since input, processing, and output can be carried out without human intervention. Input is prepared on a keyboard and is stored on a magnetic tape, which is then processed on a typesetter. Type (output) appears after development. Because of the intelligence of this equipment, several typesetting functions can be performed automatically that have to be manually performed in direct-input systems. One such function is automatic hyphenation of divided words.

Figure 4-13  DIRECT-INPUT PHOTOCOMPOSITION UNIT

Source: Courtesy of Itek Graphic Products, Division of Itek Corporation

The use of typeset materials, as opposed to regular typewritten materials, is advantageous for certain documents. Typesetting reduces the amount of printing space by about 40 percent—which significantly reduces paper costs. Secondly, typeset material has a more pleasant appearance than does typewritten material.

As word processing and printing technologies continue to develop, a closer relation between the two will result. The merging of the two technologies will facilitate the development of more efficient, better quality, and lower cost processes.

Equipment evaluation

The increasing amount of equipment used in word processing operations makes it even more important—and difficult—for equipment users to make sure they are getting the most appropriate equipment for the given situation. Without comparing equipment, it is difficult to be certain the most appropriate equipment was chosen.

One effective means of making a comparative evaluation of equipment is to use a checklist on which data about various equipment specifications and features are recorded. By completing a checklist for each brand of equipment being considered, the purchaser can make a comparative analysis. Figures 4–14 and 4–15 illustrate checklists for text-editing equipment and dictation/transcription equipment.

A variety of periodicals also contain compiled comparative data about various types of equipment used in word processing. Among the periodicals are *Administrative Management, Word Processing World,* and *Word Processing Report.* Since the information is frequently updated, it provides a useful source when comparing various brands of equipment. Figure 4–16 illustrates comparative data information.

Another source which provides data on equipment is *Datapro Reports,* a monthly publication of Datapro Research Corporation.

Review questions

1. What types of storage media are utilized by text-editing typewriters?
2. How do stand-alone text editors and interactive text editors differ from one another?
3. What are the advantages of display text editors when compared to mechanical text editors?
4. In what respects do discrete media dictation equipment and endless loop equipment differ?
5. What is the primary function of the voice-operated relay device?
6. Explain the uses of facsimile in word processing systems.
7. What are the advantages of using optical character recognition in word processing operations?
8. What is telephone interconnect?
9. What printed sources of information are available for use in comparatively evaluating word processing equipment?

Figure 4-14 EVALUATION CHECKLIST FOR TEXT-EDITING EQUIPMENT

TEXT-EDITING EQUIPMENT CHECKLIST

MACHINE CONFIGURATION

Storage
- ☐ Single ☐ Dual ☐ Card ☐ Tape ☐ Standard diskette ☐ Mini diskette ☐ Hard sectored
- ☐ Soft sectored

Number of characters _____, Pages _____

Buffer capacity _____

Video Display
- ☐ Black/white ☐ Green/white ☐ Other
- ☐ Single line ☐ Partial page ☐ Full page
- ☐ Reverse video ☐ Wide screen ☐ Variable brightness
- ☐ Scrolling ☐ Graphics capabilities
- ☐ Number of characters per line _____, Lines per screen _____

Printer
- ☐ Impact ☐ Matrix ☐ Ink jet ☐ Character ☐ Line
- ☐ Separate from Keyboard

Speed _____

SPECIFIC APPLICATIONS

Type of job _____

Comments:

Set up _____

Input _____

Proofing _____

Editing _____

Printing _____

SERVICE

Maintenance

Size of organization _____, How long in business _____, Location and staffing of closest service point _____

Promised response time for emergency service _____, Hours during which service available _____

Nature and frequency of preventive maintenance _____, Size and location of spare parts inventory _____

STANDARD CAPABILITIES

Functions

☐ Insert ☐ Delete ☐ Center ☐ Underscore ☐ Decimal alignment ☐ Move ☐ Copy ☐ Sort ☐ Search and replace ☐ Forms fill-in ☐ Repagination ☐ Footer and header control ☐ Footnote placement ☐ Right-hand margin adjust ☐ Automatic hyphens ☐ Glossary ☐ Mathematical capabilities

Intelligence

☐ Hard wired ☐ Microprocessor based ☐ Terminal has own processing capability ☐ Processing capability in host computer only

Ease of reprogramming to perform additional functions: ☐ Replace circuit board ☐ Insert program from floppy disk ☐ Key in changes on function keys ☐ Main memory expandable ☐ Initiates more than one task at a time

Communications

Code: ☐ ASCII ☐ Baudot ☐ Correspondence ☐ EBCDIC ☐ Other
Convention: ☐ Asynchronous ☐ Synchronous
Protocol: ☐ Bisynchronous
Emulation: ☐ IBM 2741 ☐ IBM 2770 ☐ IBM 2780 ☐ IBM 3780 ☐ TTY ☐ Univac 1100 ☐ Other

Procedure for handling engineering change orders
_____

Scope of vendor's training program for service technicians _____, Who does _____, How long _____, Follow up _____

Additional Services

Machine delivery time _____
☐ Basic training ☐ Advanced training ☐ Help with difficult applications ☐ Supplies available
Cost of ribbons _____, Media _____, Print wheels _____
Peripherals available
Cost of OCT _____, Photocomposition _____,
Other _____
Names of vendor's customers using this type of equipment
_____
_____
_____

PRICE FACTORS

Outright purchase _____, Purchase/leaseback _____, Option arrangement _____, Rental _____

Includes: ☐ Service ☐ Installation fees

Figure 4-15 EVALUATION CHECKLIST FOR DICTATION/TRANSCRIPTION EQUIPMENT

DICTATING AND TRANSCRIBING EQUIPMENT ANALYSIS

MFGR. _____ MODEL _____ PRICE _____ TYPE: □ Desktop □ Portable

SIZE _____ WEIGHT _____

POWER

□ Electric _____ Volts
□ Ground Cord
□ On Demo
  □ yes □ no
□ Available
  □ yes □ no

□ Batteries
  Number _____
  Type _____
  Life _____
  Cost _____
  Battery Strength Indicator □ yes □ no

RECORDING MEDIA

1. Belt □ embossed
      □ magnetic
2. Disc □ embossed
      □ pre-grooved
      □ magnetic

3. Tape □ spools
      □ cartridge
      □ cassette

Re-usable □ yes □ no

Price _____
Weight _____
Mailing Information: _____

Adaptable to other equipment: □ yes □ no
Kind _____

Tape Speed: _____
Record Time (one side): _____
Ratio: Rewind to Record _____ to 1

Rewind Time: _____
Fast Fwd. Time: _____
Ratio: Fast Fwd. to Record _____ to 1

CONTROLS

On Machine

☐ Automatic Backspace ☐ Variable Backspace ☐ Record ☐ Playback ☐ Rewind
☐ Fast Fwd. ☐ Fast Erase ☐ Fast Rewind ☐ Volume Control ☐ Digital Counter
☐ End of Tape Signal ☐ Tone Control ☐ Speed Control

Foot Pedal Controls _____

Correction Method: ☐ Erase and redictate
              ☐ Notes on index strip
              ☐ Other _____

Microphone: ☐ Remote ☐ Self contained ☐ Dual microphone speaker
Visual indicator to show that dictation is being recorded ☐ yes ☐ no

On Microphone

☐ Record
☐ Playback
☐ Rewind
☐ Index correction
☐ Index end of letter
☐ Other _____

Reproduction Quality _____

Machine can be used to record conferences ☐ yes ☐ no

If portable—is it comfortable to hold ☐ yes ☐ no
           —convenient to use ☐ yes ☐ no

Accessories: ☐ Carry Case $ _____
            ☐ Stethophone $ _____
            ☐ AC Converter $ _____
            ☐ Battery Recharger $ _____

☐ Telephone Pickup $ _____
☐ Foot Control $ _____
☐ Other $ _____

Warranty (parts and labor): _____
Cost of Annual Service Contract: $ _____

Source: Walter A. Kleinschrod, _Management's Guide to Word Processing_, Chicago: The Dartnell Corporation, 1977, p. 160.

Figure 4–16 PRINTED EQUIPMENT EVALUATION DATA

BUYER'S GUIDE TO WORD PROCESSORS

MANUFACTURER / Reader Service Card No.	MODEL	PRICE	Information Stored On	Storage Capacity	Words Per Minute	Auxiliary Input	Auxiliary Output	Stored Information Locator	Visual Display	Line Counter	Automatic Underlining	Changeable Type	Half Spacing	Keyboard Error Corrector	Justification
Addressograph Multigraph Corp. Circle No. 584	AMtext 225	$3,995.00	1	120,000[3]	15.5[4]	2	2, 6, 7	9	•	•	•	•	•	•	•
	AMtext 425	14,500	2	250,000	660	1, 2, 5	1, 5, 6, 8	10	•	•	•	•	•	•	•
Anderson Jacobson, Inc. Circle No. 585	1522	18,150	11, 12	635,000–[3] 2.6 million	45-120[4]	8, 14, 15, 16	8, 17, 18, 19		•		•	•	•	•	•
	1562	27,270	11, 12	10-40 million[3]	300[13]	8, 14, 15, 16	8, 17, 18, 19		•		•	•	•	•	•
Applied Computer Systems Circle No. 586	SA400-WP	15,000	20	1 million[3]	300	14	19	23	•	•	•	•	•	•	•
	SA300-C	7,000.00	21	64,000[3]	300	22	22	23	•	•	•	•	•	•	•
	SA300-WP1	8,000.00	20	500,000[3]	300	14	22	23	24	•	•	•	•	•	•
	SA300-WP2	9,000.00	11	1 million[3]	300	14	22	23	24	•	•	•	•	•	•
Digital Equipment Corp. Circle No. 599	WS78-AA	9,995.00	11	125[53]	540	31, 51	6, 54	14, 48	•	•	•	•	•	•	•
	WS78-CA[51]	10,495	11	125[53]	540	31, 51	6, 54	14, 48	•	•	•	•	•	•	•
	WS200	15,495	29, 52	125–[53] 2000	540	31, 51	6, 54	14, 48	•	•	•	•	•	•	•
Documation, Inc. Circle No. 600	DOC 5000	12,500	35	5100–[3] 10,200	500						•	•	•	•	•
Edit Systems, Inc. Circle No. 601	Text Ed II	55	20, 56	500,000–[3] 788,000	700-1200	15, 16, 31, 57	6, 16, 19, 26, 43, 57	58		•	•	•	•	•	•
	Text Ed III	55	20, 56	500,000–[3] 788,000	700-1200	15, 16, 31, 57	6, 16, 19, 26, 43, 57	58		•	•	•	•	•	•
Four-Phase Systems, Inc. Circle No. 602	ForeWord	59	32, 25	100,000[53]	500	32	32	60		•	•	•	•	•	•
General Computer Systems, Inc. Circle No. 603	DT IV/8	61	25	10-80[3] million	540–3000	16, 32	32	63		•	•	•	•	•	•
	DT 11/8	62	25	10-80[3] million	540–3000	16, 32	32	63		•	•	•	•	•	•

Source: The Office, November, 1978, p. 105

Cases

The headquarters of Irwin Plastic Corporation, located in Des Moines, Iowa, is currently in the process of installing a word processing system. An outside consultant concluded that savings of 5 to 7 percent in operational costs could be realized by converting to a word processing system. The consultant recommended, on the basis of the needs of the organization, that a decentralized center approach be used. According to the consultant, this approach would be much better than a centralized structure, and neither the combination nor integrated approach would be suitable.

The organization's planning committee concurs with the consultant about the use of decentralized centers. The executives responsible for making all final decisions about the word processing system also agree that a decentralized structure appears to be most suitable for the organization.

The various members of the planning committee have been talking with several equipment vendors lately to try to determine which text-editing equipment would be best for the organization. The committee members are experiencing difficulty in making a valid comparison since the various pieces of equipment are evaluated on so many different factors. It has been suggested to the chairperson of the committee that an equipment comparison form be developed to help evaluate the various brands of equipment.

1. What items do you feel should be included on the form to help evaluate the various brands of text-editing typewriters?
2. How can the planning committee be certain that the evaluation results are accurate?
3. What advantages will result from the use of such an evaluation form?

• • •

The law firm of Smith and Jones, which is located in Poplar Bluff, Missouri, has been using text-editing typewriters now for nearly five years. Because of the no-erasure requirement of certain legal documents and the frequent need to revise documents as well as make multiple copies repetitively, the purchase of text-editing equipment was a logical decision. The firm has been able to expand its client load without making corresponding increases in the number of secretarial employees.

The text-editing equipment purchased five years ago falls under the classification of mechanical text editors. It has been very serviceable and has required only insignificant maintenance and repairs. Because of the amount of use of the equipment and its extent of depreciation, the law firm is now contemplating the replacement of the original text editors with new equipment.

Before deciding on the most appropriate equipment for the firm, the administrative office manager decided that the equipment of several vendors should be evaluated. The vendors who sell the mechanical text editors claim their equipment would best meet the needs of the firm while the vendors who sell display text editors, of course, favor their equipment. The administrative office manager has a dilemma—which type of equipment to choose.

1. What are the unique characteristics of mechanical text editors? Of display text editors?
2. What are the advantages and disadvantages of each type of equipment?
3. What type of equipment do you favor? Why?
4. Do you feel the use of shared-logic equipment in this situation has merit? Why?

CHAPTER 5

Input-output processes in word processing

To thoroughly understand the word processing concept, familiarity with various aspects of input and output processes is very important. The success of the word processing system is often determined by the efficiency with which the various input and output processes are carried out.

Input

In word processing, input refers to raw information, which, when processed, results in the preparation of a document.

CATEGORIES OF INPUT

Several categories of input are used in word processing, including the following: longhand, machine dictation, form letters, dictation at the typewriter, and form dictation.

Longhand. Reports indicate that when using traditional procedures for processing information, executives write out as much as 85 percent of their correspondence. The use of longhand has the advantage of permitting the principal to outline thoughts, to draft the material, and in some cases, to refine the material before it is keyboarded.

Disadvantages include the high cost that results from the time involved and the waste of the typist's time in transcribing longhand that is often difficult to read.

Research shows that greater efficiency can be achieved when principals use machine dictation rather than longhand, especially when originating short-to-moderate length documents that have an uncomplicated format.

Machine dictation. With the growing concern for increasing productivity and reducing operational costs, the use of machine dictation in word processing is very desirable. In today's offices, the use of dictation/recording equipment plays a major part in the communication cycle, and the number of dictating machines used in the business world is expected to more than double between 1976 and 1986.

Machine dictation provides these advantages:

1. Improves executive creativity and productivity
2. Improves productivity of office employees
3. Increases flexibility in personnel utilization
4. Enhances the cost effectiveness of the operations

The fourth advantage merits special emphasis. In many cases, implementation of word processing is a direct effort to cut costs within the organization. The dictation component is crucial to the success of the word processing system. Since the cost of preparing and sending an average length business letter can be reduced as much as 20 to 25 percent when using machine dictation rather than longhand, machine dictation is the more cost effective of the two alternatives.

The primary disadvantages of machine dictation result from the improper selection and use of the equipment and the lack of a commitment by principals to follow established procedures when using the equipment.

Form letters. Form letters, which are repetitive letters sent to a number of people, are very efficiently prepared on the text-editing typewriters found in word processing installations. The body of the letter is stored on an appropriate magnetic medium. The constant material that appears in each letter is played out automatically, while the word processing specialist manually keyboards the variable information. Such items as the date, inside address, salutation, and dollar amounts are examples of variable information.

The use of form letters enables organizations to achieve economy and efficiency as well as to experience the advantage of having an originally typed letter containing personalized information.

Dictation at the typewriter. Some executives dictate isolated tasks to a word processing specialist who keyboards the material as it is being dictated. Dictation at the typewriter results in rough-draft copy. After the dictation is completed, the final copy is prepared. This infrequently used input format is generally designed to accommodate a special need of a principal.

Form dictation. As the principal dictates, the word processing specialist types information on printed form documents. Form dictation, which is used rather infrequently, is most likely to be used in processing work of a rush nature.

When principals input material into the word processing system, it is crucial that established procedures be followed. Because input procedures are often custom designed for the organization, they are efficient and justifiable in terms of costs. To assure compliance, procedures should be outlined in the principals' user manual.

DEVELOPING EFFICIENT INPUT PROCEDURES

Developing efficient input procedures requires the cooperation of principals and word processing specialists. While some of the data gathered during the feasibility study will be helpful in designing efficient input procedures, additional information may also have to be gathered. The procedures outlined in the following sections will be helpful when developing efficient input procedures.

Analyzing work flow. To help meet changing needs and to reduce operating costs, analysis of work flow should be a continuing process in developing efficient input procedures. It is especially significant in word processing to analyze work flow when organizational procedures change or when new equipment is installed.

Analysis of work flow in word processing involves examining the type and frequency of documents and the distribution of documents within the word processing center. Where applicable, the analysis may be extended to the administrative support service areas as well. Information to be gathered is based upon such records as the following:

1. Total count of each category of work completed, including letters, reports, statistical documents, etc.
2. Time involved in completing each category of work.
3. Breakdown of time for the various steps involved in each type of work to be completed.
4. Number of times each category is changed, edited and retyped, and the amount of repetitive typing.

Certain basic considerations applicable to analyzing the flow of work may be summarized as follows:

1. Record work flow on a chart depicting the layout of the office as a means of identifying backtracking and crisscrossing operations.
2. Prepare flow process charts of major procedures involved in the study, paying particular attention to the distances mapped and the delays recorded.
3. Measure the total work production involved in each process and compare this information with other related information. For example, compare longhand input, rough draft, prerecorded documents, dictated documents with stored variables, etc.
4. Observe the workloads of employees. Determine whether or not some employees seem to be constantly under heavy workloads while others have little or no work to process.
5. Determine the work flow pattern for major jobs or high-volume documents. As nearly as possible, work should flow forward in a straight line.

Designing work flow. When an organization makes a decision to convert to word processing, the application of office layout principles is important because of space needs, equipment costs, and supervisory considerations. When work flow changes, the layout of the center may also have to change. This is one of the reasons many organizations have installed portable work stations in word processing centers.

When designing the work flow in a word processing center, the following points should be considered:

1. Design work flow so backtracking is held to a minimum.
2. Locate the word processing center as close as possible to the principals who use it.
3. Allocate adequate space allowances to enhance work flow and employee comfort.
4. Provide adequate space in work stations to accommodate the employee and the employee's need for specialized equipment.
5. Locate supervisory personnel near the entrance to the center if they are responsible for input-output functions.

Outlining work flow. Work flow begins with the principal who originates words that comprise a document. This process may be quite direct in a small organization where the correspondence flows from principal to word processing supervisor, to, perhaps, an assistant supervisor who is responsible for controlling and scheduling work, and finally to the word processing specialist who processes the document.

Figure 5-1 FLOW CHART

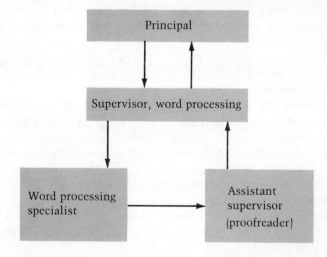

In many organizations, the correspondence is routed directly to the word processing specialist from the supervisor, and the assistant supervisor is responsible for proofreading before the completed work leaves the word processing center. This procedure is illustrated in Figure 5-1.

The following outlines the flow of work in a centralized word processing system in a law firm:

> The work flow starts with an attorney (principal) who originates a legal document. In the case of a complex agreement (international construction or a large manufacturing purchase, for example), the first document draft is usually a rough draft, rarely close to final form. The attorney sends the first draft to the center supervisor who logs the work, schedules it, fills out a work assignment card, and assigns the job to a word processing specialist.
>
> The specialist keyboards the document and stores the material on a magnetic medium. The first typed draft of the document is then returned to the attorney, who makes changes or additions, or places new instructions on the document. The document is returned to the center where the supervisor logs and schedules the revision work. The word processing specialist (most likely the one who first keyboarded the material) then retrieves the magnetic medium on which the material is stored. The unchanged portions of the document are automatically played out, while the specialist manually keyboards the changes desired by the principal.
>
> The new draft is returned to the attorney who either makes additional changes on this draft or approves the document for final distribution.

Figure 5-2 illustrates this work flow design. A variation of the work flow process, illustrating a plan used in a hospital, is presented in Figure 5-3. This outline provides for establishing work priority immediately after the document enters the word processing center.

After the material is sent to the word processing center, the word processing specialist determines whether the material is original or whether it is to be revised. After keyboarding, proofreading, and correcting, the final copy of the document is returned to the principal.

PROCEDURES INVOLVED IN THE INPUT OF MATERIAL INTO THE WORD PROCESSING CENTER

Material to be processed in the word processing center typically arrives in either of two ways: as dictation recorded on a recording device or on

Figure 5–2 WORK FLOW

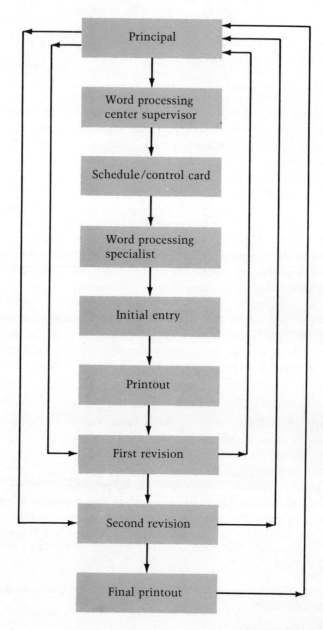

paper delivered by either mechanical or human means. Most word processing installations make extensive use of both methods.

When discrete media dictation/recording equipment is used, the equipment has to be closely monitored to assure the availability of a sufficient quantity of recording media (belts, disks, diskettes, or cassettes). If no media are available, the principal is unable to record dictation. For materials that are carried in, an employee (usually the supervisor) has to be available to receive the materials.

When production jobs are received in the word processing center by either of the two means discussed above, they are generally entered into a log book. This makes it possible to determine rather quickly and easily the status of any given job as well as helps identify the nature and number of production jobs to be processed at any given time.

Another important aspect of the procedures involved in the input of material is the assignment of each production job to a word processing specialist. The supervisor, assistant supervisor, scheduler, or some other designated individual is often responsible for assigning jobs to specialists. The unique qualifications of the word processing specialists are likely to be considered in assigning nonroutine jobs.

IMPROVING DICTATION SKILLS OF PRINCIPALS

Since dictation/recording equipment is essential to word processing, principals must become familiar with the use of this equipment. If, for example, a centralized dictation system interconnected with the organization's telephone is used, principals must first dial a number (usually three to seven digits) to access the recorder in the word processing center. A one-digit number is used to activate the recorder, another one-digit number is used to review the material, and so on. Specific instructions for beginning to record, reviewing, and making changes in dictation as well as for giving special instructions and ending dictation are usually provided by the equipment vendor.

In addition, instructions may be provided to help principals prepare for dictation and to communicate effectively with the word processing specialist. Such instructions may include tips on preparing for dictation and giving instructions at the beginning of, during, and after dictation. The checklist presented in Figure 5–4 illustrates points the dictator may wish to review. Figure 5–5 provides an example of how errors can occur, increasing the turnaround time of the document being prepared.

Since a major portion of the dictated material is to be transcribed in either standard letter format, memorandum format, or tabular format, the following instructions may be helpful:

Figure 5–3 WORK FLOW

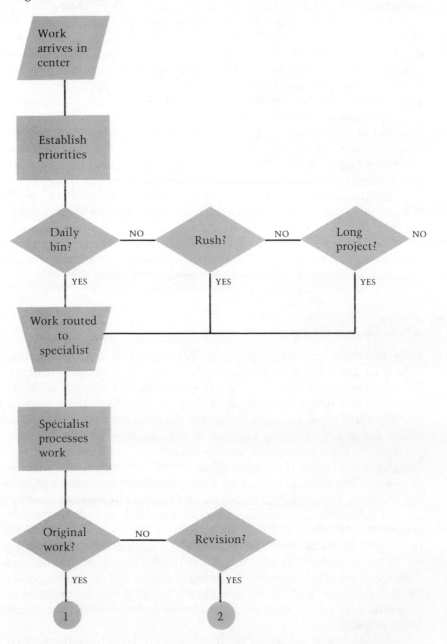

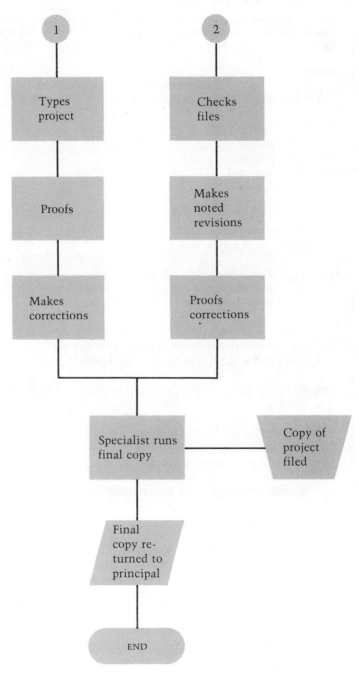

Source: Courtesy of Lincoln General Hospital, Lincoln, NE.

Figure 5-4 DICTATOR'S CHECKLIST

This is a checklist of instructions to be given before, during, and after your dictation:

BEFORE:
  1. Identify yourself—name, position, and department.
  2. State type of document dictation:

> Letter
> Memo
> Report
> Proposal
> Contract
> Form number

  3. State number of copies.
  4. State type of transcription.

> Rough draft
> Revision
> Final draft

  5. State type of stationery to be used (letterhead, plain, etc.).
  6. State special instructions—format, spacing, etc.
  7. Name and address of recipient—spell out.

DURING:
  1. Spelling:

> All names and addresses
> Technical/unusual words
> Words commonly confused

  2. Special punctuation and format, such as:

> Underscoring
> Capitals
> Tabulations
> Indentations
> Paragraphing

  3. Closing, only if differing from Item 1, "Before" section.

AFTER:
  1. Names and addresses of persons receiving copies.
  2. Enclosures.
  3. Instructions for retention of magnetic medium.

How to dictate a standard letter

1. This is (your name) of (department).
2. This is a letter to be typed on letterhead, with (number) copies required.
3. It is addressed to (spell proper names, give full address).
   For example,

   Mr. John Carey (C-A-R-E-Y)
   The James Hugghoffer (H-U-G-G-H-O-F-F-E-R)
       Company
   4316 (four-three-one-six) Grand Avenue
   Lincoln, Nebraska 68512 (six-eight-five-one-two)

4. Dear John.
5. Dictate body of the letter, indicating paragraphs and punctuation when possible.
6. Dictate the complimentary closing and your name and title.
7. There will be (number) enclosures.
8. A copy is to go to (name and title).

How to dictate a memorandum

1. This is (your name) in (office/division).
2. (Number) copies will be required.
3. This is a memorandum.
4. It is to be addressed to (name/title/department).
5. It is from (your name and title).
6. Dictate the subject and message, indicating paragraphs and punctuation when possible.
7. There will be (number) of enclosures/attachments.
8. Address an envelope to (name[s] and address[es] of recipient[s].

How to dictate tabular format

1. This is (your name).
2. This is an (external letter). The body will contain (a short three-column table indented from the left).
3. It is addressed to (name and address of recipient).
4. Dictate salutation.
5. Dictate body of letter to point of tabular material.
6. The following will be in three columns. Underline the headings. The headings are: First column, *Model*; second column, *Serial Number*; third column, *Age in Years*. Next line. Column 1, 1123; Column 2, 123456; Column 3, 10. Next line.

Figure 5–5 ILLUSTRATION OF HOW ERRORS ARE MADE

DICTATION VS. TRANSCRIPTION EXAMPLE

The letter on the left (below) appears as the principal thought it would appear at the time of dictation. However, because of incomplete dictation instructions, the secretary transcribed it as it appears on the right (below).

Dictated: *Transcribed:*

Ms. M. R. Pierre
7510 Hale
St. Louis, Missouri 67890

Dear Melissa:

I heartily share your belief that effective communication is one of the biggest problems of business today.

I am convinced that a great deal of effectiveness is lost in the simple mechanics of dictation. Perhaps a good communications training program would have some value in your organization.

Mr. Pitt, of the X-L Company, has developed an excellent dictation training course. If you will contact him at MU 7-8018, he will be happy to give you some suggestions.

I am looking forward to seeing how you approach this problem in your company.

Sincerely,

Jack Fieden

JF:jaf

Ms. M. R. Peer
75 Tin Hail
St. Louis, Missouri 67890

Dear Ms. Peer:

I hardly share your belief that effective communication is one of the biggest problems of business today. I am convinced that a great deal of effectiveness is lost in the simple mechanics of dictation. Perhaps a good communications training program would have some value in your organization. Mr. Pit of the Excell Company has developed an excellent dictation training course. If you call him at MU 7-8810 he will be happy to give you some suggestions. I am looking forward to seeing how you approach this problem in your company.

Sincerely,

Jack Fiden

JF:jaf

Column 1, 1238; Column 2, 987654; Column 3, 9. Next line. Column 1, 4567; Column 2, 459823; Column 3, 12.
7. Dictate remainder of message.
8. Dictate complimentary closing and your name and title.

Proper use of the specialized dictation system within an office, together with the dictator's skill in dictating clearly and giving understandable instructions to the word processing specialist, contribute immeasurably to the efficiency and effectiveness of the word processing system.

Output

In word processing, output is the final product. To maximize the efficiency of output processes, word processing and administrative support personnel as well as the principals must understand one another's situations. Management's responsibility is to establish communication, to set policies, and to develop procedures that will enable word processing personnel to produce output that meets desired performance objectives.

NATURE OF OUTPUT

While input refers to raw information, output refers to the documents that have been prepared in the word processing system. Output consists of letters, memoranda, reports, drafts, forms, statistical information, and so forth.

Figure 5-6 illustrates input, processing, storage, and output in a word processing system.

Quantity and quality of output are affected by several factors, including the following:

1. Quality of original input.
2. Type of original input (longhand, machine dictation, etc.).
3. Language and keyboarding skills of word processing personnel.
4. Type of equipment used in the word processing installation.

In addition, many human factors, such as morale, motivation, and attitudes, have an impact on quantity and quality of output. These human factors frequently require management and supervisory attention.

CATEGORIES OF OUTPUT

Output is categorized as follows: (1) repetitive, (2) combined repetitive and variable, (3) transcription, (4) editing and revising, and (5) photocomposition. Each category has special uses.

Repetitive. The repetitive category of output is probably the easiest of the categories of output to process. Repetitive material, which is constant from one document to the next, contains no variable information.

When a principal feels that future use might be made of material that has been keyboarded and stored on a magnetic medium, the medium is permanently retained. Each medium that is placed in storage is assigned a document identification number.

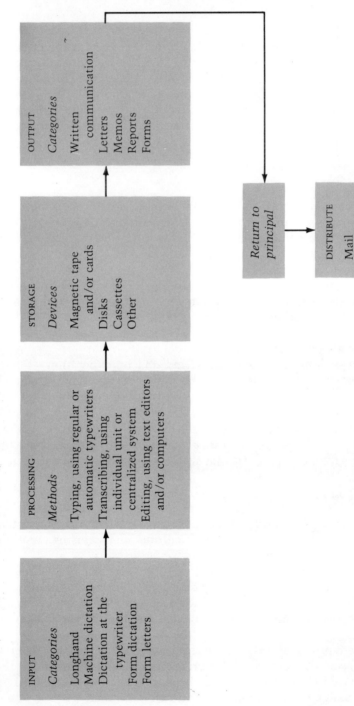

Figure 5-6 INPUT, PROCESSING, STORAGE, OUTPUT IN WORD PROCESSING

INPUT

Categories

Longhand
Machine dictation
Dictation at the
   typewriter
Form dictation
Form letters

PROCESSING

Methods

Typing, using regular or
   automatic typewriters
Transcribing, using
   individual unit or
   centralized system
Editing, using text editors
   and/or computers

STORAGE

Devices

Magnetic tape
   and/or cards
Disks
Cassettes
Other

OUTPUT

Categories

Written
   communication
Letters
Memos
Reports
Forms

*Return to
principal*

DISTRIBUTE

Mail
Facsimile
Electronic

When the principal desires an original copy of a document that has already been keyboarded and stored on a magnetic medium, the identification number of the medium is given to the word processing supervisor (or some other designated individual). The appropriate medium is retrieved from storage and assigned to a word processing specialist who uses the medium to activate the typewriter to print the document. The word processing specialist logs playback production, returns the medium to storage, and gives the completed copy to the word processing supervisor. The document is then either prepared for distribution or delivered to the principal.

Combined repetitive and variable. The combined repetitive and variable output format is used for processing documents that consist of constant material as well as material that varies from one document to another. A common use is letters that contain identical basic paragraphs but differ in terms of names, addresses, and perhaps numerical information.

Typically, when the combined repetitive and variable procedure is used, each word processing station has a reference book with hard copies of all prerecorded letters. Blank spaces in the text of each letter indicate where variables are to be inserted, as shown in Figure 5–7.

When a principal wants to send a combination repetitive/variable letter, a form is prepared for each letter that identifies the prerecorded letter and number and the variable information to be inserted. The variable information is inserted in the appropriate places on the form, which is then sent to the word processing center. After the letter is prepared, the copy of the form and the completed letter are returned to the principal. This procedure eliminates the need for proofreading the entire letter since only the variable information has to be proofread. It also provides the principal with a follow-up system for repetitive/variable correspondence.

Another common application of the combined repetitive and variable information category involves the use of prerecorded paragraphs to construct letters. This application is frequently found in collection departments in organizations, for example.

To illustrate, perhaps fifty different paragraphs have been keyboarded and are stored on a magnetic medium. Principals who have a reference manual that contains these paragraphs simply determine which paragraphs they wish to put in the letter. The variable information (name, address, dollar amounts, etc.) is provided the word processing specialist, along with the numbers of the desired paragraphs. The media on which the standard paragraphs are recorded are retrieved from storage. While the standard paragraphs are played out automatically, the variable information is manually keyboarded.

Figure 5-7 EXAMPLES OF STORED INFORMATION

Date _____

1 _____
_____
_____

Dear _____2_____ :

Your reservation for _____3_____ Tour, depart-
ing _____4_____ is confirmed; and a receipt for
your deposit is attached.

We welcome you to our American Delight Tours. Our on-site tour
representative will meet you on your departure date and remain
with you throughout your trip. We've planned an exciting trip,
accommodations at top-rate hotels, and special activities at your
option to complete your memorable holiday.

You will receive additional information and tour credentials
approximately ten days before departure. Final billing will be made
approximately 30 days before departure.

If you have any questions during your trip planning, please call or
write us.

Cordially,

5 _____
6 _____

ADT/07

Transcription. The transcription category involves the specialists'
transcribing dictation that has been recorded on a dictation/recording
device. The recording medium on which the dictation is recorded is
amplified, and the word processing specialist keyboards while listening to the dictation. The transcription category also involves keyboarding longhand input. The end result is the same as when dictation is
transcribed.

The type of recording medium on which the dictation is stored
will determine the type of transcription device that the word processing specialist will use. For example, if the dictation/recording device
uses magnetic belts, the transcription device used by the word processing specialist will also have to use a belt.

Editing and revising. The editing and revising category of output is used for production jobs that are quite complex or that might benefit from extensive amounts of editing and revision. Its use is especially suited to the preparation of long reports, legal documents, and so forth.

The following outlines the procedures that are characteristic of this output category. The raw information is assigned to a word processing specialist for keyboarding. Once the rough draft has been completed, it is returned to the principal who revises the material. The revised rough draft is then returned to the word processing specialist who originally keyboarded the material. Using the magnetic medium that was prepared during the original keyboarding, the typewriter automatically plays out the unchanged portions of the document. The changes, which are manually keyboarded by the specialist, are also recorded and stored on this magnetic medium. When completed, this draft is returned to the principal for additional editing and revising. The cycle is repeated until the principal is satisfied with the document, at which time the final draft is prepared.

Although the categories of repetitive, combined repetitive and variable, and transcription production jobs may involve rather limited editing, the editing and revising category involves extensive amounts of editing and revision. In some instances, as many as four or five drafts might be prepared before the document is released for distribution. With the first three categories, the first draft may be the final draft; however, in some instances, one revision may take place.

Photocomposition. Photocomposition refers to that process in which each character is exposed photographically on light-sensitive paper that is developed into a reproduction-quality proof. A wide variety of photocomposition equipment is available for use in word processing systems. Typically, photocomposition results in the preparation of masters that are used in offset duplication processes or in some other type of duplication process.

Photocomposition is a rapidly increasing application of word processing.

OUTLINING EFFICIENT OUTPUT PROCEDURES

Just as a user manual is important for the principals who use word processing, a procedures manual is important for the word processing specialists. A well-designed manual, which must be updated as changes occur in output procedures, often contributes significantly to the efficient operation of a word processing system.

The procedures manual should contain information dealing with output procedures, and many contain additional information as well. Inclusion of material should be determined by the specific needs of the organization and the structure of the word processing function. The following list identifies topics frequently included in the procedures manual:

1. Purpose of word processing.
2. Hours of operation.
3. Priorities of document processing.
4. Storage systems.
5. Cycle of work processed.
6. Sample formats.
7. Confidential documents.
8. Equipment operation and maintenance.

The following outlines a portion of a procedures manual:

PROCEDURES FOR WRITTEN COMMUNICATION

SUMMARY   Three categories of written communication are processed by the center: original dictation, prerecorded material, and special requests. (Specific procedures appropriate for each category are explained in the appropriate section of an actual procedures manual. An example of the procedures for original dictation is presented in Figure 5–8.)

CATEGORY	DESCRIPTION
Original dictation	Consists of documents original in content: *Letters/memos*: Includes standardized formats to speed processing. *Reports*: With simplified or standardized formats. *Original letter for several people*: The same original letter is sent to several people.
Pre-recorded material	Includes information stored on magnetic medium that facilitates automatic playback. *Stored documents*: Only variable information is manually keyboarded. *Stored paragraphs*: Merged with original dictation to complete final document.
Special requests	Consists of items that do not fall into the normal dictation flow and thus require special handling. *Reports*: Those with unusual formats. *Proposals*: Those with technical terminology. *Updates*: Those which appear in periodic reports. *Extensive statistical tables.* *Large numbers of form letters.*

Figure 5-8 OPERATIONAL PROCEDURES

SUBJECT: Original dictation (letters, memos, reports)

RESPONSIBILITY	ACTION
Principal	1. Identifies self by name and department.
	2. Indicates type of communication (letter, memo, report).
	3. Identifies number of copies needed.
	4. Dictates material.
	5. Gives copy distribution.
Supervisor	6. Removes belt and indexing slip from recorder and places in input file. Marks indexing slip with: Date and time of removal from recorder Recorder number
Word Processing Specialist	7. Removes belt from first folder of input file.
	8. Prepares a job assignment card.
	9. Transcribes material on continuous form paper using standard formats and recording instructions.
	10. Proofreads recorded copy before playback.
	11. Corrects any errors.
	12. Logs playback production and sends completed copy to supervisor.
Supervisor	13. Reviews copy, inserts in routing envelope for distribution to principal.
Routing Clerk	14. Delivers to department.
Principal	15. Proofreads, signs, and prepares copy for outgoing mail *or:*
	16. Edits and revises material and returns document to center where changes are made.

Figure 5-8 illustrates specific procedures for handling original dictation.

Handling priority and confidential jobs in word processing. The procedures for handling rush jobs and confidential material vary from organization to organization. The operating procedures of the word processing installation often have an impact on the handling of priority and confidential jobs. Usually, priority and/or confidential materials are sent directly to the supervisor (or some other designated individual) and are processed either by one of these individuals or by a word processing specialist. If these materials are processed by a word processing specialist, the job description for this position should specifically mention responsibility for handling priority or confidential materials.

The procedures for handling priority or confidential material should be stipulated in the organization's procedures manual for the specialists and the user manual for the principal. Such procedures might be outlined as follows:

PRIORITY ITEMS: Keep priority requests to a minimum. When an item is needed immediately
Principal notifies the center supervisor. Supervisor immediately assigns a job to a word processing specialist.

CONFIDENTIAL ITEMS: Principal notifies the center supervisor. The medium on which the dictation is recorded is removed from the recorder by the supervisor who transcribes the material.

Another example of procedures used for special requests follows:

PRIORITY ITEMS: Please keep priority requests to a minimum. When an item is needed immediately, the following procedures will be followed:

1. The principal's department head must approve the request.
2. When dictating priority items, call the center supervisor immediately afterwards to schedule the project for immediate transcription.
3. The principal will be notified upon completion of the project.

CONFIDENTIAL ITEMS: The following procedures should be followed in submitting confidential items to the supervisor:

1. Place the material in an envelope.
2. Submit the material to the center supervisor.
3. When dictating confidential material, call the center supervisor so the recording medium on which the material is dictated can be removed from the recorder and marked as confidential.
4. The principal will be notified when the confidential project has been completed.

Some of the new dictation/recording devices automatically eject the recording medium after confidential or priority material has been dictated.

Distribution methods

Once the output is in final form and approved by the principal, it is ready for distribution. Internal documents are often distributed by messenger or by interdepartmental mail. External documents may be distributed by any of the following distribution methods: mail, facsimile, or electronic document distribution.

MAIL

Although external transmission of written messages is one of the fastest changing methods of communication involving business correspondence today, the most widely used method of distribution is still the U.S. Postal Service. Currently, business firms alone are transmitting more than seventy billion pieces of mail annually, and the volume is increasing steadily, even with the increasing mail costs.

Several types of services for first-class mail are provided by the postal service. Most first-class mail now travels by air when the destination is more than three hundred miles. Priority mail (which is first-class mail weighing more than twelve ounces) provides next-day delivery to nearby ZIP code areas, second-day delivery within another radius, and third-day delivery to distant points.

Express mail guarantees next-day delivery to designated post offices. When the sender transports the mail to the post office by 4:30 P.M., delivery at the destination post office is guaranteed by 10:00 A.M. the following day. If post-office pickup is not requested for destination delivery, post-office delivery to the local address is guaranteed by 3:00 P.M. the day after an item is mailed.

While the Mailgram is not used extensively for external messages, the U.S. Postal Service and Western Union jointly operate the Mailgram network, which involves transmitting messages between post offices via Western Union equipment. The messages are delivered by the postal service the following day. This technique is made more convenient by allowing customers to store names, addresses, and text in Western Union computers as a means of facilitating repetitive production of documents.

Those responsible for administrative services are taking a new look at the relationship between mailroom functions and word processing functions, with a view toward increasing mechanization, integrating the two functions, and improving control. For some functions, electronic equipment is available for addressing, collating, folding, inserting, sorting, stacking, tying, sealing, weighing, metering, and conveying operations.

The procedures for handling outgoing mail usually include the following:

1. Follow a regular schedule in collecting mail from the mail distribution points in the organization.
2. Sort by class of mail and by destination.
3. Use adequate equipment to expedite work.
4. Dispatch outgoing mail to the post office if volume justifies and coordinate times with plane schedules.

FACSIMILE

Wire communication, which overcomes some of the limitations of mail transportation, is a viable alternative to using the mails for document distribution. The use of wire communication, such as facsimile, is expanding rapidly. Although facsimile should not be used for the distribution of all external documents, in appropriate situations its use is very beneficial for many organizations.

In some organizations, the word processing center is responsible for the facsimile unit while in other organizations, the mailroom is responsible.

ELECTRONIC DOCUMENT DISTRIBUTION

The current trend of increasing technology at lower costs will no doubt continue. While the use of communicating text-editing equipment as a communications device is receiving considerable attention, it must be cost effective to justify its use. Standardization of communications and computer technology will contribute to continued development of economical electronic distribution.

Telecommunications is becoming increasingly important as word processing moves words quickly internally and externally. And the integration of word processing into telecommunications will mark another milestone in the development of an effective office communications system.

Figure 5–9 presents a page from a law firm's procedures manual which includes instructions for personnel in the home office and six branch offices when using electronic distribution devices.

Figure 5-9 PAGE FROM PROCEDURES MANUAL

COMMUNICATION PROCEDURES
ALL OFFICES

1. All material to be communicated will have been recorded using format features.

2. A summary sheet should *always* be sent with each project.

3. All projects communicated will *not* have page numbers or any top margin text unless specifically designated otherwise.

4. Always have Remote Device 2. This will insure that the project will be put on cards at the remote location.

5. Material communicated should be scanned before it is sent. Any stop codes should be for footnotes or double underscoring *only.* Make sure you tell the remote station what the stop codes are for.

6. When you place a call, tell the remote station how much you are sending them and see if they may have something to send you.

7. The *called* party goes to data first.

8. If the line gets disconnected, the party who called originally should replace the call. This avoids confusion as to who calls back when disconnected.

9. If you need to talk to the remote station during the transmission, wait until the job(s) have been transmitted, depress and hold the stop/talk button. the remote station should answer. You can line stop the transmission, depress and hold the stop/talk button until the remote station answers and then continue transmission.

10. Play back documents using the Legal Courier 72 10 pitch element. The number on the silver part on top should be 177. This will insure that the keyboards are the same and that the material will play back as recorded.

11. If you have trouble playing back communicated material, let the remote station know what the trouble was.

Source: Courtesy of Nelson & Harding, Lincoln, NE

CHOOSING THE APPROPRIATE DISTRIBUTION METHOD

Several factors should be considered when deciding which of the distribution methods to use. These factors include the following:

1. The relative importance of the document.
2. The amount of time available for document distribution.
3. The length of the document.
4. The number of copies of the document to be distributed.

Review questions

1. Discuss each of the various categories of input.
2. Discuss the considerations that should be present when analyzing the flow of work.
3. What factors have an impact on the quantity and quality of output?
4. How do repetitive and combined repetitive and variable categories of output differ?
5. What subjects are frequently covered in procedures manuals?
6. How are priority or confidential jobs frequently handled in word processing?
7. Discuss the electronic document distribution concept.
8. What factors should be considered in choosing the appropriate distribution method?

Cases

You are the word processing supervisor in the home office of Gregory Manufacturing Company, which is located in Chicago. Your firm has six branch offices, which are located in San Francisco, Houston, Atlanta, New York, Kansas City, and Denver. Small word processing centers are in operation in each of the branch offices. However, at present, no intracommunication channel exists among the Gregory Manufacturing Company offices.

Volumes of correspondence and data are transmitted daily between the various offices by means of priority and express mail. A considerable amount of the correspondence has a time-value element. As supervisor of word processing, you are aware that excessive costs and delays may be attributed to the current method of distributing the intraoffice correspondence.

The top management of the firm recently issued a "cut costs" memorandum to all supervisory and executive personnel.

1. Besides using the U.S. Postal Service, what other alternatives might be considered for distributing the correspondence? Assess the desirability of each of the alternatives you list.
2. What factors should be considered in determining which alternative to use?
3. Which alternative do you recommend? Why?
4. How might the organization evaluate the usefulness of the alternative you recommend once it has been utilized for six months?

• • •

You are the word processing supervisor in Bradley Publishers, which is located in Detroit. Forty principals dictate through a centralized dictation system. The word processing specialists have been making a number of transcription errors. Much of their transcription seems to be based on guesswork.

After speaking to three of the specialists about their work, you sense that a major part of the problem is due to inefficient dictation. For example, John Elbon's words are clipped because he speaks very fast; Alva Lacey slurs her words; Jack Axton practically whispers. With a branch office in Tokyo, some of your correspondence is addressed to names with which the specialists are unfamiliar. They therefore have to guess at the correct spelling of the name. In addition, the specialists do not always insert correct punctuation, especially where unusual punctuation is expected.

Most of the correspondence to be transcribed is original; however, sometimes an original letter goes to several people. A large amount of dictation involves material that should be transcribed in tabular format.

1. Prepare a list of instructions to be given to the principals to help them improve their dictation habits.
2. Prepare a list of techniques that can be used to train the principals to become more effective in the dictation process.
3. Of the techniques you provided in number 2, which do you recommend as being the most appropriate? Why?

CHAPTER 6

Word processing personnel

The word processing/administrative support concept, a major thrust in the development of a new office technological system that began in the middle to late sixties, is responsible for the development of new office careers. These careers are discussed in this chapter and the one that follows.

The word processing/administrative support concept

Word processing, in the broadest sense, began with the first communicating and recording processes. The more recent vintage of the word processing concept includes the components of personnel, equipment, and procedures.

In the early 1960s, the word processing concept began to crystallize through the use of automatic typewriters and a division of the functions of the traditional secretary. One area of emphasis was the use of high-speed text-editing equipment, while the other area was concerned with such nontyping activities as handling the mail, telephoning, filing, and receiving office callers. The latter involved duties more adequately termed administrative support. The word processing/administrative support concept requires a manager who can administer and lead such a multifaceted system.

It is possible that the current perspective of word processing and administrative support is too narrow. Word processing and administrative support are evolving toward becoming management's major source of support for all office and communication services. The management of the word processing and administrative support system continues to assume increased responsibility for providing a high quality, cost-effective office system capable of interacting with other facets of the organization.

Regardless of whether word processing and administrative support are centralized or decentralized, they provide a vehicle for communication. Much of the technology used to process managerial paperwork is highly automated. This technology automates the creation, distribution, storage, retrieval, and destruction of a vast amount of communication previously handled by nonautomated processes. Word processing, which is being interfaced with data processing systems, provides a sound vehicle through which future office technological communication can be channeled.

The word processing/administrative support concept continues to evolve. Word processing and its support services provide an effective channel through which office efficiency can be increased and operating costs decreased.

SPECIALIZATION OF LABOR

While the equipment and procedures components are necessary to the success of a word processing/administrative support system, the personnel involved—from top management to the word processing specialist—represent a basic component in word processing/administrative support. The division of labor within previously generalized tasks is encompassed within the people component of the word processing/administrative support concept.

In word processing/administrative support, the traditional job of the secretary is divided into two. The word processing specialists perform keyboarding tasks, duplication, and transmittal services; and the administrative secretary provides input, maintains records, assists with travel and conferences, gathers information, and assumes other nontyping duties and responsibilities traditionally performed by the secretary. While the word processing specialist generally is task-oriented, enjoys typing and working with machines, and is interested in producing a finished written document, the administrative secretary typically is people-oriented, enjoys the human side of the office, and functions efficiently in a nonstructured office.

It should be pointed out, however, that while a word processing system consists of these two basic functions—typing and all secretarial duties other than typing—these two jobs may be split in several ways. Originally, word processing installations consisted of a single typing center and a single administrative support center. The current trend is to have clusters of word processing and administrative support personnel strategically grouped to provide their services when and where needed. Recently, too, for management personnel who need a traditional secretarial arrangement for one reason or another, word processing equipment is made available to the secretaries.

A study of the organization's needs can provide information on how the word processing and administrative support function should be organized. Answers to the following questions are needed: What are the functions of the secretaries? What duties and responsibilities do the principals have? How can their secretaries best perform their work?

JOB TITLES OF PERSONNEL INVOLVED IN WORD PROCESSING AND
ADMINISTRATIVE SUPPORT CONCEPT

Job titles of personnel involved in word processing and administrative support services may vary according to the needs of the organization. The *Dictionary of Occupational Titles* (Fourth Edition, 1977) lists these job titles which may be applicable to word processing:

Supervisor, Word Processing (clerical) or supervisor, communication center.

Supervisor (clerical).

Supervisor, Transcribing Operators (clerical) or transcribing operator, head.

Magnetic-Tape-Typewriter Operator (clerical).

Transcribing-Machine Operator (clerical) or dictating-machine transcriber or dictating-machine typist.

Magnetic-Tape-Composer Operator or composing-machine operator.

Although the functions of many of the word processing positions in organizations are very similar to the functions of the D.O.T. positions, the titles may be quite different.

CAREER PATHS OF WORD PROCESSING/ADMINISTRATIVE SUPPORT PERSONNEL

The career-pathing concept provides opportunities for personnel within a word processing system to train for increasingly more responsible positions. Word processing is frequently thought to provide greater career opportunities than those offered in the traditional office.

The following career pathing illustrates three levels of responsibility for word processing positions:

Supervisor, word processing: The supervisor is responsible for day-by-day operation of the center. This supervisory position involves an emphasis on human relations skills. The supervisor's accountability can be expressed in terms of the volume of documents, the number of people under supervision, and the dollar volume of word processing equipment in the center. In some organizations, the supervisor is known as a team leader. The supervisor of word processing is also responsible for keeping the word processing system up to date.

Senior word processing specialist: This individual will have diversified experience and may serve as assistant to the supervisor.

Word processing specialist: The person filling this position demonstrates above-average production on specialized documents.

Senior word processing operator: At this intermediate level, a fully trained experienced word processing operator produces a satisfactory level of work.

Word processing operator: This is an entry-level position and the job holder frequently is assigned noncomplex jobs while learning job responsibilities.

An increasing number of organizations are utilizing proofreaders and schedulers. Although the hierarchical levels of these positions vary from one organization to another, the positions are often placed hierarchically above the senior word processing specialist position. The following identify some of the common job responsibilities.

Proofreader: This individual, who has excellent skills in English usage, grammar, and punctuation, is responsible for proofreading all final revised documents and spot proofreading daily correspondence.

Scheduler: This individual distributes the workload among the word processing specialists and operators and maintains current production records.

On the administrative support side, career pathing might include the following positions:

Supervisor, administrative services: This individual is responsible for the coordination of administrative support within an organization. Generally, the supervisor provides for training, promotion, reassignment, and other developmental opportunities for personnel in the administrative support area.

Senior administrative secretary: The senior administrative secretary may serve as assistant to the supervisor. This person may dictate correspondence, handle all records management, make travel arrangements, conduct library research, or handle other specialized functions.

Administrative secretary, level II: At level II, the administrative secretary may be responsible for filing, telephone communications, report writing, and other assignments as needed or as specified by the job description.

Administrative secretary, level I: This is an entry-level position. The person filling the position files, routes mail, and serves as receptionist.

The supervisors of word processing and administrative support are likely to be responsible to a manager of word processing/administrative support, especially in a large business firm.

While the career pathing illustrated above for word processing and administrative support is not intended to provide detailed job descriptions, the pathing does illustrate varying levels of responsibility. Detailed descriptions are presented later in this chapter.

The word processing/administrative support concept has created several other indirectly related positions. Included are the following: manufacturer's sales representatives, manufacturer's marketing support representatives, word processing consultants, owner/manager of independent service bureaus, and in-house word processing/administrative support systems analysts.

Increasingly, individuals who have experience in either word processing or administrative support are moving into these indirectly related positions. While directly related work experience is not a job prerequisite in most instances, these positions do create additional job opportunities for individuals involved in word processing/administrative support.

Perhaps the most obvious social impact of word processing/administrative support is the creation of additional career opportunities for women in managerial positions. The level of responsibility in managerial positions in word processing centers and in administrative support can be a key step upward in career movement. For those with initial managerial experience, opportunities may be available to move into other management areas of the organization.

Personnel involved in word processing

Basic considerations relating to personnel involved in word processing are not unlike those concerning personnel in other areas of the organization. Job descriptions outline the expectations the employer has of the employee. Certainly, prospective employees must be aware of the characteristics needed of them to succeed on the job. Procedures and techniques for selecting, training, and promoting personnel contribute immeasurably to the success or failure of any functional area, whether it is word processing, marketing, or production.

JOB DESCRIPTIONS OF WORD PROCESSING PERSONNEL

Job descriptions serve as a basis for an understanding of the performance expectations the employer has of the employee. Descriptions also prevent misunderstandings between employees and their supervisors as to the nature of job duties and responsibilities.

Figure 6-1 JOB DESCRIPTION FOR WORD PROCESSING CENTER SUPERVISOR

JOB DESCRIPTION FOR WORD PROCESSING CENTER SUPERVISOR

Primary function

The word processing center supervisor reports to and is accountable to the vice president of the administration division. He/she is accountable for the performance of personnel in the center and coordinates the work of the center with the various divisions of the organization.

Typical duties

1. Evaluates each division by gathering samples of material that have been standardized by the division.
2. Studies volume of all major typing applications in each division to be processed by the center. Looks for additional material that can be standardized and stored on magnetic medium.
3. Writes procedures for processing each application—for the principal as well as the processor.
4. Assumes responsibility for printing and binding the procedures.
5. Works closely with equipment manufacturer (vendor) in training processors and maintains liaison with manufacturer.
6. Acts as a liaison between word processing specialists, operators, and users of the center.
7. Keeps production records and other reports.
8. Establishes priorities. Controls the distribution of workload, including special requests or special projects; analyzes and supervises rush items; proofreads all material to be sent out of the center; and prepares finished items for routing to principals.
9. Maintains the dictation recorders, orders all center supplies, and keeps principal list current.
10. Instructs and trains new employees on word processing center procedures including use of dictation equipment.
11. Studies and suggests better ways of programming materials.
12. Handles all incoming calls to the center; acts as host/hostess for visitors touring the word processing center.

General

1. Is familiar with all functions and operations of the center.
2. Possesses knowledge of other divisions and maintains a favorable image for the center.
3. Has proficiency in use of words, formats, machine operations, letter-writing techniques and etiquette.
4. Guides and controls the word processing specialists and operators.
5. Keeps the word processing system and procedures up to date.

Figure 6-2 JOB DESCRIPTION FOR ASSISTANT WORD PROCESSING CENTER SUPERVISOR

JOB DESCRIPTION FOR ASSISTANT WORD PROCESSING SUPERVISOR

Primary function

The assistant word processing center supervisor reports and is account-able to the word processing center supervisor. He/she assists in coor-dinating the work of the center with various divisions and, in the supervisor's absence, is responsible for the performance of the person-nel in the center.

Typical duties

1. Aids the supervisor in evaluating each division by gathering samples of standardized material from the division.
2. Looks for additional material that can be standardized and stored on magnetic medium.
3. Assists in acting as a liaison between word processing specialists, operators, and users of the center.
4. Helps keep production records and other reports.
5. Controls distribution of workload, supervises rush items and special projects in supervisor's absence. Assists in proofreading material to be sent out of the center and in routing to principals.
6. Studies and suggests better ways of programming materials.
7. Handles all incoming calls and acts as host/hostess to visitors tour-ing the center in the supervisor's absence.
8. Aids in setting up procedures for new applications to be processed in the center.
9. Transcribes dictation and plays out material on composer. (Rotates regularly with word processing specialists and operators.)

General

1. Is knowledgeable of all functions and operations of the center.
2. Possesses knowledge of other divisions and helps maintain a favorable image for the center.
3. Guides and assists word processing specialists and operators when the center's supervisor is absent.

The job descriptions shown in Figures 6-1 through 6-3 provide illustrations of typical jobs for personnel in word processing and ad-ministrative support operations. Figures 6-4 and 6-5 present descrip-tions of the proofreader and scheduler positions. The descriptions would, of course, vary according to the needs of each company.

Figures 6-6 through 6-10 illustrate position descriptions found in the *Dictionary of Occupational Titles* that apply to word processing. Figure 6-6 illustrates the titles of Supervisor, Transcribing Operator

Figure 6–3 JOB DESCRIPTION FOR WORD PROCESSING SPECIALIST

JOB DESCRIPTION FOR WORD PROCESSING SPECIALIST

Primary functions

The word processing specialist reports to and is accountable to the word processing center supervisor. He/she performs stenographic and clerical duties in the center with the primary duty of transcribing dictation of all divisions. In addition, he/she will answer an unattended telephone, greet visitors, maintain files, and attend to routine and administrative details of the center. He/she must be aware that all items processed in the center are to be considered of a confidential nature.

Typical duties

1. Transcribes dictation of formal correspondence, memoranda, reports, bulletins, and related material and types from penciled copy reports and memoranda including statistical tables.
2. Maintains proficiency in general secretarial skills including vocabulary, letter writing forms, and techniques.
3. Evaluates daily transcription to determine similar and repetitious material that can be standardized and stored on magnetic medium.
4. Maintains a daily log of production activity.

General

Possesses a complete knowledge of word processing center procedures, functions, work traits, files, records, and operation of equipment. A knowledge of the various divisions is helpful and expected. An attentive attitude with an eagerness to learn must supplement typing, transcribing, and general stenographic skills and is required to fulfill this assignment.

(clerical) or transcribing operator, head; Supervisor (clerical) section chief, section head; and Supervisor, Word Processing (clerical) or supervisor, communication center.

While a Terminal-System Operator (clerical) may not necessarily be included in word processing operations, the title is included because of the trend toward the blending of word processing, data processing, and telecommunications (see Figure 6–7).

Another job title now included in word processing is that of the Magnetic-Tape-Composer Operator or printing and publication composing-machine operator, shown in Figure 6–8.

Still another position often found in a word processing operation is that of a Magnetic-Tape-Typewriter Operator, as described in Figure 6–9.

Figure 6-4 JOB DESCRIPTION FOR PROOFREADER

JOB DESCRIPTION FOR PROOFREADER

Primary functions

The proofreader reports to and is accountable to the word processing center supervisor. He/she proofreads all final revised documents. In addition, he/she will answer an unattended telephone, greet visitors, maintain files, and attend to routine and administrative duties in the center. He/she must be aware that all items processed in the center are to be considered of a confidential nature.

Typical duties

1. Proofreads all final revised documents.
2. Spot proofs daily correspondence.
3. Keeps current on English usage, grammar, and punctuation rules, as well as special vocabulary or technical terms used in the organization.
4. Coordinates with the supervisor in plans and policies for improvement.
5. Establishes and meets quality goals and objectives.
6. Works with word processing specialists in helping them improve their grammar.

General

Possesses a thorough, complete knowledge of the English language and grammar usage, including punctuation, capitalization, spelling, and word choice.

Since machine transcription is basic to the word processing/administrative support center, a Transcribing-Machine Operator (clerical) station will be found in all organizations using word processing. However, the job title may reflect that of a word processing specialist. The D.O.T. description of such a position appears in Figure 6-10.

CHARACTERISTICS NEEDED OF WORD PROCESSING/ADMINISTRATIVE
SUPPORT PERSONNEL

Several characteristics needed of word processing/administrative support personnel can be identified. These characteristics are discussed in the following section.

Word processing specialist. A very important characteristic or qualification of the word processing specialist is skill in English usage. The

Figure 6–5 JOB DESCRIPTION FOR SCHEDULER

JOB DESCRIPTION FOR SCHEDULER

Primary functions

The scheduler reports to and is accountable to the word processing supervisor. He/she distributes the workload among the word processing specialists and operators to ensure the meeting of deadlines. In addition, he/she will answer unattended telephones, greet visitors, maintain files, and attend to routine and administrative duties in the center. He/she must be aware that all items processed in the center are to be considered of a confidential nature.

Typical functions

1. Distributes the workload among the word processing specialists and operators to ensure that deadlines are met.
2. Maintains current production records. Notes turnaround times, deadline schedules, and interferences with productivity.
3. Coordinates with the supervisor on status of jobs or projects.
4. Informs word processing personnel of unusual requirements of special situations—i.e., heavy workloads.
5. Analyzes input and output problems pertaining to content or dictation techniques, etc.
6. Maintains records on personnel schedules—absences, vacations, work schedules—to coordinate work volume.
7. Coordinates with supervisor on special scheduling requests.

General

Possesses a good understanding of work flow principals, of working with others, and of word processing concepts. In addition, an understanding of systems analysis and design is helpful.

word processing specialist must understand and correctly use words. Since the specialist often must transcribe without an opportunity to ask questions of the principal, an understanding of vocabulary unique to the organization is also important.

Correct spelling, correct punctuation, and correct grammar usage are essential. Ability to operate equipment, such as dictation/transcription machines and text-editing typewriters, as well as good keyboarding skills, help to insure a prospective employee an opportunity to work in a competitive job market. Word processing specialists generally need at least a high school diploma or its equivalent.

Word processing supervisor. Supervisory position requirements in word processing also include a thorough knowledge of the English

Figure 6-6 JOB DESCRIPTION

203.132–014 *Supervisor, Transcribing Operators (clerical) or transcribing operator, head:*

Supervises and coordinates activities of Transcribing-Machine Operators (clerical) in a bank or other business organization, performing duties as described under Supervisor (clerical).

Supervisor (clerical) section chief; section head is listed as follows:

Supervises and coordinates activities of clerical workers: Determines work procedures, prepares work schedules, and expedites workflow. Issues written and oral instructions. Assigns duties and examines work for exactness, neatness, and conformance to policies and procedures. Studies and standardizes procedures to improve efficiency of subordinates. Maintains harmony among workers and resolves grievances. Prepares composite reports from individual reports of subordinates. Adjusts errors and complaints. May perform or assist subordinates in performing duties. May keep time and personnel records, and oversee preparation of payrolls. May hire, train, and discharge workers. Classifications are made according to type of work or functions of unit supervised. . . .

A more appropriate title listed in the DOT may be:

203.137–010 *Supervisor, Word Processing (clerical) or supervisor, communication center*

Supervises and coordinates activities of workers engaged in preparing correspondence, records, reports, insurance policies, and similar clerical matter and in operating specialized typing machines, such as magnetic-tape typewriting and composing machines. Advises other departmental personnel in techniques and style of dictation and letter writing. Recommends changes in procedures to effect savings in time, labor, costs, and to improve operating efficiency. Assigns new workers to experienced workers for training. Assists subordinates in resolving problems in nonstandard situations. Evaluates job performance of subordinates and recommends appropriate personnel action. Performs duties as described under Supervisor (clerical).

Source: Dictionary of Occupational Titles

language, grammar, spelling, and punctuation. In addition, supervisors need a knowledge of the following: modern office methods and procedures; equipment utilized in word processing; and functions to be performed in word processing operations.

Figure 6-7 JOB DESCRIPTION

203.362–018 *Terminal-System Operator* (clerical)

Operates computer terminal and compiles data to produce business, scientific, or technical reports and publications in printlike format. Reviews source documents, such as correspondence, company records, statistical tables, and accompanying instructions to determine computer operations required to produce texts in format requested. Confers with source document originators to clarify instructions, such as paragraphing, indentation, line spacing, and other style requirements. Arranges data input sequence according to manuals. Types coded commands on computer terminal keyboard to enter, store, retrieve, or delete data, using knowledge of coding system. Proofreads printout of draft copy to correct errors and verify format specifications. Types coded command to computer to produce finished copy on paper, magnetic tape, or punched cards for subsequent reproduction as completed texts by peripheral equipment, such as high-speed printers.

Source: Dictionary of Occupational Titles

Supervisors of word processing operations also need the following skills and abilities: Ability to (1) organize and supervise the work of others; (2) determine management, administration, and secretarial needs in developing a strong communication system; (3) establish and maintain effective working relationships with administrative personnel and with subordinates; and (4) maintain a favorable image for word processing networks.

Word processing supervisory positions generally require that the incumbent possess as a minimum a high school education or its equivalent, as well as have experience in office operations. Usually, at least one year's experience which includes supervision of other staff members is preferred. College-level training is also very desirable.

Administrative secretaries. Administrative secretaries located within the administrative support areas of the word processing/administrative support organization are expected to have the characteristics exhibited by the traditional secretary. The administrative secretary must also be skilled in the use of the English language because of the possibility of being responsible for dictating material, as well as for composing, editing, and proofreading correspondence. Usually, the administrative secretary performs all secretarial tasks other than typing; however, this individual may also be expected to know how to operate word processing equipment.

The administrative secretary must be able to handle details of recordkeeping, gather information, and assume public relations respon-

Figure 6-8 JOB DESCRIPTION

203.382–018 *Magnetic-Tape-Composer Operator (print. & pub.)*
composing-machine operator

Operates magnetic-tape recording and typographic composing machine
to prepare copy used for offset printing of forms, documents, adver-
tisements, and other matter, following copy and layout instructions
and using knowledge of typesetting and typing techniques: Clips copy
and instructions to copyholder. Inserts blank tape cartridges on tape-
station hubs and starts recorder to thread tape. Selects and attaches
specified type-font element to typewriter carrier. Adjusts margins and
other spacing mechanisms to set line justification. Types from marked
copy, using electric typewriter that simultaneously produces proof
copy and master tape. Types in composer control codes according to
program sequence to allow change of type font and format. Proofreads
copy. Makes corrections by strikeover on proof copy, automatically
correcting identical material on master tape, or retypes corrected portions only, generating correction tape. Reference codes correction tape
to error location in original copy and tape. Removes tape cartridges
from recorder and installs cartridges, with correction tape, if any, into
composer-output printer. Installs specified type font and sets escape-
ment and vertical spacing controls. Keys in layout and composing
codes on control panel, following program sequence. Inserts coated
paper and starts composer. Operates composer controls in response to
function-light indicators and changes type font and format as work progresses. Removes copy from composer, examines copy for errors, and
makes necessary corrections. May specialize in operation of recorder or
composer units. May operate varitype machine to set headline copy.

Source: Dictionary of Occupational Titles

sibilities. The administrative secretary is apt to be more people oriented
than the word processing specialist. The administrative support position reflects an emphasis on human relations within the office and in
dealing with people outside the company.

SELECTION OF WORD PROCESSING PERSONNEL

The selection process for word processing personnel is not unlike the
selection process for other office personnel. Depending on the organization, certain selection activities may be performed by the supervisor
while others are performed by the personnel department. A comprehensive selection program involves certain basic steps, which are outlined in the following section.

Figure 6-9 JOB DESCRIPTION

203.582-034. *Magnetic-Tape-Typewriter Operator (clerical)*

Operates magnetic-tape typewriter and tape console to type positive proof copy and simultaneously to produce master tape for automatic reproduction of finished texts, such as letters, reports, and other data from manuscript or pretaped material: Positions blank cartridge on tape spindle head and peg in tape station of console. Presses button to load tape into console. Inserts proof paper into typewriter carriage, sets controls for margins, spacing, and tabulation and turns dials for automatic preparation of magnetic tape. Types from draft and reads proof copy for errors. Backspaces and strikes over or presses line-return button and retypes entire line to correct individual character or line errors on both proof copy and tape. Presses button to stop tape or to mark end of tape section. Removes proof copy from carriage and completed tape cartridge from tape-station housing. Frequently combines or transfers data between two tapes, one with standard text and the other with personalized data, to prepare individualized correspondence. Keeps log of reference numbers and data recorded on each tape. Files tapes, correspondence, and reports. May transcribe data from recorded message, using earphones and recording unit. May use typewriter equipped with magnetic card rather than tape and be designated Magnetic-Card-Typewriter Operator (clerical).

Source: Dictionary of Occupational Titles

Figure 6-10 JOB DESCRIPTION

203.582-058 *Transcribing-Machine Operator (clerical)* or *dictating-machine transcriber; or dictating-machine typist.*

Operates typewriter to transcribe letters, reports, or other recorded data heard through earphones of transcribing (voice reproducing) machine: Positions record or tape on machine spindle and sets needle on record, or threads tape through machine. Depresses pedal to rotate record or tape. Turns dials to control volume, tone, and speed of voice reproduction. Types message heard through earphones. Reads chart prepared by dictator to determine length of message and corrections to be made. May type unrecorded information, such as name, address, and date. May keep file of records. May condition records for reuse, using wax-shaving attachment. . . . May be designated by subject matter transcribed as Legal Transcriber (clerical); Medical Transcriber (clerical).

Source: Dictionary of Occupational Titles

In a self-paced program, each student progresses at his or her own speed, learning to operate word processing equipment and to apply skills in a business environment. Students may also practice their skills through the provision of a transcription service to supervisors and administrators within the school system. In such an arrangement, emphasis is placed on quality work, ability to work independently, and responsibility for meeting deadlines. Students are expected to complete assigned projects in an acceptable, businesslike manner.

In-house training. Despite the growth of secondary- and college-level offerings in word processing, in-house training is still the most widely used procedure for training word processing personnel. The on-the-job training experiences take place within the actual jobs, and the equipment involved is the equipment which the employee will be expected to operate. Because of the sophistication and complexity of equipment used in word processing operations, in-house training is especially appropriate.

Such training includes every aspect of word processing—explaining what it is, how it operates, how it benefits principals in the organization, and the guidelines or procedures it involves. Special training sessions may be conducted for top management, middle management, and secretarial personnel to orient each to the concept. In-depth training may be provided for word processing specialists and administrative support secretaries. Special sessions for training principals in dictation techniques are especially helpful in word processing training programs.

Many firms have installed training programs for new specialists. The orientation program gives the new specialist an opportunity to become familiar with the company, the equipment, and the word processing procedures. The new employee may spend six weeks in orientation, and an additional one to two weeks in operating the equipment unique to that word processing operation. Such a program contributes to development of keyboarding skills and increased productivity.

APPRAISING WORD PROCESSING PERSONNEL

One of the most important factors involved in word processing, as in any other office function, is the appraisal of employee performance.

Techniques. Any method appropriate for appraising other office personnel may be applied to word processing employees. However, because of the cost-effectiveness basis for the implementation of word processing and the necessity for measuring productivity in word processing, the results-oriented technique is especially useful in appraising performance.

The results-oriented appraisal generally involves both the supervisor and the subordinate in setting employee performance goals that are measurable. The next step is to determine specific courses of action to reach the established goals. At interim intervals, the supervisor and subordinate review progress being made toward reaching these goals.

At the end of the appraisal period (perhaps three to six months for word processing personnel), the supervisor and subordinate officially evaluate the degree to which specific goals were accomplished. Goals for the next time period are then set.

Objectives should be achievable within a relatively short time, and those objectives should consist of three elements: (1) the desired results, (2) the quantity or amount of change, and (3) the day by which the objective should be achieved.

Some of the other techniques that might be used to appraise employee performance are the following: traditional (merit) rating scale, checklists, forced choice, and paired comparison.

PROMOTING WORD PROCESSING PERSONNEL

Managers and supervisors who are responsible for personnel assignments and promotion are obligated to base their decisions upon objective, sound evidence. The use of subjective factors often causes morale problems.

Techniques. Valid and reliable evidence, usually taken into consideration in employee performance appraisals, is often considered when promoting employees. Productivity rates, established by various formulas, are usually maintained, and data obtained from productivity records may be used in establishing bases for promotion.

Within a word processing center, the promotion steps might be from word processing operator to senior word processing operator and then to word processing specialist. The next promotion might then be to scheduler or proofreader, or perhaps to senior word processing specialist. Also, in some centers, the senior word processing specialist is responsible for the transcription of dictation and other materials from high-level executives. Much of their correspondence is confidential, which necessitates the use of employees who can be trusted with the work.

The highest level job within the word processing center is typically the supervisor, manager, or director of the center.

Just as the word processing center has several different levels of positions, so does the administrative support area. The administrative secretarial levels, from the lowest to the highest, may include the following: administrative secretary, trainee; administrative secretary, level I; administrative secretary, level II; senior administrative secretary; executive administrative secretary; and administrative support supervisor. In a large word processing organization, the word processing supervisor and administrative support supervisor are likely to be responsible to a manager of word processing/administrative support.

Human relations in word processing

One of the functions of management is to provide working conditions that employees find comfortable, enjoyable, and satisfying. Human relations is an important aspect of a word processing system at any time, but especially during the first few months the installation is operational.

When an organization converts from a traditional system to word processing, employees' jobs must change, some quite drastically. It takes time for the office employees to adjust to this new system, and it is management's responsibility to help employees make the adjustment. Effective human relations can play an important role in helping facilitate the transition from the traditional system to the new system.

Some office employees have difficulty accepting the fact that traditional secretarial positions may be replaced by word processing and administrative support positions. It is quite unlikely that all office employees will adjust equally well to the new system. It is reasonable to expect that some employees will react negatively—at least for a minimum time—to the new system. Human relations is often used in helping employees adjust more quickly.

Human relations is an ongoing process. It is not an activity that suddenly ends. Several techniques have been used by organizations to help improve human relations in the word processing/administrative support system. Included are such techniques as job rotation, job enrichment, motivation, and rewards.

JOB ROTATION

With the advent of word processing, job rotation, which has been used in many organizations, has taken on a new face. With this plan, employees rotate from one area to another, performing duties in a variety of functional areas.

To maximize employee utilization, some organizations have begun rotating secretaries between word processing and administrative support areas. Such programs give secretaries an opportunity to handle and learn several job functions. Through cross-training, cross-utilization, and rotating assignments, employees have an opportunity to develop skills and knowledge other than those involving only the typing function. On a planned rotational basis, employees may rotate from correspondence to administrative functions.

While rotation schedules may vary depending upon the organization, word processing specialists usually spend three months on the equipment initially. After that time, rotation might vary from three to six weeks. When production pressures are heavy, six weeks seems to be an appropriate rotation period because of the fatigue factor.

Administrative support jobs can be rotated on a wide time span because of the nature of the work. Rotation creates an awareness of the total organization and the departmental functions. Helping employees improve their performance results in higher output.

The advantages of job rotation may be summarized as follows: improved morale, quality production and increased volume, and minimal personnel turnover.

JOB ENRICHMENT

Another method for improving human relations in word processing is job enrichment, which involves giving employees additional responsibility, control, and planning opportunities in their jobs.

Job enrichment results in the following advantages:

1. Increases overall performance—work output.
2. Increases employee motivation and commitment.
3. Reduces employee turnover, absenteeism, and complaints.
4. Facilitates the introduction of new equipment, methods, or procedures.

In essence, job enrichment provides word processing employees an opportunity to do the following: (1) perform more challenging and meaningful work, (2) utilize skills and knowledge to a greater extent, (3) assume more authority and responsibility in planning, directing, and controlling work, (4) receive feedback on performance, and (5) prepare for jobs with greater responsibility.

An example of job enrichment is the redesign of a word processing specialist's position to enable the incumbent to communicate directly with the principal when a question arises about the material being processed. Increasingly, the specialist is also given responsibility for directing output. This change enables the specialist to communicate directly with management, to ask questions about incoming dictation, to assume responsibility for proofreading, and to receive direct feedback on performance.

MOTIVATION TECHNIQUES

Several techniques have been successfully employed by organizations to motivate word processing specialists. One technique is to pay word processing specialists more than other secretarial classifications.

As in any office organizational structure, one of the most effective motivational devices is open communication. Keeping employees informed of what is happening or about to happen or has already occurred is the responsibility of management.

In addition, various other communication devices may be effective. One word processing manager reported that weekly situation-improvement sessions were effective morale-boosters. When employees were in charge of these sessions, an atmosphere of openness contributed to their discussion of problems, procedures, and whatever else they wished to discuss. Any activity that permits employes to relieve pressures, to realize small goals, to be recognized as part of the organization's team, can be used as a motivator in the word processing/administrative support concept.

REWARDS

The technique probably most successfully used in developing effective human relations in word processing is that of recognizing word processing specialists for outstanding performance. The need for recognition is a basic human need, and any reward that singles out an individual for doing a job well contributes to his or her overall effectiveness in word processing.

Types of rewards include the following: selection as the outstanding specialist of the month; merit salary increases; faster-than-average promotions; and public recognition in organization publications.

Review questions

1. How may career opportunities for word processing and administrative support personnel differ from those of the traditional secretary?
2. In general, what qualifications are required for entry-level positions in word processing?
3. Discuss the career paths found in word processing and administrative support.
4. What indirectly related positions has word processing created?
5. What characteristics should the effective word processing supervisor possess?

6. Discuss the steps that frequently take place in hiring word processing personnel.

7. What are the objectives of programs designed to train word processing personnel?

8. What advantages result from job enrichment?

9. What types of rewards are made available to word processing personnel?

Cases

Jane Plunkett has been employed for two months as a word processing specialist in the word processing center in the Acme Oil Company, which is located in Oklahoma City. You, the supervisor of the center, notice that Jane's production output is low, often 20 to 30 percent less than the other specialists.

Another employee, Mary Wilbur, recently resigned from her position in the word processing center. You are attempting to fill the position Mary left as well as add another word processing specialist to help process the increasing volume of correspondence coming into the center.

You have interviewed several prospective applicants and note that grammar, punctuation, and spelling skills seem to be deficient among recent high school graduates whom you've interviewed. Because of the great need in your city for personnel with word processing skills, you find yourself in a highly competitive market for the few available skilled word processing specialists.

You are considering a remedial training program for Jane, as well as a training program for new employees.

1. How can you determine whether Jane's poor performance rate is due to inadequate training or to some other cause?

2. If you determine that Jane needs additional training, what steps will you take to introduce a new training program?

3. On what basis will you recommend a remedial training program to other new employees?

4. How can you evaluate the effectiveness of the training program once it has been functioning for six months' time?

• • •

You are the word processing supervisor in Midwest Insurance Company, a large insurance firm located in Chicago. You have been interviewing individuals for word processing specialists' positions in the word processing center, but you are finding it difficult to locate prospective employees with the qualifications you want. You have recently interviewed two applicants, though, who seem to meet the requirements. You are considering employing one of them.

Velma typed ninety words a minute with only two errors on your three-minute timed writing test. She also made a score of ninety on a hundred-word spelling test. Velma indicated on her application that she had been very active in high school extracurricular activities, having been president of the pep club, president of the Spanish club, and secretary of the student council, and having served in other leadership roles. She also graduated third in a class of 150.

Jill, the other applicant whom you are considering, typed only fifty words but had no errors. She missed only two words on the spelling test. Jill told you that she had an "A" average in English in high school. She had been a member of Future Business Leaders of America. Her career goal was "to work in an office."

Since costs in training personnel are increasing, you want to hire the person who will have the best production rate, who will assume responsibility for getting work out on a fast turnaround time, and who will probably not require a replacement soon.

1. In hiring a new word processing specialist, what qualifications are you going to look for?
2. Which of the two applicants seems to be the best qualified for the position? Why?
3. What alternatives are available for training the applicant who is hired (assuming some training may be needed)?

CHAPTER 7

The administrative support concept

One of the important aspects of the word processing/administrative support concept is the specialization of labor resulting from the separation of office functions into typing and nontyping positions. While the previous chapter covered in detail the positions involved in the word processing component, this chapter is devoted to discussion of the administrative support component.

Objectives of the administrative support concept

The administrative support concept has several important objectives, including the following: developing specialization of labor, increasing the level of administrative effectiveness, providing for job recognition, and providing greater promotional opportunities than those found in traditional office structures.

DEVELOP SPECIALIZATION OF LABOR

The position of administrative secretary consists of nontyping tasks formerly handled by general office clerks, messengers, stenographers, and secretaries. The position may also include certain tasks previously handled by managers.

The traditional secretarial position has been divided, with the word processing specialist performing typing and related activities and the administrative secretary specializing in such areas as composition, telephoning, receptionist services, scheduling work, mail distribution, and records management, in addition to other activities assigned by principals. Many of the duties of the administrative secretarial staff are often considered beyond the typical duties of the traditional secretary. Such duties include conducting research, writing speeches, developing manuals and handbooks, evaluating and selecting equipment, and studying space requirements and work flow.

Administrative secretaries often work in clusters of three or four. Since they are no longer responsible for typing or related activities, they essentially become assistants to managers (principals), usually numbering from two to six.

Managerial needs determine the number of administrative secretaries required for efficient operations. For example, six administrative secretaries may serve as many as twenty or twenty-five principals. They may perform all secretarial tasks other than typing, or they may be assigned special areas in which they excel. For example, an administrative secretary might handle all travel arrangements, receptionist duties or records management for all of the principals within a unit.

INCREASE LEVEL OF ADMINISTRATIVE EFFECTIVENESS

Because of the opportunity for secretarial groups to specialize, the level of administrative effectiveness may be increased. When the administrative secretaries are relieved of typing tasks, they are free to perform more complex administrative duties. Areas of responsibility that administrative secretaries may assume include establishing work assignment priorities, time management, composing reports and letters, training principals in the utilization of dictation equipment, conference planning, and assignments requiring problem-solving and decision-making skills.

The level of administrative effectiveness can be increased through the encouragement of supervisors, through regular administrative support staff meetings designed to solve departmental problems, through encouragement of secretarial participation in decision making, and through training in communication.

Principals recognize the value of the administrative support concept. The results of the initial feasibility study and an appreciation for the concept are instrumental in principals' acceptance and utilization of administrative support. Managers responsible for administrative support centers should meet with department heads to explain the benefits of administrative support. The principals need to recognize that the word processing/administrative support system is based on a team concept. Strong top-management support of the concept also facilitates principals' acceptance of word processing/administrative support.

In administrative support, cross-training of administrative secretaries is important. When familiar with each other's activities, administrative secretaries are able to work with one another's principals should the need arise.

Supervision is basic to the effectiveness of administrative support. In selecting supervisory personnel, fundamental qualities to look for include oral and written communication skills, human relations skills, ability to handle pressure and to cope with stressful situations, and a willingness to accept change.

The administrative support supervisor, to be effective, must first determine the individual needs of the executives to be served by the center. In addition, the supervisor must develop a good working relationship with each subordinate administrative secretary. It is also essential that administrative secretaries be given challenging work that stimulates a sense of individual responsibility.

In conjunction with his or her responsibility for the quality and quantity of work produced in the administrative support area, the administrative support supervisor must establish specific attainable goals that correspond to the needs of the principals. Through periodic appraisals and evaluation of the performance of administrative secretaries, an administrative support supervisor can contribute to overall operating effectiveness. The supervisor is also responsible for motivating subordinates, for maintaining high levels of morale, and for recognizing achievement of subordinates.

Probably the most valuable contribution an administrative support supervisor can provide is efficient organization of the work flow to optimize individual and center productivity. The system must be designed to meet the needs of both principals and the department.

In smaller centers where a supervisor may not be designated, the coordination responsibility rests with the individual secretaries and with the principals who must work together as a team.

PROVIDE JOB RECOGNITION

Another major objective of the administrative support concept is to provide greater job recognition for administrative secretaries. Because administrative secretaries work directly with principals, often on a daily basis, the performance of the administrative secretaries is observed continually. The executives are aware of the capabilities of the administrative secretaries to perform their responsibilities.

Before the emergence of the word processing/administrative support concept, the secretary's recognition was dependent upon the position of the executive for whom he/she worked. Often, the secretary's salary was dependent upon the boss's position within the organization. The word processing/administrative support concept, however, incorporates the viewpoint of performance-based job recognition. Positions are classified on the basis of job evaluation and individual performance, and the establishment of salaries is independent of the position of the boss. Job enrichment also provides the high-achieving administrative secretary an opportunity to reach new levels on the career ladder.

PROVIDE PROMOTION OPPORTUNITIES

The higher-level administrative secretaries, who perform numerous decision-making tasks, often have greater opportunities for promotion to middle management positions than traditional secretaries have had. With the increased interest in moving women into management, administrative secretaries now have a valuable vehicle to prepare them for promotion into managerial positions.

It should be pointed out, however, that *opportunities* for promotion to management positions may be available, but in order to take advantage of those opportunities, administrative secretaries must *prepare* to enter competition for upper-level managerial positions. While many of the capabilities and skills necessary to fill the role of an effective administrative secretary are also necessary in supervisory and management positions, the emphasis does shift. Training in such areas as accounting, statistics, finance, management, budgeting, human relations, and economics is often needed by administrative secretaries who advance to managerial positions.

Evidence of the acquisition of managerial proficiency is provided through the attainment of the Certified Administrative Manager designation, a program sponsored by the Administrative Management Society. The content of the CAM examination covers personnel management, financial management, control and economics, systems and information management, and administrative services.

Another alternative which contributes to career options for the administrative secretary is often the attainment of the Certified Professional Secretary designation. Candidates must pass a two-day examination covering six broad areas: (1) behavioral science in business, (2) business law, (3) economics and management, (4) accounting, (5) secretarial skills and decision making, and (6) office procedures and administration. While individuals who pass this examination usually have a goal of attaining the highest degree of professionalism as a secretary, many do find that the CPS designation also contributes to other career options.

Personnel involved in the administrative support concept

The specialization of labor characteristic of the word processing/administrative support concept has resulted in the creation of the administrative secretary career path. These positions are typically more varied than the word processing specialist positions.

JOB DESCRIPTIONS OF ADMINISTRATIVE SECRETARIAL PERSONNEL

The performance of administrative secretarial personnel depends upon management's commitment to efficiency. Accordingly, job descriptions must be developed, the work of administrative secretaries must be measured, and their performance must be evaluated.

Specific duties of an administrative secretary may include the following:

1. Evaluates adequacy of current equipment, space, and furniture.
2. Advises on utilization of space and on selection of new equipment and furniture.
3. Assists in planning and scheduling workload.
4. Composes and dictates correspondence.
5. Gathers information.
6. Researches and prepares reports.
7. Requisitions supplies and equipment.
8. Schedules appointments, meetings, and conferences.
9. Assists with meetings and conferences.
10. Develops efficient work flow procedures.
11. Maintains records.
12. Handles telephone communications.
13. Assumes responsibilities in decision making.
14. Greets visitors.
15. Prepares travel itineraries and handles arrangements.
16. Prepares budgets.
17. Assumes responsibility for administrative details as delegated.
18. Assumes responsibilities for reproduction work.
19. Processes mail.
20. Maintains principals' accounts.
21. Establishes priorities in work production and principals' requests.
22. Supervises work of others.

Contrast the current description of the administrative secretary with the traditional secretarial position as described in Bulletin 1804 (p. 63) prepared by the U.S. Department of Labor, Bureau of Labor Statistics:

Secretary—assigned as personal secretary, normally to one individual. Maintains a close and highly responsive relationship to the day-to-day work activities of the supervisor. Works fairly independently, receiving a minimum of detailed supervision and guidance. Performs varied clerical and secretarial duties usually including most of the following:

a. Receives telephone calls, personal callers, and incoming mail; answers routine inquiries, and routes technical inquiries to the proper persons;
b. Establishes, maintains, and revises the supervisor's files;
c. Maintains the supervisor's calendar and makes appointments as instructed;

    d. Relays messages from supervisor to subordinates;
    e. Reviews correspondence, memoranda, and reports prepared by others for the supervisor's signature, to assure procedural and typographic accuracy;
    f. Performs stenographic and typing work.

The transition from a traditional office structure to a word processing/administrative support system necessitates only two changes in this traditional secretarial position. Normally, the administrative secretary will work with several principals rather than one, and in most cases the administrative secretary will not perform stenographic and typing work. However, in some decentralized word processing systems, administrative secretaries sometimes perform typing as well as nontyping functions.

Figure 7–1 provides a detailed discussion of job descriptions for administrative support personnel at Eastern Airlines. As one moves from the lower-level positions to the higher-level positions, the levels of achievement and responsibility increase.

CHARACTERISTICS NEEDED OF ADMINISTRATIVE SUPPORT PERSONNEL

Whenever an office is converted to a word processing/administrative support system, proper selection of administrative support personnel is crucial. The following qualifications may be considered in hiring or in assessing current employees for administrative support positions:

Has basic knowledge of office functions.
Demonstrates initiative.
Readily assumes responsibility.
Is skilled in oral and written communication.
Is sensitive to the needs of others.
Has ability to view company from overall perspective.
Is flexible and adaptable to change.
Has ability to make decisions and to assume responsibility in the absence of principals or supervisors.
Demonstrates a desire to upgrade skills and continue professional growth.
Has basic knowledge of operating and administrative systems.

The administrative secretary must be capable of making decisions as well as be able to exercise good judgment. The administrative secretary must also be skilled in human relations, understand organizational interrelationships, and be aware of the word processing/administrative support concepts and operational procedures.

Figure 7-1 ADMINISTRATIVE SUPPORT JOB DESCRIPTIONS (EASTERN AIRLINES)

ADMINISTRATIVE SUPPORT JOB DESCRIPTIONS
Supervisor

Reports to: Manager of secretarial services.

Basic functions: Serves the company by:

Providing administrative and secretarial support for departments designated to use the services.

Providing necessary training and motivation of personnel within the unit.

Providing liaison and maintaining good working relationships with those being served to insure that users' objectives are being met.

Responsibilities:

Provides work direction and training for one or more groups of administrative secretaries composed of from 5 to 15 employees.

Provides complete administrative support, including telephone coverage, reservations, filing, developing and handling of correspondence, and all other administrative details required of a function or group of functions.

Determines financial objectives for the unit including budget planning.

Establishes and maintains unit objectives concerning quality of administrative support.

Determines manpower requirements and best use of resources, including temporary help, overtime, special assignments, and cross-utilization of resources.

Designs and revises secretarial job assignments in cooperation with the management supported.

Recommends space needs for present and future administrative support requirements.

Establishes standards of performance for quantity and quality of output.

Determines work priorities between units.

Provides orientation and makes presentations to new users of the secretarial services output.

Resolves customer dissatisfactions.

Figure 7–1 CONTINUED

Interviews and selects personnel for unit staffing, appraises performance, and administers company merit program.

Relationships:

Internal: Confers with management personnel who are supported by the administrative services unit in the coordination, procedural development, and operation of the administrative support function.

External: Demonstrates the concept of administrative support services to interested outsiders, at Administrative Management Society and other professional seminars. Contacts management personnel in other companies employing the concepts of word processing and administrative support services; provides and exchanges information. Keeps abreast of the latest systems, procedures, and equipment in this area.

Supervision: The administrative support supervisor delegates responsibilities to and supervises personnel in the following positions:

Administrative support unit supervisor.

Administrative support coordinator.

Senior administrative support secretary.

Administrative support secretary.

Administrative support secretary trainee.

Coordinator

Reports to: Administrative support supervisor.

Basic functions:

Serves the company by acting as procedural specialist in the area of administrative support services.

Provides guidance, training, and assistance to all administrative support personnel in the accomplishment of the unit's objectives.

Responsibilities:

Provides guidance to all administrative support secretaries in the areas of work procedures such as filing systems, telephone answering, reservations, itineraries, mail procedures, correspondence handling, dictation procedures, and other administrative details.

Acts as section supervisor in absence of incumbent.

Screens, analyzes, and categorizes supervisor's mail in order of priority and importance.

Figure 7-1 CONTINUED

Exercises judgment with respect to urgency, confidential status, and relative importance of all inquiries or messages intercepted for principals. Follows up to adhere to established or increasing response requirements.

Initiates and dictates over own signature frequent requests for routine information of an administrative, technical, or personal nature and incorporates into reports, correspondence, and presentation material as directed, or uses same in continuing reports or files for which the administrative support coordinator is exclusively responsible.

Correlates and reviews work prepared by administrative support secretaries and presents for supervisor's signature or use.

Maintains liaison between supervisor and staff personnel, arranging appointments and relaying information.

Resolves work priorities between groups.

Assists administrative support secretaries in organizing and controlling work at administrative workstations.

Prepares individual productivity reports on administrative support secretaries, consolidates for unit report for manager of secretarial services.

Relationships:

Internal: Resolves problems with departments served, seldom requiring evaluation, and interpreting data and drawing conclusions. Problems usually self-evident.

External: Maintains contacts through professional organizations with peers in other companies and industries applying the administrative support concept.

Supervision: In the absence of section supervisor, directs the following classifications of personnel:

Senior administrative support secretary.

Administrative support secretary.

Associate administrative support secretary.

Administrative support secretary trainee.

Senior Administrative Support Secretary

Reports to: Administrative support unit supervisor.

Figure 7–1 CONTINUED

Basic functions: Serves the company by performing administrative support duties of a complex nature or otherwise requiring exercise of initiative and judgment.

Responsibilities:

In addition to performing all the duties of the lower-level administrative support secretaries, performs more complex work involving a high level of quality, quantity, and speed.

Handles correspondence for a function or group of functions.

Opens, screens, and routes mail.

On own initiative, compiles from files, or other sources, pertinent facts to assist supervisor or staff personnel in handling inquiries and incoming mail. Follows up to adhere to response requirements.

Acknowledges and/or on own initiative summarizes replies requested by correspondence. Initiates timely and appropriate follow-ups as supervisor or staff personnel delegates.

Performs telephone services, makes appointments, receives and screens callers.

Establishes and maintains filing system.

Independently prepares and dictates drafts of finished correspondence for signature by supervisor or staff personnel.

Assists or, in accordance with supervisor's general instructions, prepares statistical reports requiring correlation of facts or figures from one or more sources.

Incorporates statistical data into presentation data as directed.

Anticipates and responds to detailed needs of supervisor.

Maintains awareness of activities within supervisor's scope of operation and on own initiative, through outlines, briefs, or other suitable means, keeps supervisor informed.

Administrative Support Secretary

Reports to: Administrative support unit supervisor.

Basic functions: Serves the company by performing varied secretarial and administrative duties specified below. Uses such office equipment as adding machines, calculators, dictation machines, copiers, and other such units.

Figure 7–1 CONTINUED

Responsibilities:

In addition to performing all the duties of the lower-level administrative support secretarial positions, performs functions of a more complex nature requiring further training in general office practices.

Correlates and distributes incoming mail to proper individual for follow-up. May screen mail for supervisor and draft replies.

Establishes follow-up files and gathers material for supervisor in handling incoming mail.

Maintains and sets up file systems, where necessary, based upon the company's records management program.

Performs telephone answering services.

Schedules appointments and maintains supervisor's calendar, alerts others to operational or administrative commitments.

Compiles and maintains continuing report requirements.

Keeps calendar of reports due, with adequate advance notice to supervisor for preparation.

Prepares and dictates routine correspondence, prepares and dictates varied correspondence from verbal outlines and submits for approval and signatures.

Prepares presentation material from drafts or detailed instructions.

Associate Administrative Support Secretary

Reports to: Administrative support unit supervisor.

Basic functions: Serves the company by performing secretarial and administrative duties using general office procedures. Uses office equipment such as adding machines, calculator, Codacom, copiers, and other such units.

Responsibilities:

Performs routine duties such as handling correspondence and miscellaneous administrative functions.

Greets visitors and escorts them to the appropriate area.

Answers telephones, makes appointments, and receives callers.

Obtains and assembles information requested by supervisor.

Figure 7-1 CONTINUED

> Maintains and/or establishes filing system based upon company's records management program. Protects confidential material in an appropriate manner.
>
> Prepares reports on own initiative or general instructions; verifies calculations, collates, proofreads, and distributes as necessary.
>
> Prepares material for presentation as requested.
>
> Arranges for travel reservations.
>
> Operates general office machines, such as copiers, calculators, and adding machines.
>
> With direction, schedules conference meeting times and conference room reservations, inspects room for arrangements and equipment.
>
> Under direction, prepares and/or processes cash advances, expense accounts, checks vendor's invoices for accuracy, and maintains records where required.

Source: Walter A. Kleinschrod, *Management's Guide to Word Processing*, Chicago: The Dartnell Corporation, 1977.

Organization of the administrative support concept

The administrative support system may be organized in several ways. In the early installations of word processing, administrative support was viewed as a function entirely separate from word processing. While all typing tasks were channeled through word processing, the nontyping tasks were performed by the administrative support personnel. Later, when it became apparent that the system should be designed to meet the needs of each organization, several alternatives emerged.

In some offices, administrative secretaries perform only administrative functions; in some, they work as teams performing interdepartmental administrative jobs; and in others, they are organized into teams performing both typing and nontyping activities.

MODES OF ADMINISTRATIVE SUPPORT

Three commonly used organizational structures of administrative support—the augmented mode, the work-group mode, and the centralized mode—are identified in Walter A. Kleinschrod's *Management's Guide to Word Processing*, pp. 50–51, a Dartnell Corporation publication.

Augmented mode. This structure refers to that office organization which enables the secretary to perform the duties of an administrative assistant. Through this approach, the word processing component of the system is generally located in or near the administrative support area. This structure handles the typing function of the office operation within the physical area of the administrative support services. The augmented structure has been effectively used in introducing word processing because of the minimum change required in the physical and social office structure.

Work-group mode. A work-group mode structure utilizes the division of labor principle but at the same time encompasses only one department or unit. All personnel become familiar with the vocabulary, functions, personnel, and procedures of a single division. Because of the variety of jobs and responsibilities of each employee, motivation poses few problems.

Centralized mode. The centralized mode represents to the greatest degree the original theory of the division of labor with respect to the typing and nontyping functions within the office. Personnel whose responsibilities are within the administrative support area perform no typing tasks. Usually the administrative support personnel perform tasks associated with executive correspondence, such as drafting communications, editing, proofreading, and preparing materials for dispatch. Usually, the centralized mode operation includes a supervisor who is a key member of the team.

Figure 7–2 illustrates the application of these modes. In executive row, an augmented arrangement provides both typing and administrative support, with part of the typing function being performed in word processing. In a marketing department, for example, a work-group mode may meet the need for productivity as well as for giving consideration to the principals. With productivity of major importance in engineering, the work-group arrangement with a higher principal-to-secretary ratio may be preferred. In manufacturing, where productivity is the priority, a centralized administrative support system has the highest principal-to-secretary ratio, with all typing processed through the word processing center.

OTHER ALTERNATIVES FOR ORGANIZING ADMINISTRATIVE SUPPORT

Another organizational pattern of the administrative support component, developed by IBM, is the System I, II, III, IV concept.

System I represents the most complete division of labor between administrative work and correspondence work. This was the system

Figure 7-2 MODES OF ADMINISTRATIVE SUPPORT

PRINCIPAL GROUP	PRINCIPAL GROUP	SECRETARIAL SUPPORT SYSTEM DESIGN

PRINCIPAL GROUP
Performance criteria:
1. Job satisfaction 3. Responsiveness
2. Productivity 4. Convenience
  5. Quality

EXECUTIVE ROW

Job satisfaction — 2 3 4 5

MARKETING

Job satisfaction — 2 3 4 5

ENGINEERING

Job satisfaction — 2 3 4 5

MANUFACTURING

Job satisfaction — 2 3 4 5

EXECUTIVE ROW
Principals
Secretaries
Com Com Com

MARKETING
Com Com / Com Com

ENGINEERING
Adm Adm / Com Adm

MANUFACTURING
Adm Adm Adm / Adm Adm

EXECUTIVE ROW
Ungrouped combination typing and administrative
Com Com Com Com
Coordinator activity oriented   Principal oriented
Typing overload to word processing center

MARKETING
Grouped
Com Com Com Com
Principal oriented combination stations
NO TYPING TO WORD PROCESSING CENTER

ENGINEERING
Grouped
Adm Com Adm Adm
Coordinator activity oriented   Principal oriented   Activity oriented   Activity oriented
Most typing to word processing center

MANUFACTURING
Grouped
Adm Adm Adm Adm
Coordinator activity oriented   Activity oriented   Activity oriented   Activity oriented
All typing to word processing center

LEGEND: Typ TYPING STATION   Adm ADMINISTRATIVE STATION   Com COMBINATION STATION (Typing and administrative)

Source: Walter A. Kleinschrod, *Management's Guide to Word Processing*, Chicago: The Darnell Corporation, 1977.

most often used in the earlier plans, when it was thought that a center for all typing activities separated from the administrative roles would be most productive. Administrative work continued to be performed by individuals specifically assigned to principals.

System II came into being early in the historical development of the word processing/administrative support concept. Based on the experience of a limited number of business organizations, it became apparent that the word processing/administrative support concept could be even more productive when one individual or several individuals were assigned to a small group of executives. The typing functions were still centralized in a word processing center or, in some instances, in a functional area.

System III, which reflects the next change in the evolving process of the word processing/administrative support concept, combines administrative services and correspondence services into the same centers. The secretaries have at their work stations the necessary equipment that enables them to provide both correspondence and administrative functions as a means of supporting the principals.

System IV, or the mixed configuration, makes it possible for some centers to provide both correspondence and administrative support. Other centers serve exclusively as correspondence centers for document reproduction especially suited to that organization—high-volume correspondence, long turnaround typing jobs, manuscripts, and so forth.

Obviously, plans in addition to those described here are being used where organizations have found other divisions of workloads to meet their needs best. When designing a word processing/administrative support system, it is important that the organizational structure of the concept meet the needs of the organization. Therefore, the organizational structure will not necessarily parallel the various patterns discussed in this text.

The administrative support center

As evidenced in the foregoing organizational patterns of the administrative support functions, the division between administrative support and word processing may, in fact, be less distinctive in terms of physical environment than the original concept of word processing/administrative support envisioned. Generally, however, the administrative support function encompasses those tasks and duties other than transcribing dictation and typing. With vendors now providing specialized electronic equipment for administrative support, the functions of the administrative support areas may shift.

LAYOUT

The layout of the administrative support area, which is based upon organizational design, should contribute to convenience in carrying out functions of the area. If support personnel are organized into teams, then the team members should be located where they can easily assist each other.

An administrative support area should be located near the principals it serves, and the size should provide for approximately eighty to ninety square feet per work station. Although office landscaping can create a design which may give the illusion of privacy, care should be exercised to give the administrative secretary a sense of belonging.

Each administrative secretary's work station should provide for flexibility to meet changing needs, which is easily accomplished through office landscaping, movable partitions, and modular furniture. Acoustically treated dividers contributing to a harmonizing color scheme can provide a spacious, pleasant atmosphere in the administrative support area. At the same time, these dividers, modular furniture, and work stations can be rearranged easily to accommodate a change in personnel or work flow needs.

The physical appearance of an administrative support center can be structured to meet the needs of specific jobs and the employees who perform those jobs. The wide range of options of specialized, tailor-made units, which include the partitions, furniture, and accessories, often result in considerable cost savings. With the addition of effective lighting, coordinated colors and designs, proper work flow, and efficient personnel, office landscaping has been quite successful when applied to administrative support areas.

A common configuration of administrative support is to cluster team members so they can easily assist one another, as well as be able to work with other principals served by the team. The receptionist's desk is located near the entrance to the center to provide easy access to visitors. The supervisor's desk should be positioned to provide easy access to both principals and administrative secretaries when needed. The supervisor must be located where he/she is able to schedule work loads among the administrative teams to assure efficient work flow procedures.

Figure 7–3 illustrates the layout of an administrative support center.

Evaluation of administrative support

The tremendous increase in the implementation of word processing systems and the creation of administrative support positions has

Figure 7-3 LAYOUT OF ADMINISTRATIVE SUPPORT CENTER

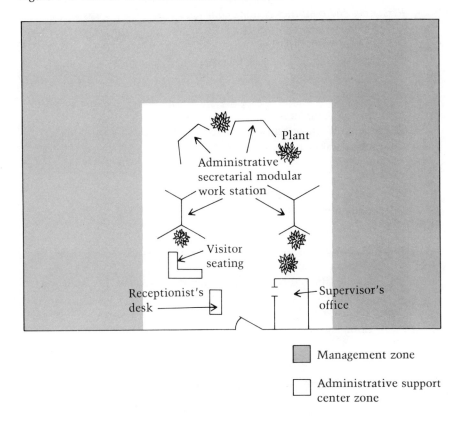

Management zone

Administrative support center zone

brought about significant changes. These changes necessitate the need for the evaluation of various aspects of administrative support.

EVALUATION TECHNIQUES

In moving ahead with a functioning, productive word processing/administrative support system, Kleinschrod, in *Management's Guide to Word Processing*, pp. 190–191, suggests the use of the following operational checklist, which is helpful to management in evaluating both word processing and administrative support.

OPERATIONAL CHECKLIST

During the start-up phase

( ) Monitor learning curves.
( ) Provide, if needed, for additional support.
( ) Plan attrition.

When fully operational

Personnel and communications consideration:

( ) Appraisal and counseling.
( ) Information bulletins.
( ) Management/employee meetings.
( ) Activity reports for management.

Productivity considerations:

( ) Charge-back system for prorating center costs.
( ) Reports and controls.
( ) Job descriptions.
( ) Training.
( ) Work assignments.
( ) Adjustments within the system.

Possible problem situations:

( ) Addition of new principals.
( ) Inflexibility to accommodate principal movement, i.e., staff and job-level changes.
( ) Too fast a rate of secretarial attrition.
( ) Unionization.

Possible solutions:

( ) Realistic plan for career-path mobility.
( ) Night shifts, part-timers, temporaries.
( ) Attitude feedback systems.
( ) Management reports and controls.

JOB ANALYSIS

Word processing/administrative support has brought about significant changes not only in procedures but also in the structure of jobs. Job descriptions, which are written statements outlining the duties and responsibilities of a job, are based upon job analyses, the formal process of collecting information about a job. The job specification provides a statement outlining the personal qualifications required of an individual in order to perform the duties and responsibilities identified in the job description.

The success of the job analysis program is greatly affected by the reliability of the information collected. Two techniques appropriate for use in collecting information are the questionnaire and the interview.

The questionnaire. The questionnaire typically consists of short-answer questions to which those individuals who are most familiar with a particular job respond. The integrity of the questionnaire technique depends upon the employee's ability to interpret correctly the questions and to respond to those questions with accurate answers that are easy to classify.

Largely, the design of the questionnaire is determined by the number of administrative support employees to be included in the study. In organizations with a small number of word processing/administrative support employees, a simplified questionnaire relating to the job title, description of duties, schedule of tasks, special requirements for the job, and special work performed on the job may be adequate.

Human relations is an important factor in the administrative support concept. Because it may be difficult for employees in certain positions to assess human relations or personality factors that comprise their jobs, the questionnaire technique may not be suitable in certain instances.

However, by using the questionnaire technique, a large amount of information can be obtained rapidly. A potential disadvantage of the questionnaire technique involves the construction of the questionnaire. Because questionnaires may be complex and long, employees sometimes provide inaccurate information because of their difficulty in completing the questionnaire. Too, employees may over- or under-estimate the importance of the jobs they perform. To help assure the collection of accurate information, the supervisor may want to review the employees' responses.

To overcome these disadvantages, some organizations also use interviews to gather needed information about jobs.

The interview. The interview method assures the interviewer of collecting all the needed information about a particular job. Less-than-complete information, which may be a result of the questionnaire technique, is partially avoided by the interview. This technique, which involves questioning employees about the duties and responsibilities of their jobs, may also include observation when the interview is conducted at the work station.

Based upon a job information worksheet, the interview technique can increase accuracy and completeness of information by reading the employee's responses back to him or her for confirmation. The interview technique is especially appropriate when the job being analyzed includes human relations and personality factors, two traits common in administrative support positions.

EMPLOYEE APPRAISAL

In addition to an overall evaluation of operations, as well as using job analyses and developing job descriptions and specifications, supervisors and manager/principals are responsible for the appraisal of employee performance. While each supervisor continuously evaluates employees' performance on an informal basis, many organizations utilize formal appraisal systems.

An appraisal technique especially useful for administrative secretaries is the results-oriented technique. This technique is especially useful because of the broad nature of such positions. The results-oriented technique, originally used in evaluating managerial employees, requires the employee's active participation in establishing goals for which the employee will be held accountable.

A typical results-oriented appraisal form includes the employee's name and position, the supervisor's name, title of the department, and period of evaluation. Records are maintained as follows: Target, criteria for measurement, results achieved, and percent of target.

Records are also maintained of the employee's long-range future goals and his or her training needs to reach each of these goals. This aspect of the evaluation is especially important for administrative support personnel who want to take advantage of promotion opportunities. Although career paths for administrative support personnel are evident, many employees need additional training to qualify for upper-level positions.

Figure 7–4 illustrates a form that may be used in results-oriented appraisal.

Several advantages of the results-oriented system of employee evaluation for administrative support personnel may be noted:

1. The employee knows management's expectations of his/her performance.
2. The employee's progress is based upon measurable goals.
3. Attention is directed to specific results in work performance.
4. Communication between supervisor and employee provide better understanding in working relationships and achievement of goals.
5. Career development of the employee is encouraged.
6. Overall performance is usually improved.

Regardless of the system of evaluation used, performance appraisal of the administrative support personnel is extremely important to the success of the total word processing/administrative support concept.

Figure 7-4 RESULTS-ORIENTED PERFORMANCE REVIEW

Name _____   Date_____

Position _____   Department _____

Supervisor _____   Evaluation period_____

GOALS

Target	Criteria for measurement	Results achieved	Percent of target
1.			
2.			
3.			
4.			
5.			

FUTURE GOALS	TRAINING NEEDS

One year   Area: _____
             Specific: _____
1.   _____
                           _____
2.   _____

3.

4.

Two years

1.

Employee signature: _____   Supervisor's signature: _____

Review questions

1. Define the term "specialization of labor."
2. In what ways has the word processing/administrative support structure contributed to increased administrative effectiveness?
3. What major benefits seem to derive from the administrative support organization?
4. How do the duties of secretaries in administrative support services differ from secretarial duties as defined by the U.S. Department of Labor?
5. What special characteristics are needed by administrative support personnel?
6. Compare the augmented mode, the work-group mode, and the centralized mode of organizational structure.
7. How do Systems I, II, III, and IV differ in procedures?
8. Discuss the advantages and disadvantages of the questionnaire and interview methods of job analysis.
9. Discuss the results-oriented method of employee appraisal.

Cases

You are the administrative secretary to Edward Jones in the firm, Jones and Shelling, Certified Public Accountants, which is located in Washington, D.C. Your responsibilities include not only gathering reference material for research studies and preparing reports and statistical analyses, but also proofreading correspondence from the word processing center. Mr. Jones dictates outgoing correspondence (much of it urgent) each morning with the expectation that turnaround time in the word processing center provides for your proofreading, his signature, and distribution, all in the same day. During the past month, you have worked overtime at least three times a week to retype letters that were not mailable.

You have noticed no special pattern in the types of errors that are occurring, but as you recall they seem to consist mainly of incorrect addresses, misspelled names, wrong figures quoted, and sentences that are unclear. As far as you know, personnel in the word processing center has not changed during the past month when errors have been increasing noticeably.

Although you report directly to Mr. Jones, Elizabeth Ashley supervises the word processing center.

1. What actions might you take to solve the problems mentioned above?
2. Do you feel that you should continue to have to work overtime to assure the completion of urgent work? Why?
3. What specific recommendations might you make to Elizabeth Ashley?
4. Do you feel you should make recommendations to Mr. Jones enabling him to improve his dictation? If so, what might your recommendations be?

• • •

Nearly six months ago, the executive committee of the Johnson Company, a hardware supplier located in Scottsday, Arizona, decided that the use of word processing would be desirable. Accordingly the decision was made to install a decentralized word processing/administrative support system.

Progress on installing the word processing component has been more rapid than in developing the administrative support area. Because the changeover to the new system is now about two months away, the coordinator for the installation of the new word processing/administrative support system feels that action on the administrative support component needs to take place immediately.

Accordingly, she has asked for your help in certain phases of the process.

1. Of the three modes—augmented, work-group, and centralized—which do you feel would be most appropriate for this situation? Why?
2. When hiring individuals for the administrative secretarial positions, what qualifications or characteristics should the organization look for?
3. Once the administrative support system is installed and has been functioning for a period of time, what factors should be considered when assessing the effectiveness of administrative support?

CHAPTER 8

Control in word processing systems

Control is as important in word processing systems as in any other business system. The overall purpose of control is to assure compliance of actual results with anticipated results. In developing and maintaining cost-effective word processing, the following are important control devices: work measurement; production records and standards; cost controls related to personnel, equipment, and supplies; and work scheduling controls. This chapter presents a discussion of control as it relates to quantity of output; quality of output; costs of personnel, equipment, and supplies; and work scheduling.

Quantity control

Quantity control varies among word processing systems and organizations. Control involving work measurement, development of standards, and maintenance of production records is usually a basic consideration in word processing. Through quantity control, the efficiency of the word processing operation may be evaluated on the basis of both total production and individual performance.

NATURE AND CHARACTERISTICS OF QUANTITY CONTROL

Control is a follow-up process identifying results, particularly those of an unsatisfactory nature, that require the application of certain measures of correction. In word processing, control is essential for assuring the success of the operation and for meeting goals and expectations.

When a word processing system is installed, devices for controlling the work program should be developed during the planning stages. The person responsible for word processing in an organization will find control especially crucial in achieving desired results in the operation.

Quantity control in word processing has several important objectives, including the following:

1. To provide a mechanism for assessing the conformity of anticipated results with actual results.
2. To assure the achievement of the goals and objectives of the word processing system.
3. To maximize the cost effectiveness of the word processing system.
4. To increase the efficiency of the operation of the word processing system.
5. To provide a mechanism for coordinating the various elements of word processing.

6. To help the word processing/administrative support employees perform their jobs as efficiently and effectively as possible.

When instituting a quality control program in word processing, the following steps are utilized:

1. Identification of the specific functions of the work to be controlled.
2. Determination of production goals.
3. Assessment of actual production.
4. Comparison of actual production with production goals.
5. Application of corrective measures when and where needed.

Before a quantity control program can be instituted, those responsible for its use must be familiar with its various components. The success of the quantity control program is more often determined by the human element than any other factor.

WORK MEASUREMENT

As increasing numbers of business, government, and educational organizations are becoming more cost-efficiency conscious, the measurement of office activities is receiving considerable attention. Many office managers and word processing managers view work measurement as a means of controlling office operations and especially word processing functions. When using production standards to compare actual results with anticipated results, efficiency can be improved.

Nature of work measurement. One of the greatest challenges facing the word processing supervisor is that of work measurement, a system designed to assess employee productivity and to provide a basis for determining work standards. Various work measurement approaches should be carefully investigated to ensure that performance among personnel is maximized, that workloads are equitable, and that productivity is accurately measured. Care should be exercised to assure that work measurement itself does not entail undue amounts of employee and supervisor time in recordkeeping activities.

Techniques of setting standards. Several work measurement techniques may be used to set work standards in word processing. In selecting the appropriate technique to use, factors to be considered may include the following: (1) The degree of accuracy desired; (2) The cost of developing the standards; (3) The nature of the work for which standards are needed; (4) The use to be made of the standards; and (5) The personnel involved and their understanding of the work measurement program.

Although other techniques might be adapted to word processing, those discussed in this chapter are production records, time study, and predetermined standard time data.

Production records. Production records is a widely used technique for measuring work to develop standards in word processing. This technique incorporates the use of employee production records to determine the time needed to complete a particular job or project.

The advantages of using the production records technique are its simplicity, understandability, and low cost. A potential disadvantage, however, may result from inaccurate standards caused by an employee's failure to maintain precise time logs or because of the nonuniform projects that are completed in a word processing operation.

Production measurement systems are based on character, word, line, unit, or page counts. Character or word counts are very precise, but the cost of collecting the data may be prohibitive. Page counts present a disadvantage since unfair weights may be assigned. Generally, the size of a page is not considered (8½-by-11-inch or 8½-by-14-inch), and the amount of type on a page may not be considered. For example, one page may have only three or four lines, and another page have forty or more lines, but both would be counted the same.

A line count may be determined rapidly with an overlay for either elite or pica type. The overlay allows the typist to measure standard pages as well as irregular size pages. Allowance, too, may be made for variation in vertical linespacing.

Another alternative is the unit count, made by an overlay of four sections, each referred to as a unit. A section containing any typewritten material is counted as one unit, with page computations based upon total units divided by four. This same technique could be successfully used by dividing a page into eight sections and making the computations in the same way as when using four sections. Although line counts have been widely used in the past, quarter-page as well as one-eighth page counts are rapidly increasing in popularity.

Time study. The time study technique may be adapted to word processing measurement. This technique involves three steps:

1. Identifying and dissecting into its basic components the job involved.
2. Recording the time taken by each component of the job on a time-study sheet.

3. Determining appropriate standards on the basis of the amount of time taken by each component of the job.

Sometimes termed stopwatch study, this technique can produce highly accurate and reliable time standards. Essential preliminaries to such a study are standardization of methods and conditions under which the work is performed. The technique, used appropriately, is regarded as an objective, scientific approach to establishing time standards for units of work. Time study is appropriate for measuring work processes containing minute elements, and the resulting standards can be readily used in measuring employee performance.

This method does require well-trained analysts and objectives that protect employee interests as well as clear communication of program objectives.

Predetermined standard time data. Predetermined times are often used to set standards for general office operations. This approach affords a high degree of accuracy and is generally accepted by employees. Predetermined time systems include body motions and time values, while standard data refer to the grouping of the basic elemental times into larger blocks. Predetermined standard time data are generally purchased from management consulting firms or from work measurement associations. These standards are used to guide the setting of work standards within the organizations that use the predetermined standard time data.

Data are developed by trained analysts, using the following steps:

1. Breaking the work process down into minute elements.
2. Analyzing each element according to the motion involved.
3. Comparing each motion of the work process with the purchased predetermined standard time data to determine the appropriate standard for each of the motions.
4. Establishing standards for the entire process by adding the standard times for each of the motions.

Several predetermined standard time data systems are available. The Master Clerical Data, which is adapted from Methods Time Measurement (MTM), may also be adapted for certain categories of word processing activities.

The use of predetermined standard time data provides accurate standards that, because of the exactness with which standards are developed, are more readily accepted by employees than standards developed by other techniques. Another advantage of this technique is that it is not as time consuming as other devices. The cost, however, is considerable because of the need for highly trained analysts and the necessity of purchasing the standard time data.

The charts in Figure 8-1 contain predetermined standard time data designed to assure consistent and representative work that is performed in both routine clerical operations and in standard office operations. The basic time values were developed with standard data, which were then correlated to these time data.

Before material is evaluated, steps must be taken to define the characteristics of the material being evaluated. The following information is needed:

> Total current workload by typing category, i.e., letters, memos, abstracts, forms, and other documents.
> Amount of statistical or columnar typing and nonstatistical typing in the workload.
> Number of lines per page and the number of characters per line.
> Average number of lines per page in each category, i.e., the total number of lines typed divided by the number of pages in that particular category.
> Number of retyped revisions for each category and the average number and kinds of revisions for each page.
> Average hourly salary rate for the typists and professional proofreaders who will be performing the work.
> Volume information on backlog work and overtime used and any expected increase in staff.
> Projection of the future workload by category.

For each individual application, the following instructions must be used to calculate the typing time:

> Determine the particular machine to be used: text editor, display text editor, etc.
> Determine into which category the particular document fits— letter, memo, legal document, or form.
> Determine whether or not the material is considered statistical (columnar typing, which may or may not include numbers) or nonstatistical typing.
> Determine whether or not erasures or strikeovers are permitted on the material being typed.

At this point, the correct charts to be used are determined by reading the headings in Table 1 of Figure 8-1. All time standards are in minutes and include a 15 percent allowance.

Figure 8-1 PREDETERMINED STANDARD TIME DATA

FIGURE 1

Chart A. Manual typing of addresses, salutations, date, and closures for letters, memos, legal documents, and forms

	Standard time in minutes
Erasures permitted:	
1. Letters from typed material	3.20
2. Letters from hand written material	3.35
3. Letters from dictation (steno or machine)	3.35
4. Memos from typed material	2.37
5. Memos from hand written material	2.57
6. Memos from dictation (steno or machine)	2.57
7. Legal documents from typed material	1.34
Erasures not permitted:	
1. Letters from typed material	1.63
2. Letters from hand written material	1.89
3. Letters from dictation (steno or machine)	1.89
4. Memos from typed material	1.77
5. Memos from hand written material	1.97
6. Memos from dictation (steno or machine)	1.97
7. Legal documents from typed material	0.94

Figure 8-1 CONTINUED

TABLE 1

Typing system	Machine	Type of document	Classification of documents for text editor typing	S:statistical NS:nonstatistical	E:erasures permitted NE:no erasures permitted	Chart to be used for calculating typing time
Non-automatic	Nonautomatic electric typewriters	Body of letters		E NS S NS	E E NE NE	C D E
		Body of memoranda		S NS S NS	E E NE NE	B C D E
		Body of legal documents		S NS S NS	E E NE NE	B C D E
		Body of forms		S NS S NS	E E NE NE	B C D E
	MT/ST and Punched paper tape	Body of letters, memoranda, legal documents, forms				F
Automatic	Text editor	Body of letters	Form			G
			Paragraph selection			H
		Body of memoranda	Form			G
			Paragraph selection			H
		Body of legal documents	Form			G
			Paragraph selection			H
		Body of forms	Form			G
			Paragraph selection			H

Chart B. Manual typing from dictation, long-hand manuscripts, or statistical typing of bodies of letters, memoranda, legal documents, and forms with erasures and strikeovers permitted.

Number of lines typed — Standard time in minutes, Average characters per line

Number of lines typed	25	30	35	40	45	50	55	60	65	70	75	80	85
5	0.52	0.63	0.73	0.84	0.94	1.04	1.15	1.25	1.36	1.46	1.57	1.67	1.81
10	1.04	1.26	1.46	1.68	1.88	2.08	2.30	2.50	2.72	2.92	3.14	3.34	3.62
15	1.56	1.89	2.19	2.52	2.82	3.12	3.45	3.75	4.08	4.38	4.71	5.01	5.43
20	2.08	2.52	2.92	3.36	3.76	4.16	4.60	5.00	5.44	5.84	6.28	6.68	7.24
25	2.60	3.15	3.65	4.20	4.70	5.20	5.75	6.25	6.80	7.30	7.85	8.35	9.05
30	3.12	3.78	4.38	5.04	5.64	6.24	6.90	7.50	8.16	8.76	9.42	10.02	10.86
35	3.64	4.41	5.11	5.88	6.58	7.28	8.05	8.75	9.52	10.22	10.99	11.69	12.67
40	4.16	5.04	5.84	6.72	7.52	8.32	9.20	10.00	10.88	11.68	12.56	13.36	14.48
45	4.68	5.67	6.57	7.56	8.46	9.36	10.35	11.25	12.24	13.14	14.13	15.03	16.29
50	5.20	6.30	7.30	8.40	9.40	10.40	11.50	12.50	13.60	14.60	15.70	16.70	18.10
55	5.72	6.93	8.03	9.24	10.34	11.44	12.65	13.75	14.96	16.06	17.27	18.37	19.91
60	6.24	7.56	8.76	10.08	11.28	12.48	13.80	15.00	16.32	17.52	18.84	20.04	21.72

Using the letter in Figure 1 as an example, the production time of the letter typed on automatic equipment, with paragraph selection, consisting of nonstatistical material, and permitting erasures on manually typed portions, will be determined. In Figure 8-1, Table 1 directs reference to Chart G for the body of the letter and Chart A for the other parts of the letter (address, salutation, enclosures, etc.).

Figure 8-1 CONTINUED

Chart C. Manual nonstatistical typing, from typewritten material, of bodies of letters, memoranda, legal documents, and forms with erasures and strikeovers permitted.

Number of lines typed	Standard time in minutes Average characters per line												
	25	30	35	40	45	50	55	60	65	70	75	80	85
5	0.44	0.53	0.62	0.70	0.79	0.87	0.96	1.05	1.13	1.22	1.31	1.40	1.48
10	0.88	1.06	1.24	1.40	1.58	1.74	1.92	2.10	2.26	2.44	2.62	2.80	2.96
15	1.32	1.59	1.86	2.10	2.37	2.61	2.88	3.15	3.39	3.66	3.92	4.20	4.44
20	1.76	2.12	2.48	2.80	3.16	3.48	3.84	4.20	4.52	4.89	5.24	5.60	5.92
25	2.20	2.65	3.10	3.50	3.95	4.35	4.80	5.25	5.65	6.11	6.55	7.00	7.40
30	2.64	3.18	3.72	4.20	4.74	5.22	5.76	6.30	6.78	7.33	7.86	8.40	8.83
35	3.08	3.71	4.34	4.90	5.53	6.09	6.72	7.35	7.91	8.55	9.17	9.80	10.36
40	3.52	4.24	4.96	5.60	6.32	6.96	7.68	8.40	9.04	9.77	10.84	11.20	11.84
45	3.96	4.77	5.58	6.30	7.11	7.83	8.64	9.45	10.17	10.99	11.79	12.60	13.32
50	4.40	5.30	6.20	7.00	7.90	8.70	9.60	10.50	11.30	12.21	13.10	14.00	14.80
55	4.84	5.83	6.82	7.70	8.69	9.59	10.56	11.55	12.43	13.43	14.41	15.40	16.28
60	5.28	6.36	7.44	8.40	9.48	10.44	11.52	12.60	13.56	14.65	15.72	16.80	17.72

Chart D. Manual typing from dictation, long-hand manuscripts, or statistical typing of bodies of letters, memoranda, legal documents, and forms with no erasures or strikeovers permitted.

Number of lines typed	Standard time in minutes Average characters per line												
	25	30	35	40	45	50	55	60	65	70	75	80	85
5	0.84	1.01	1.18	1.35	1.52	1.68	1.85	2.02	2.19	2.36	2.53	2.69	2.93
10	1.20	1.44	1.69	1.91	2.16	2.38	2.62	2.87	3.09	3.34	3.58	3.82	4.08
15	2.16	2.61	3.03	3.36	3.91	4.32	4.77	5.20	5.65	6.07	6.52	6.93	7.52
20	3.08	3.74	4.33	4.97	5.56	6.16	6.82	7.41	8.06	8.64	9.09	9.90	10.73
25	3.80	4.60	5.34	6.14	6.87	7.60	8.40	9.20	9.94	10.67	11.48	12.21	13.23
30	4.32	5.24	6.07	6.98	7.82	8.64	9.56	10.39	11.31	12.13	13.05	13.87	15.04
35	4.84	5.86	6.80	7.82	8.75	9.67	10.70	11.63	12.66	13.59	14.62	15.55	16.85
40	5.36	6.50	7.52	8.66	9.69	10.71	11.86	12.89	14.02	15.06	16.18	17.22	18.66
45	5.85	7.12	8.25	9.50	10.63	11.76	13.01	14.14	13.39	16.51	17.76	18.89	19.48
50	6.40	7.76	8.98	10.34	11.57	12.81	14.16	15.40	16.74	17.98	19.32	20.56	22.28
55	6.92	8.38	9.72	11.18	12.51	13.85	15.31	16.64	18.10	19.43	20.90	22.23	24.09
60	7.44	9.02	10.44	12.02	13.45	14.89	16.45	17.89	19.46	20.89	22.46	23.90	25.93

Next, determine the number of characters per line in the letter. To do this, draw a vertical line at the righthand side of the body of the letter to indicate the average length of line. Measure or count the individual characters, including spaces between words and punctuation, in the average line. Round the number off to the nearest five characters. In this example, the average is sixty-nine, which is rounded off to seventy.

Measure or count the number of typed lines in the body of the letter, rounded to the nearest five lines. In this example, the number of typed lines is eighteen, rounded off to twenty.

Figure 8-1 CONTINUED

Chart F. Form letters, memoranda, legal documents and forms typed on text editor, automatic mode.

Number of lines typed	Standard time in minutes Average characters per lines												
	25	30	35	40	45	50	55	60	65	70	75	80	85
5	0.24	0.26	0.29	0.32	0.34	0.37	0.40	0.43	0.45	0.48	0.51	0.53	0.56
10	0.37	0.42	0.48	0.53	0.59	0.74	0.70	0.75	0.80	0.86	0.91	0.94	1.02
15	0.51	0.59	0.67	0.75	0.93	0.91	0.99	1.07	1.16	1.24	1.32	1.40	1.48
20	0.64	0.75	0.86	0.97	1.07	1.18	1.29	1.40	1.51	1.62	1.72	1.83	1.94
25	0.78	0.91	1.05	1.18	1.32	1.45	1.59	1.72	1.86	2.00	2.13	2.26	2.40
30	0.91	1.07	1.24	1.40	1.56	1.72	1.89	2.05	2.21	2.37	2.54	2.70	2.86
35	1.05	1.24	1.43	1.62	1.80	1.99	2.18	2.37	2.56	2.75	2.94	3.13	3.32
40	1.18	1.40	1.52	1.83	2.05	2.26	2.48	2.70	2.91	3.13	3.35	3.56	3.78
45	1.32	1.46	1.80	2.05	2.29	2.54	2.78	3.02	3.27	3.51	3.75	4.00	4.24
50	1.45	1.62	2.00	2.26	2.54	2.81	3.08	3.35	3.62	3.88	4.16	4.43	4.70
55	1.59	1.89	2.18	2.48	2.78	3.08	3.37	3.67	3.97	4.27	4.56	4.86	5.16
60	1.72	2.05	2.37	2.70	3.02	3.35	3.67	4.00	4.32	4.65	4.97	5.29	5.62

Chart G. Paragraph-selection typing of bodies of letters, memoranda, legal documents, and forms on the text editor on automatic mode. Standards are based on the selection of two paragraphs. For each additional paragraph selected, add 0.10 minutes to the standard.

Number of lines typed	Standard time in minutes Average characters per line												
	25	30	35	40	45	50	55	60	65	70	75	80	85
5	0.34	0.36	0.29	0.42	0.44	0.47	0.50	0.52	0.55	0.58	0.61	0.63	0.66
10	0.47	0.52	0.58	0.63	0.69	0.84	0.80	0.85	0.90	0.96	1.01	1.04	1.12
15	0.61	0.69	0.77	0.85	1.03	1.01	1.09	1.17	1.26	1.34	1.42	1.50	1.58
20	0.74	0.85	0.96	1.07	1.17	1.28	1.39	1.50	1.61	1.72	1.82	1.93	2.04
25	0.88	1.01	1.15	1.28	1.42	1.55	1.69	1.82	1.96	2.10	2.23	2.36	2.50
30	1.01	1.17	1.34	1.50	1.66	1.82	1.99	2.15	2.31	2.47	2.64	2.80	2.96
35	1.15	1.34	1.53	1.72	1.90	2.09	2.28	2.47	2.66	2.85	3.04	2.23	3.42
40	1.28	1.50	1.62	1.93	2.15	2.36	2.58	2.80	3.01	3.23	3.45	3.66	3.88
45	1.42	1.56	1.90	2.15	2.29	2.64	2.88	3.12	3.37	3.61	3.85	4.10	4.34
50	1.55	1.72	2.10	2.36	2.64	2.91	3.18	3.45	3.72	3.98	4.26	4.53	4.80
55	1.69	1.99	2.28	2.58	2.88	3.18	3.47	3.77	4.07	4.37	4.66	4.96	5.26
60	1.82	2.15	2.47	2.80	3.12	3.45	3.77	4.10	4.42	4.75	5.07	5.29	5.72

Calculate the total typing time for the letter by adding the separate values found in the appropriate charts. Following is the calculation of the standard time for the example letter:

Heading and closure of letter (Chart A)	3.35 minutes
Body of letter (20 lines at 70 characters per line) (Chart G) (1.72 + .10 for third paragraph)	1.82 minutes
TOTAL TIME	5.17 minutes

Had this same letter been typed manually, the time consumed in the typing of the body of the letter would have been 4.89 minutes (Chart C), which combined with the time for typing the heading and

Figure 8-1 CONTINUED

Chart H.   Automatic typing of bodies of letters, memoranda, legal documents, and forms on the text editor and punched paper tape machines.

Number of lines typed	Standard time in minutes Average characters per line												
	25	30	35	40	45	50	55	60	65	70	75	80	85
5	0.14	0.16	0.19	0.22	0.24	0.27	0.30	0.32	0.35	0.38	0.41	0.43	0.46
10	0.27	0.32	0.38	0.43	0.49	0.54	0.60	0.65	0.70	0.76	0.81	0.84	0.92
15	0.41	0.49	0.57	0.65	0.73	0.81	0.89	0.97	1.06	1.14	1.22	1.30	1.38
20	0.54	0.65	0.76	0.87	0.97	1.08	1.19	1.30	1.41	1.52	1.62	1.73	1.84
25	0.68	0.81	0.95	1.08	1.22	1.35	1.49	1.62	1.76	1.90	2.03	2.16	2.30
30	0.81	0.97	1.14	1.30	1.46	1.62	1.79	1.95	2.11	2.27	2.44	2.60	2.76
35	0.95	1.14	1.33	1.52	1.70	1.89	2.08	2.27	2.46	2.65	2.84	3.03	3.22
40	1.08	1.30	1.52	1.73	1.95	2.16	2.38	2.60	2.81	3.03	3.25	3.46	3.68
45	1.22	1.46	1.70	1.95	2.19	2.44	2.68	2.92	3.17	3.41	3.65	3.90	4.14
50	1.35	1.62	1.90	2.16	2.44	2.71	2.98	3.25	3.52	3.78	4.06	4.33	4.60
55	1.49	1.79	2.08	2.38	2.68	2.98	3.27	3.57	3.87	4.17	4.46	4.76	5.07
60	1.62	1.95	2.27	2.60	2.92	3.25	3.57	3.90	4.22	4.55	4.87	5.19	5.52

Chart I.   Standards for typing inserts in form letters or selected paragraphs for letters, memoranda, legal documents, and forms on an automatic typewriter.

Number of lines typed	Standard time in minutes Average characters per line												
	25	30	35	40	45	50	55	60	65	70	75	80	85
5	0.57	0.69	0.81	0.91	1.03	1.13	1.25	1.37	1.48	1.59	1.70	1.83	1.95
10	0.88	1.00	1.24	1.40	1.57	1.73	1.91	2.09	2.26	2.43	2.61	2.82	2.95
15	1.43	1.82	2.00	2.26	2.57	2.80	3.10	3.39	3.64	3.93	4.22	4.53	4.74
20	2.07	2.49	2.91	3.28	3.71	4.07	4.50	4.93	5.29	5.71	6.15	6.56	6.93

Source: Excerpted from *Word Processing Report,* copyright © 1974 by Geyer-McAllister Publications, Inc., New York.

closure (Chart A) would have been a total of 8.24 minutes. Thus, 3.07 minutes were saved by using the automatic equipment for this particular job. By determining the annual volume of letters and multiplying this number by the time saved per letter, the total number of hours saved per year can be determined. The hours saved multiplied by the average hourly rate of the typist will determine in monetary terms what is being saved.

At this point in the analysis, the time saved in revisions and proofreading as well as the elimination of overtime can be determined.

Quantity output information is desirable for determining the efficiency and effectiveness of a word processing system, and cost information helps determine the amount of time that will be consumed to process a given amount of work. This information is necessary for scheduling work, which is discussed in a later section of this chapter.

MAINTAINING PRODUCTION RECORDS

In order to monitor the word processing center and to be able to present meaningful reports to top management, the word processing supervisor must devise a means for determining the center's productivity. These reports are often used by management to provide a basis for making changes in the word processing system—adding more work stations, installing higher speed equipment, and so forth.

Records in word processing centers are usually maintained on a daily basis. Data are gathered on the basic kinds of work processed by the center, such as correspondence, form fill-in, long reports, statistical typing, and other documents unique to each organization. Once productivity rates have been obtained for the center, as well as for each employee, performance standards may be established. Changes in procedures may have to be made to maintain standards.

Techniques. The techniques for maintaining production records vary from one word processing system to another, depending upon the organization of the word processing activities, the types of equipment used, and the categories of communication processed.

One large organization reported implementation of an operations analysis plan which eliminated previous manual systems used to gather data on production, quality, and client usage. Previously, the company spent three to four hours a day calculating production from the previous day and maintaining cumulative monthly figures for eighteen typists in two centers.

Now, principals fill out a requisition form, consisting of three sections, as shown in Figure 8-2. The top section is completed by the principals submitting new work. The middle section is used when revisions are needed. The last section accumulates all information. At the end of each day, requisitions are gathered from centers and the raw data in the last section are recorded on a tape cassette by an electronic typing system equipped with a communicating feature. The data on the tape are computerized under a predetermined file name. When a record of performance is desired, the word processing supervisor simply contacts the computer via the communicating terminal and asks for a report, which is received on a high-speed printer.

Figure 8-3 illustrates a word processing production report that provides detailed information of each employee's weekly production rates. Information includes the principal for whom the work was performed; a description of the document; time required for processing; type of input (machine dictation, longhand, or copy typing); total lines based upon rough draft or final, original copy; lines of revision; or lines of stored data (standard); turnaround time; and total pages. From this

Figure 8-2 REQUISITION FORM

South Central Bell

ASD09X
APRIL, 1977

ADMINISTRATIVE SERVICES WORD PROCESSING CENTER TYPING REQUEST
(To Be Filled Out By Author)

Document No. _____

Hq. _____ State _____

Job Description _____

Today's Date _____

Name _____

Date Needed _____

Room/Floor Number _____

( ) Rush Approval for priority handling

Ext. Number _____

Day/Hour Requested _____ (am) (pm)

Responsibility Code _____

District Level Supervisor _____

Function Code _____

Environment Code _____

Special Instructions: _____

Rate Area & Rate Group _____
(where appropriate)

Account Number _____

Retention: Yes _____ No _____

How Long: Days _____ Permanent _____

Final _____
Draft _____
Original _____ Carbon _____ Blue _____
Bond _____ Letterhead _____
Form _____

ADMINISTRATIVE SERVICES WORD PROCESSING TYPING REVISION
(To Be Filled Out By Author If Returning Job)

Document No. _____

Date Needed _____

Date Returned _____

Please revise the attached material.

Additions/Deletions _____

Spelling _____

Misinterpretation _____

Typographical Error _____

Punctuation _____

Revision & Error _____

Other _____

Name _____

Retention: Yes _____ No _____

Room/Floor _____

How Long: Days _____ Permanent _____

Extension _____

Account Code _____

Hq. _____ State _____ Environment Code _____

Responsibility Code _____ Function Code _____ Rate Area & Rate Group (where Appropriate) _____

194

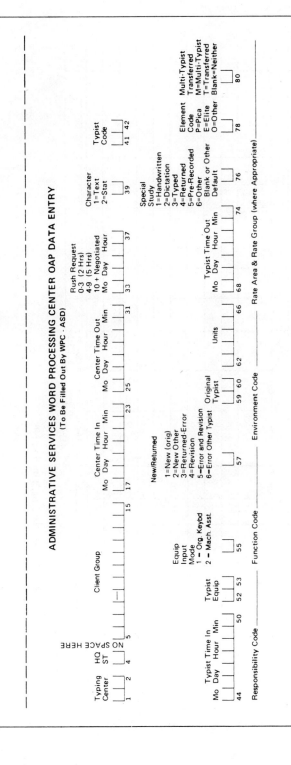

The word processing requisition form is divided into three sections.

Source: The Office, November, 1977.

Figure 8–3 WORD PROCESSING PRODUCTION REPORT

WORD PROCESSING PRODUCTION REPORT WEEKLY SUMMARY

NAME ______________________ WEEK OF ______________________

							LINES								
PRINCIPAL	DESC.	DATE	TIME IN	TIME STARTED	TIME OUT	INPUT	ORIGINAL		REVISION		STANDARD		TURN	TIME	TOTAL
							ROUGH	FINAL	REVISE PLAY	REVISE PRINT	PLAY	PRINT	TIME 1 2 3 4 6 8 24	SPENT	PAGES
						MD / LH / CT									

Average time __________ *Total pages* __________

Total lines __________

MD—Machine dictation
LH —Longhand
CT —Copy type

Source: Courtesy of Nelson & Harding, Lincoln, NE

Figure 8-4 WEEKLY PRODUCTION RATES

| | PRODUCTION FOR WEEK OF OCTOBER 2–OCTOBER 8, 1980 | | |
	Total lines	*Total pages*	*Average time*
Andrea	12,308	321	2.0
Maggie	13,500	421	4.0
Joanne	6,167	170	3.0
Carla	5,390	151	4.0
Laverne	4,997	148	3.0
Christine	2,818	77	3.5
CENTER	45,180	1,288	3.5

Source: Courtesy of Nelson & Harding, Lincoln, NE

information, the record of each employee's total line production, total page production, and average turnaround time may be charted.

From the weekly production rates, shown in Figure 8-4, comparisons may be noted and used as a basis for scheduling purposes, as well as for other considerations.

Figures 8-5 and 8-6 show how total lines produced in a word processing center may be charted and comparisons made on a yearly basis.

Some word processing centers maintain computerized daily production controls that provide the basis for weekly and monthly reports. A daily/weekly report may contain such information as units of measure (twenty-five lines of copy, jobs, or forms); activities (machine dictation; handwritten, hard copy; prerecorded, rough drafts, etc.); predetermined goals; production-goal ratios; and total volume. On the basis of these data, close control of production rates can be maintained.

Forms used. Figures 8-7 and 8-8 illustrate control forms that are used by a state agency. Figure 8-7 is completed when dictated material is processed through the center, while Figure 8-8 is a work order that is completed when a principal sends nondictated material to the word processing center.

Figure 8-5 PRODUCTION RATES (LINES)

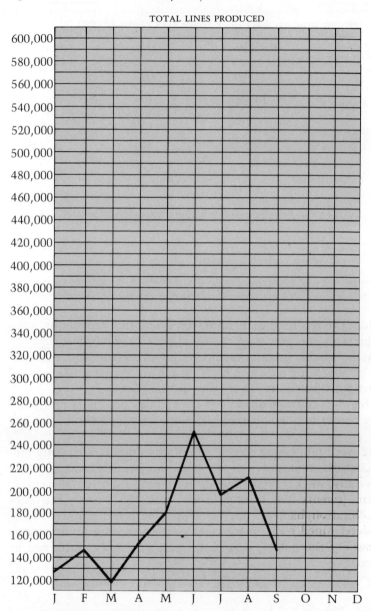

TOTAL LINES PRODUCED

Source: Courtesy of Nelson & Harding, Lincoln, NE

Figure 8-6 PRODUCTION RATES (PAGES)

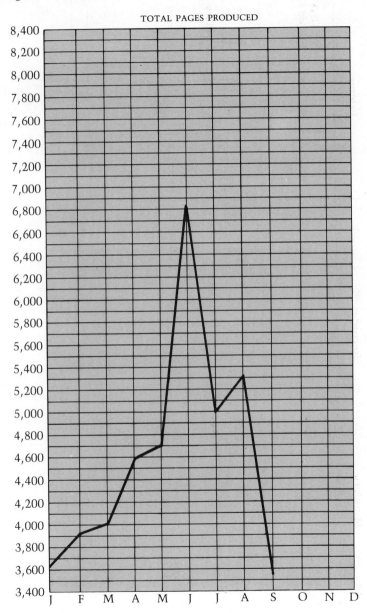

TOTAL PAGES PRODUCED

Source: Courtesy of Nelson & Harding, Lincoln, NE

Figure 8–7 CONTROL FORM

Recorder	Secretary	Recorder				Printer		
Application	Secretary	Customer	Author	Date In	Time In	Time Out	Date Out	Work Days Elapsed
1	2	3	4	5	6	7	8	9
Copy		Welfare						

Secretary		Recorder	Secretary			Printer		Secretary
Long Hand Lines	Short Hand Lines	Machine Dictation Lines	Media Time	Copy Type Lines	Rough Lines	Revised Lines	Repetitive Lines	Typed Lines	Document I.D.
10	11	12	13	14	15	16	17	18	19

DPW-15 6/77 0100

Source: Courtesy of Nebraska Department of Public Welfare

Figure 8–8 WORD ORDER

WORD PROCESSING CENTER WORK ORDER

Nebraska | Department Of Public Welfare

• Please complete this form when sending non-dictated work to the Word Processing Center.
If you would like to discuss a project, feel free to call the W.P.C. Manager.

Author	Division	Telephone Number
Title of Project	Date	Date Needed

SPECIAL INSTRUCTIONS

☐ Rough Draft ☐ Letterhead ☐ Number of Originals

☐ Final ☐ Envelopes ☐ Number of Carbons

☐ Plain Bond ☐ Labels ☐ For Permanent Storage

ADDITIONAL INSTRUCTIONS

Source: Courtesy of Nebraska Department of Public Welfare

Quality control

An important factor in the success of word processing is satisfactory quality of work. Typed material that contains a spelling error or a major grammatical error contributes to additional time and cost in proofreading and correcting. Errors in transcription result in loss of confidence by principals. Errors in proofreading on repetitive documents contribute to excessive costs in equipment use, operator time, and paper used, and—when not caught before the documents are distributed—may be damaging to company image and reputation.

On the other hand, when work dispatched from the word processing center is consistently accurate and neat and reflects good judgment, it will bring favorable recognition to the word processing operation and personnel. High quality work is a source of pride to the employee involved.

Most word processing installations have incorporated some form of quality control into their operations to assure the quality of production.

BASIC ELEMENTS

A word processing quality control procedure incorporates at least five basic elements:

1. Standards for use when completing documents.
2. Actual quality of current work.
3. Records of errors.
4. Correction of defective work.
5. When necessary, training employees as a means of improving the quality of work.

The inability of a word processing system to achieve quality goals can be caused by a variety of reasons. In some cases, poorly trained word processing specialists contribute to poor quality. In other instances, carelessness on the part of the word processing employees contributes to errors. Other reasons might include quantity standards so high that the quality of employee output suffers and carelessness on the part of principals when originating material.

Many organizations have found that keeping a log of uncorrected errors of each specialist and having the specialist who made the error responsible for correction are effective ways of helping improve the quality of output.

word processing manager is concerned with how to maintain a cost-effective operation. Because conversion to word processing was initially motivated by the need for cost-effectiveness and because the business organization is concerned with the rise in total office costs, cost control in any word processing system is mandatory. A considerable amount of the word processing supervisor's time will, therefore, involve cost-control activities.

Cost control provides several important objectives for word processing.

1. To develop standard costs for various word processing operations.
2. To develop within the word processing/administrative support employees a desire to be cost conscious.
3. To assist in the development of efficient word processing operating procedures.
4. To allocate the costs of word processing operations to the appropriate functions or departments.
5. To identify word processing operations that need improvement.

To calculate costs, the word processing supervisor should take into consideration the following: the volume of the correspondence, the degree to which the correspondence is standardized, the number of tasks involved in word processing input-output, the efficiency with which the correspondence is processed, and the level of cost incurred in processing the communications.

Data used in determining the word processing costs can be used in a number of ways:

1. Identifying the relationship between the actual costs of word processing and expected costs.
2. Identifying inefficient word processing operations and procedures.
3. Assisting in evaluating and revising work methods.
4. Assisting in selecting new equipment to meet current needs of the word processing operation.
5. Identifying the alternative word processing procedures that are most efficient in view of the costs incurred in performing the tasks.

TECHNIQUES FOR CONTROLLING COSTS IN WORD PROCESSING SYSTEMS

Major costs in word processing systems stem from personnel costs, equipment costs, supplies costs, and work procedure costs. Word processing costs have been discussed, to a limited extent, in the section of this chapter dealing with work measurement, but additional considerations are mentioned here.

Personnel costs. Because salaries of personnel account for a large portion of the costs of the word processing operations, employee cost control is a major factor in controlling costs within the organization.

One suggestion for controlling costs is to be certain that the number of employees is appropriate for the amount of work being processed. Because turnover is likely to increase if employees are unduly pressured to increase production, employee output should be based on reasonable standards. By using the standards developed during work measurement and by projecting work schedules, an estimate of the number of personnel needed to cover the workload can be made. The cost of frequent selection, placement, and training of new employees will contribute to excessive personnel costs in the word processing operation.

Another suggestion for controlling personnel costs is to hire employees who are qualified for the jobs they are expected to perform. Or, if qualified employees are not available, training experiences should be made available to new employees. Some vendors of word processing equipment provide training for employees who use their equipment. With the increasing use of word processing equipment, schools at secondary and postsecondary levels have developed curricula in this area and are providing students with appropriate learning experiences.

Management and supervisory personnel should communicate with employees and prospective employees about expected output levels. Through an awareness of employer expectations and word/document production levels, employees are more likely to establish individual production goals. When the workload exceeds the manpower available, consider which of these alternatives would result in the greatest savings: employee overtime, part-time employees, employees from temporary help agencies, or floating units.

Personnel costs must be addressed in the design and implementation of any word processing system. Proper staffing not only results in satisfactory service for the principals served but also contributes to cost efficiency. The number of personnel required for an effective word processing system depends upon the organization of the word processing system, the type of work which the system is to handle, the quantity of work to be processed, workload variation, service level expectations, productivity rates, and equipment use.

Equipment costs. While word processing equipment does not solve the problem of the high cost of office operations, it is one means by which productivity can be increased and costs reduced. Word processing equipment is expensive, and it is important that its use result in a full benefit at the lowest cost.

The equipment used in word processing depends upon the type of system that is most cost effective for the work processed by each organization. An examination of the many types of equipment and systems available is necessary to be able to choose equipment that meets the needs of the organization. Factors to be considered are cost, availability of service, vendor assistance in setting up procedures during installation of equipment, manufacturer/vendor training support, ease of equipment use, standardization and compatibility of equipment, purchase versus rental, and reliability of manufacturer.

Furniture and supplies costs. Word processing centers and administrative support areas require the kinds of supplies and accessories found in any office, such as desks, chairs, waste baskets, pencil sharpeners, and decorator accessories. Some of the major categories of furniture and supplies especially useful in a word processing or administrative support office are:

> Binders that hold magnetic cards, document formats, and the documentation for word processing routines.
> Racks and files for storing cartridges, cassettes, and diskettes.
> Media for dictation and automated typing equipment.
> Work station modules designed for word processing operations.
> Specialized paper and envelopes for continuous typing.
> Typewriter ribbons/cartridges.

Uses made of supplies can contribute to cost efficiency, especially when inventory controls are maintained through computerized requisitions. Figure 8–9 illustrates a form that may be used in such a system.

Figure 8-9 SUPPLY REQUISITION FORM

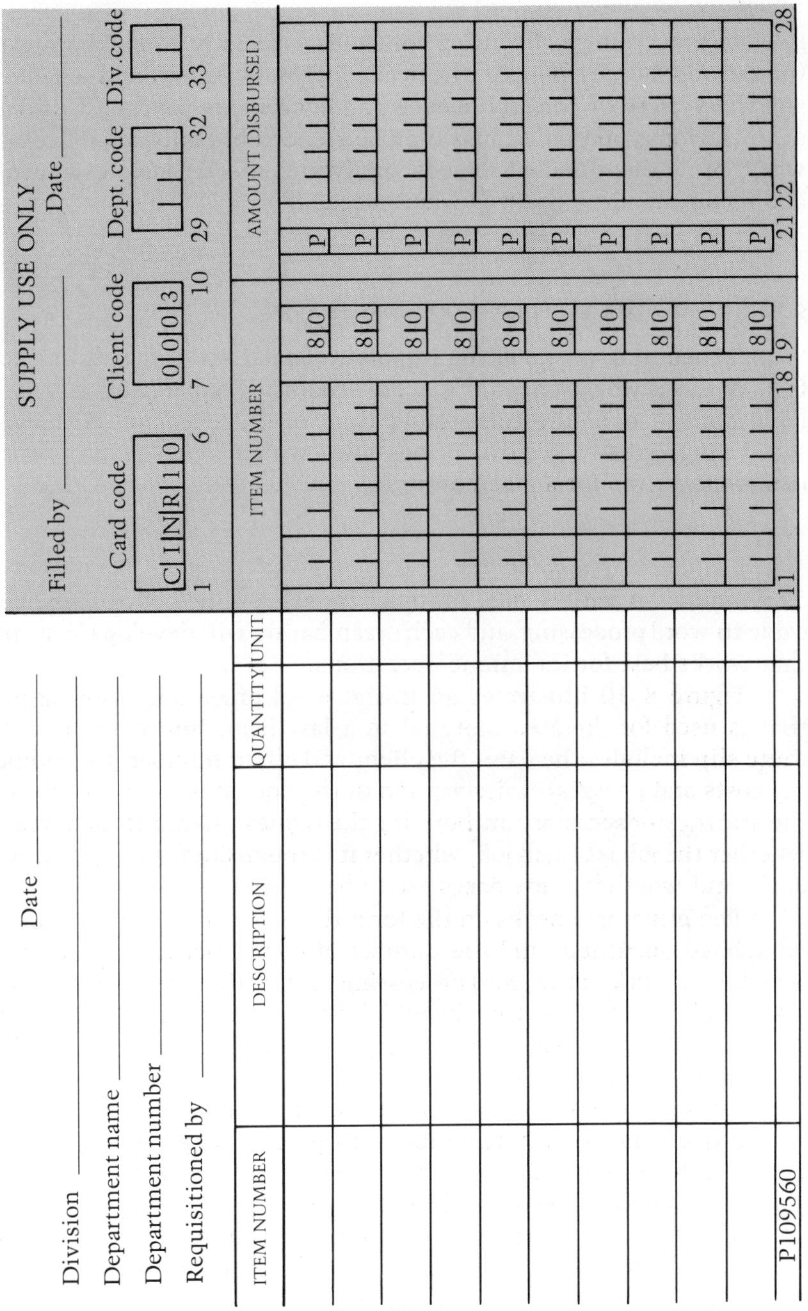

Scheduling control

In word processing, scheduling control is especially crucial because of the various sources of input, the need for prompt turnaround schedules, and the variety of correspondence and documents processed. In large organizations, one individual may be responsible only for scheduling work, providing detailed records, analyzing effectiveness of controls, and recommending changes where needed.

SCHEDULING WORK IN WORD PROCESSING SYSTEMS

Work scheduling is one of the important functions of scheduling control. Without work scheduling, word processing supervisors have very little control over the turnaround time of a document. With work scheduling, greater control is possible, which helps assure desired turnaround time for a given project.

Techniques. A variety of techniques for scheduling control are applicable to word processing, and each organization will develop the format that works best for its unique operations.

Figure 8–10 illustrates an initial word processing routing form that is used for dictated material in a law firm. Information on the route slip includes the date; the client and client number (for computing costs and charges); a description of the document; the signature of the attorney or secretary authorizing the request; name of the dictator; whether the job is a rush job; whether it is rough draft, rerough, or final copy; and whether some pages are to be revised.

The principal checks on the form the paper size requested for the completed document and the number of copies needed. As an aid in scheduling work in the word processing center, the principal (attorney) also checks an absolute time by which the document must be ready for distribution. The absolute time may be to meet express mail schedules, and the principal indicates on the routing form whether or not the completed document is to meet one of these schedules.

If overtime is authorized for word processing personnel to complete the document, that item is checked "yes" on the form. Space is also available for other special instructions.

Schedule log. Schedule logs are frequently used for scheduling work within the word processing center. The schedule log is generally completed by the word processing supervisor, or by an assistant, to provide knowledge of the stage of completion of the work in progress.

Figure 8-10 WORD PROCESSING ROUTING FORM

WORD PROCESSING ROUTING FORM

Date _____

CLIENT_____

CLIENT NO. _____

DESCRIPTION _____

_____

ATTORNEY/SECRETARY _____

DICTATED BY _____

☐ RUSH

☐ ROUGH

☐ REROUGH

☐ FINAL

☐ REVISION p. _____

PAPER SIZE

☐ 8½ x 11   ☐ 8½ x 14

☐ Letterhead   ☐ 8 x 10½

NO. OF COPIES _____

COMPLETION TIME

PREFERRED_____

ABSOLUTE _____

EXPRESS MAIL _____

AIR FREIGHT _____

IS OVERTIME AUTHORIZED

☐ YES   ☐ NO

SPECIAL INSTRUCTIONS:

Source: Courtesy of Nelson & Harding, Lincoln, NE

Figure 8–11 WORK CHART

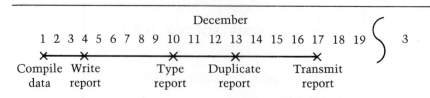

Work chart. Another technique for use in scheduling is the work chart shown in Figure 8–11. When using this technique, the word processing supervisor works backward from the required completion date. For example, if a manuscript is to be completed on December 19, the supervisor indicates the date each chapter is to be typed, to whom the project is assigned, time started, and time finished. By determining the completion date of a project and by determining the amount of time it will take to complete each phase of the project, the date on which each subportion must be started and/or completed can be readily determined.

Work schedule calendar. Another work scheduling technique is a work schedule calendar, illustrated in Figure 8–12. This day-by-day schedule for a week's duration contains jobs or projects that are to begin on a specific day. The work schedule calendar often provides a list of the names of word processing specialists so that when jobs are accepted by the word processing center, the specialist who is responsible for completing each job can be designated. As a specialist completes one project, the next one can be started without the word processing supervisor's making the assignment at that time.

Measuring the overall performance of the word processing system

A checklist might be quite helpful in measuring the overall performance of the word processing system. The management information checklist illustrated in Figure 8–13 can provide the basis for designing a tailormade performance measurement and control report. This checklist presents more than thirty measures of word processing activities typically generated as output from Benton's Performance Measurement and Control (PMC) systems. It is a compilation of the kinds of measures used in many word processing centers and incorporates specific performance measures needed to manage efficiently.

Figure 8-12 WORK SCHEDULE CALENDAR

Employee	Monday Tuesday Wednesday Thursday Friday
Jane	Year-end report (Cramer)
Lori	Sales letters (Brown) Project (Davidson)
Pat	Manuscript (Jones) Report (Smith)
Mary	

Benton states that the first step in selecting performance measures is to formulate a clear idea of the word processing center objectives —from the center manager's point of view, from upper management's point of view, and from principals' points of view. Once the center objectives have been outlined, the task of identifying performance measures to be selected becomes easier.

On the left side of the checklist appear descriptions of more than thirty measures that could be developed into a PMC system. Opposite each description is a brief statement about the use of each measure. Each of the five columns on the right side of the checklist represents a different level of importance, from "absolutely necessary" to "unnecessary." Any measure or information not listed on the chart but needed in a management report can be added at the bottom. At the bottom of each of the five columns, a suggested frequency for preparing the data is provided.

Performance measurement systems are available from vendors and word processing consultants or can be developed by in-house personnel who are trained in systems design. Generally, when designing a work measurement system, managers find it advantageous to work with a word processing consulting firm or a systems engineer familiar with word processing.

Figure 8–13 EVALUATION FORM

THE WORD PROCESSING MANAGEMENT INFORMATION CHECKLIST

MEASURES THAT COULD BE DEVELOPED IN A WORD PROCESSING PERFORMANCE MEASUREMENT AND CONTROL (PMC) SYSTEM:			FOR YOUR CENTER THE MEASURE AT THE LEFT IS (CHECK ONE):				
DESCRIPTION OF MEASURE	WHAT THE MEASURE INDICATES OR HOW USED:	REF:	**5**	**4**	**3**	**2**	**1**
			DEGREE OF IMPORTANCE 5 HIGH-1 LOW				
1. PRODUCTIVITY							
(A) Productivity of total center, e.g. work units/keyboard. hours	1. (A) Indicates **performance rate** or efficiency for overall center	I(A)					
(B) Productivity of each secretary	1. (B) Same as I(A), calculated for each secretary	I(B)					
2. TURNAROUND TIME							
(A) A single turnaround time average for all documents processed by the center	2. (A) Indicates overall **level of service** as it relates to speed of getting documents back to users	II(A)					
(B) Turnaround time average **by secretary** for all documents processed by that secretary	2. (B) Same as I(A), calculated for each secretary	II(B)					
(C) Turnaround time average **by user department** for user dept's. documents	2. (C) Same as I(A) except indicates service provided **to** each user department	II(C)					

(D) Turnaround time averages for original, revision, and rush work. Total of three averages for overall center   2. (D) Indicates level of service provided by center on three classes of work. Recognizes differences in priority of the three classes   II(D)

(E) Turnaround time averages **by secretary** for original, revision, and rush work. Three avrgs. for each secy.   2. (E) Same as II(D), calculated for individual secretary   II(E)

(F) Turnaround time averages **by user department** for original, revision & rush work. Three averages per dept.   2. (F) Same as II(D) except indicates service provided **to** each user department.   II(F)

3. WORK VOLUMES

(A) Total volume of work processed by the center, e.g. pages, documents, or other units of work   3. (A) Indicates **quantity** of work produced or through-put of center - how much was done   III(A)

(B) Total volume of work processed **by each secretary**   3. (B) Same as III(A), calculated for each secretary   III(B)

(C) Total volume of work processed **for each user dept.**   3. (C) Same as III(A) except indicates work done for each user dept.   III(C)

(D) Total volume of work processed on each type of equipment in use in the center   3. (D) Indicates how extensively each type of equipment is being used   III(D)

(E) Total volume of work processed of each major document type. e.g. vol. of letters. vol. of proposals, etc.   3. (E) Indicates how much of each **type** of work the users are producing   III(E)

Figure 8-13 CONTINUED

THE WORD PROCESSING MANAGEMENT INFORMATION CHECKLIST—CONT.

MEASURES THAT COULD BE DEVELOPED IN A WORD PROCESSING PERFORMANCE MEASUREMENT AND CONTROL (PMC) SYSTEM:

DESCRIPTION OF MEASURE	WHAT THE MEASURE INDICATES OR HOW USED:	REF:	FOR YOUR CENTER THE MEASURE AT THE LEFT IS (CHECK ONE): DEGREE OF IMPORTANCE 5 HIGH–1 LOW				
			5	4	3	2	1
(F) Total volume of original, revision, and rush work processed **by the center**	3. (F) Indicates how much of each **class** of work the users are producing. Recognizes differences in procedures and work requirements of the three classes	III(F)					
(G) Total volume of original, revision, and rush work processed **by each secretary**	3. (G) Same as III(F) calculated for each secretary	III(G)					
(H) Total volume of original, revision, and rush work processed **for each user dept.**	3. (H) Same as III(F) except indicates work produced for each user. Recognizes differences in the work habits of users	III(H)					
(I) Total **revision work** volumes separated into volumes by revision cycles, i.e. volume of 1st revision work, volume of 2nd revision work, etc.	3. (I) Indicates **quantity** of different types of revision work. Recognizes revisions can be related to quality	III(I)					
(J) Volume of **project* work** separated from total work for each volume measure above	3. (J) Recognizes that project work can frequently be used for fill-in during slack times	III(J)					

4. DISTRIBUTION OF WORK

(A) Volume of work arriving at the center distributed by hour of the day

4. (A) Illuminates **intra-day** peaks and valleys. Indicates when, during the day, staffing is needed in the center — IV(A)

(B) Volume of work arriving at the center distributed by day of the week

4. (B) Illuminates **intra-week** peaks and valleys. Indicates when, during the week, staffing is needed in the center — IV(B)

(C) Volume of processed work distributed by input method, e.g. dictation volume

4. (C) Indicates how extensively each input method is being utilized — IV(C)

(D) Volume of processed work distributed by procedure used, e.g. volume of original keyboarding

4. (D) Indicates how extensively each processing procedure is being used. Points out equipment capability needs — IV(D)

(E) Volume of stored (library) documents processed distributed by document name of code

4. (E) Indicates which of the stored documents are frequently used and which have become inactive — IV(E)

5. DISTRIBUTION OF TIME

(A) Hours spent in the center distributed as regular, overtime, or lost hours. Totals for the center

5. (A) Indicates how paid hours are spent. Factor in cost-of-operation — V(A)

*Project work is work, typically large jobs, which have a specified deadline for completion.

Figure 8-13 CONTINUED

THE WORD PROCESSING MANAGEMENT INFORMATION CHECKLIST – CONT.

MEASURES THAT COULD BE DEVELOPED IN A WORD PROCESSING PERFORMANCE MEASUREMENT AND CONTROL (PMC) SYSTEM:

DESCRIPTION OF MEASURE	WHAT THE MEASURE INDICATES OR HOW USED:	REF:	FOR YOUR CENTER THE MEASURE AT THE LEFT IS (CHECK ONE): DEGREE OF IMPORTANCE 5 HIGH-1 LOW				
			5	4	3	2	1
(B) Hours spent in the center distributed for each secretary as regular, overtime, and lost hours	5. (B) same as V(A) calculated for individual secretary	V(B)					
(C) Total working hours distributed as keyboarding or administrative hours. Totals for center	5. (C) Indicates amount of time using equipment versus amount doing administrative tasks. Types of admin. tasks can be indicated. Illuminates how people and equipment are being used	V(C)					
(D) Total working hours distributed for each secretary as keyboarding or administrative hours totals by secretary	5. (D) Same as V(C) calculated for each secretary	V(D)					
6. COSTS							
(A) Cost per unit of work, e.g. cost per page. Total for center	6. (A) Indicates **cost of operation** useful in charging back costs to user depts.	VI(A)					

(B) Cost per unit of work calculated by document type, e.g. cost of letter, cost of proposal	6. (B) Same as VI(A) except measure recognizes document costs vary according to document type	VI(B)			
(C) Total processing cost incurred by each department using the center	6. (C) Converts activity of user departments to costs incurred. Useful in charging back costs	VI(C)			
7. QUALITY					
(A) Volume of secretary-made errors. Total for center	7. (A) Indicates **level of quality** for work leaving center	VII(A)			
(B) Volume of secretary-made errors. Total for each secretary	7. (B) Same as VII(A). Calculated for individual secretary	VII(B)			
8. OTHER					
Suggested frequency for preparing above measures	(A) **Prepare these measures on a regular basis, e.g. weekly** (B) **Prepare on an irregular basis** (C) **Do not include these measures in PMC system**	**A**	**B**	**C**	

Source: Reprinted from September, 1976 issue of *Modern Office Procedures* and copyrighted 1976 by Penton/IPC, Subsidiary of Pittway Corporation.

217

Review questions

1. Define "control" as it relates to word processing operations.
2. Describe the process of "quantity control" as a function of word processing.
3. Compare the techniques of setting standards for word processing. List the advantages and disadvantages of each.
4. Why are the five basic elements of quality control especially important in an assessment of word processing?
5. How may data be used in determining word processing costs?
6. How can personnel costs be controlled in word processing?
7. How can equipment costs be controlled in word processing?
8. Compare various techniques of scheduling control that may be applicable to word processing.
9. Identify items that should be considered when measuring the overall performance of the word processing system.

Cases

The Calhoun Health Center, which is located in Calhoun, Colorado, converted to word processing last year. Two word processing specialists and three word processing operators work in the center. You were recently employed as the supervisor of the word processing center, the third since the center opened.

The five employees perform a wide variety of duties. At present, each employee operates all the equipment and processes any job which comes into the center. The work includes transcription, straight-copy typing, rough drafts, statistical copy and tabulated reports, and form fill-ins. While some of the material processed in the center is dictation that involves the preparation of an original letter addressed to several people, other jobs require the processing of prerecorded material, either stored documents (i.e., form letters, form memos, contracts, drafts of manuals, etc.) or stored paragraphs.

The vice president to whom you are responsible recently suggested that some means be devised to measure the productivity of the word processing center. The absence of such information prevents management from knowing whether or not a suitable return on the investment is being accomplished.

1. What techniques are available for measuring the productivity of the word processing center?
2. Which of the techniques do you recommend? Why?
3. What steps are involved in the technique that you recommend?

• • •

You are the newly hired supervisor of the word processing center in the Gomez Distributing Company, a supplier of automobile parts, which is located in Tucson, Arizona. The center has been operating for three years.

At the time the feasibility of a word processing center was assessed by an outside consultant, the firm was told that operating costs could be reduced by a minimum of 10 percent after two years' time. At the end of the second year, the firm had reduced its operating costs by 3.5 percent. The vice president for administration has called this to your attention. He also called your attention to the fact that various costs incurred by the center frequently exceed the budgeted amounts.

The vice president has also pointed out that the turnaround time for work processed in the word processing center is too long. In fact, in some instances, it takes longer to get work completed in the center than it did before the word processing system was installed.

1. What factors may be responsible for the inability of the center to achieve the cost-saving claim that was mentioned during the time that the feasibility study was conducted?
2. What specific suggestions can you provide as a means of helping the center achieve its cost-saving objective?
3. What changes might be made to help the center achieve the desired turnaround time on the processing of work?

CHAPTER 9

Records management

The management of records is the focus of increasing attention in many organizations. It has been estimated that the number of records presently being created is increasing at a rate of 10 percent per year. To put this in actual figures, Xerox Corporation estimates 72 billion documents are created annually. Until the paperless office of the future with all its electronic equipment emerges, the majority of these documents will be maintained in paper format. And as long as paper copies are predominant, special consideration must be given to the management of these records.

Word processing and records management applications are becoming more interrelated. Word processing adds to the number of records that are created and that ultimately have to be stored. The ease with which multiple copies of documents are made on equipment used in word processing systems adds to the total records accumulation. Efficient procedures have to be developed not only for maintaining the paper copies but also for maintaining the text-editing magnetic media that are to be permanently stored. In addition, one of the important job functions of administrative secretaries is records management. For this reason, administrative secretaries must be familiar with the procedures involved in the management of records. Word processing specialists also have some records management responsibilities.

Included in this chapter is a general discussion of records management, followed by a discussion of the specific procedures dealing with the management of records in word processing systems. As used in this chapter, "records" refers to documents that are readable (such as paper copies or micrographic images) as well as data/information that are not readable (such as the material stored on magnetic media).

The records cycle through which all records progress begins with the *creation* of a record. After creation, a record is *utilized* and subsequently *stored* for a period of time. During the time a record is held in storage, it may be *retrieved* several times for additional use. At some point, the record will move into the *disposition* stage of the records cycle. Disposition involves several alternatives: destroying records no longer needed, protecting important records against loss or damage, transferring active records into inactive storage, and microrecording documents.

The records management program

Effective records management does not just happen but rather results from the concerted effort of many individuals throughout the organization. Effective records management programs are comprised of several components, including objectives, policies, structure, filing systems, personnel, and equipment. In addition, procedures have to be developed for the retention, retrieval, and disposition of records. Other procedures involve the disposition of records and program evaluation. Since the use of micrographics is increasing, decisions have to be made about the feasibility and suitability of a micrographics system.

OBJECTIVES OF THE RECORDS MANAGEMENT PROGRAM

When developing a records management program, one of the first activities that must take place is the identification of the objectives of the program. The objectives might include the following:

1. To insure adequate control over the records cycle.
2. To develop and utilize efficient procedures in maintaining records.
3. To avoid unnecessary storing of records, including duplicate copies of records.
4. To insure an effective cost-benefit ratio in maintaining and storing records.
5. To standardize and effectively use records storage.

POLICIES OF THE RECORDS MANAGEMENT PROGRAM

Any organizational program as encompassing as records management must operate within the confines of accepted policies. The policies by which the program operates are designed to enhance the effectiveness of the program. The program policies are frequently used in making decisions about various aspects of the program.

Examples of typical policies utilized in records management programs include the following:

1. Records management, an important organizational function, has the support of top management.
2. Each record must receive a level of protection commensurate with its importance to the organization.
3. Each record created within the organization falls under the jurisdiction of the records management program.
4. Primary responsibility for the records management program lies with the program administrator, but ultimate responsibility lies with the vice president to whom the records management program administrator is responsible.

STRUCTURE OF THE RECORDS MANAGEMENT PROGRAM

The structure of the records management program involves the control and storage aspects of the program. The control component of the program can be either centralized or decentralized. With centralized control, the authority and responsibility for the program rests with one individual—typically the administrator of the program. With decentralized control, on the other hand, no one individual has overall authority or responsibility for the program. Decentralized control is not as effective because of the lack of overall direction. It is not very likely that an effective records management program will emerge when program control is decentralized.

The storage of records can be centralized for the entire organization or decentralized throughout the various work units of the organization. Centralized storage results in a centrally located records depository in which all records are stored. With decentralized storage, each work unit stores its own records. With centralized control, it is possible to use either centralized or decentralized storage or a combination of both. A majority of organizations that utilize centralized storage also use decentralized storage for certain records, such as those used very often or those of a confidential nature.

Decentralized control almost always results in decentralized storage of records. As organizations grow in size, decentralized control is less likely to enable an organization to make effective use of its records.

Several advantages result from centralized storage, including the following:

1. The storage of duplicate records can be controlled.
2. Since filing equipment will be more effectively used, less equipment will be needed.
3. Greater filing accuracy results from the use of employees specifically trained in the management of records.
4. Greater control is exerted over the various elements of the records management program.
5. The standardization of equipment and procedures possible with centralized storage is cost effective.
6. All records pertaining to one subject or topic are filed together.
7. Employee absence does not hamper the program since other employees keep the program functioning.

Centralized storage results in the following disadvantages:

1. Records are not as accessible or convenient to users since they must first be obtained from the central storage area.

2. Records are more vulnerable since they are stored in one location rather than dispersed throughout the organization.
3. The confidentiality of records may be more difficult to maintain. For this reason, organizations are more apt to store confidential records in the various work units rather than use centralized storage.

To help make the decision as to which storage alternative to use, the following factors might be considered:

Size and type of organization.
Number and kinds of records stored.
Philosophy of top management with regard to records management.
Competence of personnel with regard to records management activities.

FILING SYSTEMS

Another important aspect of the records management program is the filing system. Filing involves several activities—classifying, coding, arranging, and placing records in storage. Filing systems are comprised of alphabetic and nonalphabetic indexing methods. Alphabetic indexing methods include filing records by name, by subject, or by geographical location, while nonalphabetic indexing is comprised of numerical and chronological methods. Most organizations use two or more of the methods since each of the indexing methods has special uses for filing certain records.

The alphabetic indexing methods are used more commonly than either of the nonalphabetic methods. The filing order of documents is determined by applying filing rules. The file folders are arranged alphabetically by name, subject, or geographical location, while nonalphabetically indexing involves arranging folders either by numerial sequence or by chronological sequence.

Figure 9-1 illustrates the various indexing methods.

PERSONNEL

An important element of effective records management programs is the use of personnel who are knowledgeable about the various aspects of records management. In organizations in which the management of records is not considered an important activity, the personnel who work with records are often quite unknowledgeable. The lack of an effective records management program and knowledgeable employees is often very costly to organizations.

Figure 9-1 INDEXING METHODS

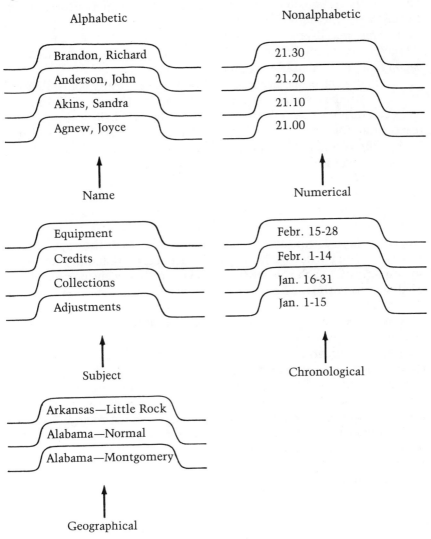

In organizations in which administrative support is used, administrative secretaries are often extensively involved in records management. This is especially true in those organizations where records are decentrally stored. In such instances, the records are stored within the various administrative support centers. Although each of the administrative secretaries should be familiar with the records management program, one or two secretaries often have primary responsibility for maintaining the records housed in the support center.

In programs with centralized control, each administrative secretary who is responsible for the records of the support center works closely with the administrator of the records management program. Thus, the overall program receives proper direction and support and there is consistency in the records management procedures utilized in each of the administrative support centers.

When records management programs are centrally controlled and utilize centralized storage, the level of responsibility of the administrative secretaries for records management is lessened since they are not responsible for system maintenance. They are, however, responsible for putting records into centralized storage. When certain records are not stored centrally because of their confidential nature or frequent use, the administrative secretaries are generally responsible for the management of such records.

Word processing specialists also have responsibilities in records management programs. Most of their responsibilities involve the proper storage of magnetic media used by text-editing typewriters. Since a certain portion of the magnetic media is permanently stored for subsequent use, each specialist has to be familiar with the procedures used in storing the media. Also, each specialist has to be familiar with the indexing system as well as retrieval procedures. Too, some organizations rotate employees between administrative secretarial positions and specialist positions. While the word processing specialist is working in an administrative secretarial position, the specialist will have records management responsibilities.

A variety of other personnel are involved in programs that use centralized storage. Included are the supervisor of the center, file clerks who are responsible for filing and retrieving records, requisitions clerks who are responsible for determining whether or not record requests are valid and legitimate, and messengers who transport records to and from the center.

Individuals who work extensively with records might consider working toward the Certified Records Manager designation as a means of providing evidence of their professional competence. This program is sponsored by the Institute of Certified Records Managers and requires the passage of a comprehensive examination covering several pertinent areas.

EQUIPMENT

Most of the storage equipment used in today's records management programs will be obsolete in the paperless office of the future, when records will be electronically stored on a variety of magnetic media. Present-day storage devices simply will not be needed.

The variety of storage equipment currently available makes it possible to use equipment suited to the specific needs of the records stored. For example, records classified as vital should be stored in a secure, fireproof cabinet. Records that are filed numerically are likely to be stored on open-shelf filing, incorporating a color-coding system to help rapidly locate misfiled folders.

Several factors should be considered in determining the appropriate kind of equipment used for storing various documents. Included are the following:

1. The nature of the records being stored, which includes the size, quantity, weight, physical composition, and value of the documents.
2. The frequency with which records are retrieved.
3. The length of time records are stored in the equipment.
4. The location of the storage area.
5. The size of the storage area.
6. The design features of the office building.
7. The degree of protection required by the various records.

Types of storage equipment. Several types of devices designed for the storage of records are on the market. The devices are classified as vertical, lateral, and power equipment. An increasing amount of the equipment is electrically operated.

At the present time, vertical equipment continues to be the most commonly used type of filing equipment, primarily because of the considerable number of four-, five-, and six-drawer filing cabinets still being used. The number of new standard cabinets now being sold is decreasing because of their poor space utilization.

While the use of standard file cabinets is decreasing, the use of open-shelf filing is increasing. Open shelves conserve space since they are available in heights up to eight feet. However, they tend to be somewhat inefficient for storing records when a few sheets are frequently removed from a folder, in contrast to the situation in which the entire folder is generally removed from the shelf. Consequently, open shelves are most useful in situations in which folders are removed with the contents intact.

Rotary files are also classified as vertical equipment. These files make effective use of floor space and they facilitate fast retrieval. Because of their cost, rotary files are not practical for storing a massive records accumulation.

Lateral filing equipment, although vertical in structure, uses lateral drawers. A distinctive feature of lateral equipment, in contrast to standard filing equipment, is the minimum amount of space it uses.

It is also easier to retrieve records from lateral equipment than from open shelving.

Several types of power filing devices that can be designed to meet an organization's specific needs are available. Although power equipment may be more expensive initially, the cost can often be offset by effective utilization of space. In some instances, the use of power equipment may reduce the number of employees needed to maintain the records accumulation.

When installing power filing equipment, answers to several questions have to be provided. Will the floor support the weight of the equipment and records? Can the system be expanded as the number of records increases? What provisions are available for operating the equipment during power outages? Does the equipment provide adequate protection of records? Are repair/service organizations readily available?

Types of power equipment available are (1) card files specifically designed to accommodate a particular size card or form, (2) structural files, and (3) mobile files.

The card files, which are rotary in nature, are frequently used to store information about customers or clients. For example, they are commonly found in doctors' offices for use in storing patient folders. The structural design of the card files generally results in effective space utilization.

Structural files are often used for storing large numbers of records. The file folders are placed in bins. To retrieve a folder, the number of the bin in which the desired folder is stored is entered into the system by means of a keyboard. An electronic eye scans the bins until the desired bin is located, and a transport mechanism moves the bin to the console operator who retrieves the folder from the bin.

Some mobile files are power operated while others are manually operated. A special feature of mobile files, which are mounted on tracks, is their ability to conserve space. To obtain access to a particular shelf unit, the other shelf units are moved in either direction to create space between two shelf units. At any one time, aisle space exists between only two shelf units. The other units are compressed against one another, which conserves space and provides an element of security.

PROCEDURES

The success of a records management program is often determined by the various procedures that comprise the system. This section contains a discussion of the procedures involved in the following areas: records retention, retrieval, transfer, and control.

Records retention. The appropriate length of time a record should be kept is identified in a records retention schedule. Retention often has an impact on the success or failure of a records management program since the schedule identifies when a record can be disposed of. Without a schedule, some records might be kept far longer than they should be while others are disposed of before they should be.

Records customarily have an active life and an inactive life. During their active life, records are used frequently. Later, when their use becomes minimal—only a few times a year—they should be placed in inactive storage. In some cases, inactive records will be stored in the same area as active records, but when storage space becomes limited, alternative locations, such as a basement or warehouse, should be considered. The records retention schedule identifies the composite length of the active and inactive life of a record. The schedule does not identify when a record should be transferred from active storage to inactive storage. The frequency of record use determines the transfer time. Specific transfer procedures are discussed in a later section of this chapter.

A records retention system provides several benefits, including the following:

1. Cost and space savings result from transferring inactive-status records to low-cost storage areas and from ultimately disposing records no longer needed by the organization.
2. Since records retention reduces the number of stored records, retrieval is made much easier.
3. Retention reduces the probability of records being destroyed before they should be.
4. Equipment is effectively utilized since only those records that have some value to the organization are stored in the equipment.

The development of the records retention schedule follows specific procedures:

1. Undertake a records inventory to determine the types of records, number of records, and location of records.
2. Determine the value of records.
3. Determine the length of time records must be kept, as specified by state or federal laws.
4. Determine the validity and reliability of the tentative schedule.
5. Seek top management approval of the retention schedule.
6. Distribute the schedule to the appropriate individuals.

The records inventory is a crucial step in the development of a records retention schedule. To facilitate this step, an inventory sheet should be used on which the following information is recorded: name or title of record; identification number of record, if present; type of record (original, carbon copy); location of record; index method used (subject, name, geographical location, etc.); volume of record (specified in linear feet); inclusive dates of record; frequency of use; and identity of users.

Once the inventory is completed, the classification of the various records can be determined. Records range in value from vital to unimportant. Vital records are those which enable the organization to exist. Important records, although not necessary for the continued existence of the organization, do serve an important function. Useful records provide a benefit, but not to the degree that vital and important records provide. Unimportant records have very little, if any, utility.

The life of many records is determined by federal and state laws. To determine the legal life of records as stipulated by federal law, *The Guide to Records Retention Requirements*, which is published annually by the U.S. Government Printing Office, is useful. Statutes of limitations, which vary from state to state, can be used to determine the legal life of records, as stipulated by state law. Certain records do not fall under the requirements of either federal or state laws. In determining the retention time of such records, the frequency of use is often the deciding factor.

Once tentative retention times have been determined, the reliability and validity of the schedule should be evaluated. The organization's accountant and attorney are useful in certifying the accuracy of the schedule. In addition, for those records that do not fall under the requirements of federal or state laws, the frequency of use in the past might be used to help determine the validity and reliability of the schedule. To illustrate, if the retention time of a document is tentatively set for four years, and in the past this document has never been used after two years, a retention time of four years is questionable.

Once the validity and reliability of the schedule has been evaluated and any necessary revisions made, the next step in the development of the records retention schedule is to seek top management approval of the retention schedule. Once this has been given, the schedule should be distributed to the appropriate individuals.

Figure 9–2 illustrates a portion of a records retention schedule.

Records retrieval. Records are stored under the assumption that they will be needed in the future. Retrieval, which involves locating and removing a record from a file, is much easier and faster if records are accurately coded and indexed. Improper coding or indexing may result in

Figure 9-2 RECORDS RETENTION SCHEDULE

Legend for authority to dispose	Legend for retention period
AD—Administrative Decision	AC—Dispose After Completion of Job or Contract
ASPR—Armed Services Procurement Regulation	AE—Dispose After Expiration
CFR—Code of Federal Regulations	AF—After End of Fiscal Year
FLSA—Fair Labor Standards Act	AM—After Moving
ICC—Interstate Commerce Commission	AS—After Settlement
	AT—Dispose After Termination
INS—Insurance Company Regulation	ATR—After Trip
	OBS—Dispose When Obsolete
ISM—Industrial Security Manual, Attachment to DD Form 441	P—Permanent
	SUP—Dispose When Superseded

Type of record	Retention period years	Authority
ACCOUNTING & FISCAL		
Accounts payable invoices	3	ASPR-STATE, FLSA
Accounts payable ledger	P	AD
Accounts receivable ledgers	5	AD
Approvals		
Authorizations for accounting	SUP	AD
Balance sheets	P	AD
Bank deposits	3	AD
Bank statements	3	AD
Bonds	P	AD
Budgets	3	AD
Capital asset record	3*	AD
Cash receipt records	7	AD
Check register	P	AD
Checks, dividend	6	
Checks, payroll	2	FLSA, STATE
Checks, voucher	3	FLSA, STATE
Cost accounting records	5AD	
Earnings register	3	FLSA, STATE
Entertainment gifts & gratuities	3	AD
Estimates, projections	7	AD

* After Disposed
** Normally
† Govt. R&D Contracts

Source: Courtesy of Electric Wastebasket Corp., New York, NY 10036.

the waste of a considerable amount of time searching for a requested document.

Depending on the formality of the records management program, retrieval may involve the following steps:

1. The individual requesting a document fills out a request slip.
2. The request slip is transported to the location of the desired record.
3. The requisition clerk approves the request.
4. The file clerk retrieves the desired record.
5. The record, after being properly charged out, is transported to the individual making the request.
6. The record is returned to the storage area on or before the due date.

Records transfer. Procedures also have to be developed for transferring records from active storage to inactive storage. Generally, inactive records are stored in low-cost storage areas. The records retention schedule identifies the length of time records are to be kept but does not indicate when records should be transferred. This decision is determined by the frequency of use of the various records.

The storage location of inactive records might also determine when records should be transferred. For example, if inactive records are stored on the premises, transfer may take place when a record is used not more than once a month. On the other hand, if inactive records are stored in a warehouse, records might not be transferred until they are used as frequently as two or three times a year.

Two common transfer methods exist—perpetual and periodic. Perpetual transfer involves continuous transfer of records. This means records are continually examined to determine which ones should be transferred to inactive storage.

Periodic transfer involves transferring records at frequent intervals —perhaps every three to five months. At transfer time, the records are examined to determine whether or not their status should be changed.

Inactive records are often stored in cardboard transfer cases placed on metal shelving. Considerable money can be saved by removing the inactive records from expensive filing equipment and storing them in inexpensive containers.

Records control. Procedures have to be developed for controlling various aspects of the records management program. For example, procedures should be developed to help identify misfiled folders. Perhaps the most effective way is to use color coding on the file folders. When a file folder is out of sequence the color grids on the folder will be different from the other folders stored in the same area. As a visual system, color coding works very well.

Another element of control involves the development of a cross-reference system. Many records or documents pertain to several secondary subjects or topics. Rather than file a duplicate of the record in each of the secondary locations, a crossreference sheet is inserted in each of the secondary folders. The crossreference sheet identifies the location of the primary document. The use of crossreferencing to control the volume of records is especially helpful when the majority of the crossreferenced documents have multiple pages.

Another important dimension of control involves the charge-out system used when records are checked out. When either an entire folder or a portion of the contents of a folder is removed, a charge-out panel should be inserted at that point. The charge-out panel is the size of a file folder and has OUT printed on the folder tab. In some cases, the charge-out panel is made from fairly heavy stock and contains lines on which the requestor's name, document name or title, today's date, and due date are printed. In other cases, the charge-out panel is made of plastic and contains a pocket into which the request slip is inserted.

A follow-up procedure also has to be devised to help track down records/folders not returned by the due date. The longer records are checked out, the greater are the chances the records will not be returned. Perhaps a tickler file might be used to identify the records that are due on any given day. Follow-up procedures can then be put into effect for those records that are still outstanding.

Control can also be applied by using performance standards. Comparing employee performance against reliable standards will provide some evidence about employee efficiency. For those employees whose performance is below the accepted standards, certain actions should perhaps take place, such as employee training, discipline, and so forth. Figure 9–3 presents an illustration of generally accepted filing standards.

DISPOSITION OF RECORDS

Disposition, which refers to the ultimate fate of records, involves permanent protection, microrecording, transfer, or destruction.

Records that are given permanent protection are those which serve a vital function in the organization. Generally, these records are necessary for the organization's survival. Protection is provided by

Figure 9–3 FILING STANDARDS

Tasks	Units per hour
Type 3 x 5 inch cards, labels, or tags	100
Code one-page letters	200
Sort 3 x 5 inch cards	300
Sort indexed or coded correspondence	250
File 3 x 5 inch cards	180
File correspondence	250
File vouchers numerically	700
Retrieve 3 x 5 inch cards	180
Retrieve correspondence and prepare charge-out forms	70

Source: Wilmer O. Maedke, Mary F. Robek, and Gerald F. Brown, *Information and Records Management,* Beverly Hills: Glencoe Press, 1974, p. 160. Reprinted with permission.

placing these records in a fireproof safe or vault. Often, duplicate copies of such records are stored in several other locations.

Microrecording involves making a micrographic image of a document. The microrecord is approximately 98 percent smaller than the original document, which may be destroyed once it has been microrecorded. Procedures for microrecording—including when to initiate coding, storage, retrieval, transfer, and retention—must be established.

Records transfer is another means of records disposition. Some records must be permanently kept, but their value after a period of time does not warrant specific protection. Such records are often placed in inactive storage in a low-cost storage area.

Several alternatives are available for destroying records, including burning, which generates heat that is often recycled to heat work areas or water. Other alternatives include recycling and shredding. Recycled or shredded paper can often be sold to paper salvage dealers. The destruction of paper records should be closely regulated.

EVALUATING THE RECORDS MANAGEMENT PROGRAM

All records management programs should be periodically evaluated to determine how well actual results compare with expected results. Evaluation should be performed more frequently in new programs than in existing programs.

Two ratios that can be used to help evaluate the program are the finding ratio and the use ratio. The finding ratio is used to determine how many requested records are actually found. A suitable finding ratio ranges from 97 to 100 percent, which means that if four records were not found in a hundred requests, problems may exist. Several conditions may be responsible for the unsatisfactory ratio: (1) records are misfiled; (2) records are not properly indexed or coded; (3) records are not properly returned to the storage area for refiling; (4) the whereabouts of records are not known because of improper charge-out procedures.

The finding ratio is as follows:

$$\text{Finding ratio} = 100 - \frac{\text{Number of records not found}}{\text{Number of records found}}$$

The use ratio determines whether or not too many records are filed that are not used. A ratio of 20 percent or higher is generally considered satisfactory. A ratio lower than 20 percent may indicate the presence of one or both of the following unsatisfactory conditions: (1) Too many records are being maintained in active storage when they should be transferred to inactive storage; (2) Individuals use duplicate records rather than request records from the central records depository. The use ratio is calculated by the following formula:

$$\text{Use ratio} = \frac{\text{Number of records used}}{\text{Number of records not used}}$$

THE RECORDS MANAGEMENT MANUAL

The records management manual is another crucial component of the records management program. The manual, which should be made available to each employee who works with records, should contain information dealing with the following topics:

1. Objectives of the program.
2. Statement of policy of the program.
3. Organizational structure of the program.
4. Filing systems used in the program and the types of records filed under each indexing system.
5. Personnel structure of the program.
6. Records retention schedule.
7. Procedures for retrieval of records.
8. Disposition of records, including protection, transfer, micro-recording, and destruction.
9. Procedures for evaluating the program.

Figure 9-4 MICRORECORD FORMATS

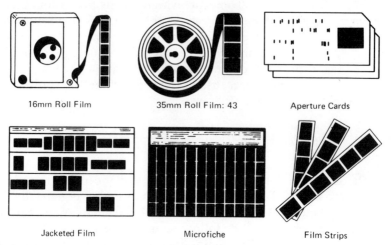

16mm Roll Film	35mm Roll Film: 43	Aperture Cards
Jacketed Film	Microfiche	Film Strips

Source: Courtesy of Hitchcock Publishing Co.

Micrographics

An increasing number of organizations are installing micrographics systems as a means of reducing the amount of space consumed by records storage. The most obvious advantage of micrographics is the space savings that result. With the typical 98:1 reduction ratio, the contents of ninety-eight file drawers can be reduced to one drawer when transformed into a microrecord format. In addition, when records are in microrecord format, duplicate copies can be easily obtained for distributed storage, should this be desirable.

Because of records density, the indexing and coding of micro-records is crucial. The absence of adequate indexing and coding procedures often results in the inability to locate quickly the desired microrecords.

A fairly new development merges micrographics and facsimile technologies. The process works in the following way: By means of a special facsimile device, a microrecord is transmitted to the receiving end where a paper copy or a visual display image on a CRT device is prepared. Telecommunications (telephone lines, microwaves, or satellites) are used in the transmission process.

MICRORECORD FORMATS

Microrecords are available in several different formats, as Figure 9-4 illustrates. The most common formats are films, reels, and cartridges (accurately called microfilm), aperture cards, microfiche, ultrafiche, and jackets. The latter four types are accurately called microforms.

The aperture cards resemble data processing cards, except that one or more microrecords are inserted in an opening (aperture) in the card. Indexing numbers are punched into the cards by means of a keyboard device. A card sorter is used to retrieve one or more cards from a stack of cards.

Microfiche is a very popular microrecord format. Measuring four inches by six inches, the piece of film can hold many records. The number of records is determined by the reduction ratio. For example, a ratio of 24:1 enables a microrecord to hold miniature images of ninety-eight standard-size documents. Other ratios permit the recording of up to three hundred twenty-five images on a fiche.

Jackets involve the use of clear plastic holder devices into which strips of microfilm are inserted. The jackets are reuseable, simply by removing the strips of microfilm and inserting others. To make a permanent copy, the contents of a jacket are photographed, which results in the preparation of a microfiche.

A fairly new development enables microrecords to be produced in color. Because of the additional cost, the use of color is not recommended unless it will serve some unique purpose. Technology also now exists for updating microrecords by making it possible to later add microimages to undeveloped image areas on microrecords. It is not possible to delete or erase existing images, however.

RETRIEVAL OF MICRORECORDS

Several different means are available for retrieving microrecords. In some cases, an indexing process is the base for the retrieval procedure. The Micracode indexing system developed by Eastman Kodak Company is one example of an effective system for indexing and retrieving records. Adjacent to each frame on the film strip, a binary code index notation appears. To find the frame, the roll, reel, or cartridge of microfilm is inserted into a reader-printer device. A keyboard is used to enter into the device the binary code index of the desired frame. The machine automatically advances the film and in a matter of seconds the desired frame is mechanically retrieved and displayed on the screen. If a paper copy of the image is desired, the printer component of the reader-printer device can be used to prepare the copy.

Increasingly, automated retrieval using computer terminals is used to retrieve microrecords. Figure 9–5 illustrates a microrecord retrieval terminal that can be used either as a stand-alone unit or on an on-line

Figure 9-5 MICRORECORD RETRIEVAL TERMINAL

Source: Courtesy of Eastman Kodak, Co., Rochester, NY

unit. The system provides immediate retrieval and paper copy output from a library of images of source documents or computer-generated data.

COMPUTER OUTPUT MICROFILM

COM (computer output microfilm) is also being used more often in many organizations. COM bypasses computer paper printout by displaying the processed data or information on an internal CRT screen. While it is being displayed, the image is photographed in microfilm and microfiche format. The operating speed of COM, in comparison to computer paper printers, is much faster.

In the not too distant future, COM will be used extensively in electronic mail and word processing systems. Large organizations will use terminals to transmit material from station to station. Each recipient's messages will be compiled and processed onto microfiche, which will eliminate the need for paper copies of various documents.

DECIDING WHAT DOCUMENTS TO MICRORECORD

It is not feasible or practical to make a microrecord of every document. Rather, the documents that are microrecorded should be selectively chosen. The following are some questions that can be asked to help make the decision.

1. *How long is the record to be kept?* Generally, records have to be kept a minimum of four years before microrecording is financially feasible.

2. *Will the physical characteristics of a record enable it to be microrecorded?* The quality of a microrecord can be no better than the quality of the original document. Dark colors or very faint printing do not always photograph well.

3. *Will the microrecord be admissible as court evidence?* Increasingly, microrecords are admissible as court evidence, but before the original is destroyed, this should be determined.

4. *Is there a sufficient number of records to warrant their microrecording?* Generally, the greater the number of records stored, the more financially feasible microrecording is. Because of equipment cost, it generally is not feasible when the volume of records to be microrecorded is quite small. An alternative would be to hire a firm specializing in microrecording to do the photographic work.

5. *Will a microrecord be convenient to use?* Paper copies are typically easier to read than are microrecords. If a record is used very frequently, perhaps it would be more convenient to use the record in paper format than microimage format.

Records management in the word processing system

The installation of a word processing system adds a new dimension to records management. In addition to an efficient system for the storage of paper documents and micrographics, word processing creates a need for the storage and easy retrieval of the variety of magnetic media used in word processing, including cards, cartridges, cassettes, and disks.

STORAGE EQUIPMENT IN THE WORD PROCESSING CENTER

Several types of storage devices are used in word processing centers. Most work stations have a file drawer or two for materials storage. Other devices include movable standard two-drawer file cabinets

Figure 9–6 BINDER USED FOR STORING MAGNETIC MEDIA

Source: Courtesy of Ring King Visibles, Muscatine, IA

mounted on wheels, open-shelf filing, and lateral files. In many cases, this equipment is easily modified to facilitate the storage of various magnetic media.

In other instances, special binders are used to permanently store magnetic media. These binders contain pockets into which the magnetic devices are inserted, and some also contain space to store a paper copy of the material on the various magnetic devices. For example, in the case of form letters, it is often desirable to store the paper copy along with the magnetic device. These binders also help protect the magnetic media from being damaged by scratches or dirt. It is extremely important that an efficient indexing system be used to code the magnetic media that are permanently stored. Otherwise, it may not be possible to locate the medium when needed.

Figure 9–6 illustrates one of the binders available for storing magnetic media.

MAGNETIC MEDIA INDEXING IN WORD PROCESSING

One of the distinct advantages of word processing is the ability to keyboard material, record it on a magnetic medium, and store the me-

Figure 9-7 JOB REQUEST SHEET

Principal's name _____   Today's date _____

Principal's department_____

_ _

Number on magnetic medium _____/_____/_____/_____

Date to be entered on documents _____

Special instructions

No. 1:   Name _____

         Address _____

         _____

         _____

         Variable information to be added:

         A
         B
         C
         D

No. 2:   Name _____

         Address_____

         _____

         _____

dium for use in the future. This eliminates having to rekeyboard material. This advantage will not occur without an effective indexing system for the magnetic media.

The majority of the magnetic devices that are permanently stored contain form messages. These messages, which are used with some degree of regularity, are generally originated by individual principals. An effective way to index the various magnetic devices is to assign a number to each of the departments or work units in the organization.

Each principal within each of the departments or work units is also assigned a number. Each time a principal originates a document that must be permanently stored, that document is also assigned a number. The following illustrates the numbering concept:

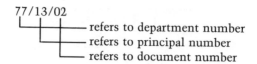

77/13/02
—— refers to department number
—— refers to principal number
—— refers to document number

This number is then entered on the magnetic medium. Each time the principal wishes to use the document, this reference number is used to retrieve the appropriate magnetic medium.

Magnetic media are also numbered serially. Some organizations use a crossreference system for indexing the magnetic media. The principal refers to the medium by the number assigned by the organization. To determine which magnetic medium is needed, the word processing specialist refers to the crossreference log. The serial number of the magnetic medium and the number are matched. The specialist then retrieves the appropriate medium from the storage file. When the job is completed, the medium is returned and refiled according to its serial number.

A job request sheet, similar to the one illustrated in Figure 9–7, is often used when working with materials permanently stored on magnetic media. The sheet provides a variety of information, including the name and address of the recipient, if appropriate; the variable information to be inserted, if appropriate; as well as other pertinent production information.

Review questions

1. What steps are involved in the records cycle?
2. Why is it important to formulate policies when designing a records management program?
3. What factors should be considered in determining whether or not records should be centrally stored or decentrally stored?
4. What factors should be considered in determining the appropriate kind of storage equipment to use in a records management program?
5. How is a records retention schedule developed?
6. Explain the differences beween periodic and perpetual transfer.

7. What types of control procedures should be developed for use in a records management program?

8. What methods are used for records disposition?

9. Explain what conditions are likely to be present when finding and use ratio levels are unsatisfactory.

10. In what formats do microrecords exist?

11. Why are efficient procedures needed for indexing magnetic media used in word processing systems?

Cases

The Bramer Corporation, located in Denver, Colorado, manufactures a variety of equipment used in hospitals and clinics. Because of a rather recent, intensive effort to capture a greater part of the market, the corporation has embarked upon a very aggressive research program. The results are beginning to pay off now through a steady increase in sales.

Nearly two years ago, the corporation installed a decentralized word processing system. After approximately six months, the system was functioning very well, meeting most standards. The corporation also uses the administrative support concept. One of the primary responsibilities of the administrative secretaries is the management of records contained in the various administrative support centers.

About a year and a half ago, it became apparent that the records management function of the Bramer Corporation was vulnerable from the standpoint that no program really existed. Each unit more or less devised its own system.

The management of the corporation is now aware of the problems created by the absence of a records management program. You, an administrative secretary, were recently appointed to a committee charged with making suggestions for improving the records management program. Obviously, the committee is recommending centralized control, but it is having difficulty deciding whether to use centralized or decentralized storage.

1. What factors should be considered in making the decision?

2. What are the advantages of centralized storage? Decentralized storage?

3. Which alternative do you feel should be chosen? Why?

• • •

Located in Rapid City, South Dakota, the Samson Corporation, a producer of wood products, has grown rapidly during the last few years. At times, business is so brisk that large work backlogs exist. Because of the increased business, the organization is well aware of the need to utilize efficient procedures.

The organization's vice president for corporate affairs has long believed that one of the best ways to increase company operating profits is to develop and utilize efficient office systems. For this reason, the organization was one of the first in the area to use word processing/administrative support. The organization's records management program has often been a model for other companies in the area when installing a new records management program. Almost without exception, the Samson Corporation is the community pacesetter with regard to operating systems.

A committee was recently formed to determine the desirability of installing a micrographics system. You, an administrative support center supervisor, have been appointed to that committee.

1. What factors should be considered in making the decision?
2. What outcomes should result from the installation of the system?
3. Once the system has been installed, what factors can be evaluated to determine whether or not the correct decision was made?

CHAPTER 10

Word processing and the office of the future: A preview

The office of the future is the subject of much speculation. Although no one at this time can identify with total certainty the exact nature of tomorrow's office, some fairly realistic predictions can be made. It is quite likely that offices in the year 2000 will be as different from today's offices as today's offices are different from those of a hundred years ago.

Word processing will be a definite component of the office of the future. However, the broadening nature of the word processing concept and the evolution of the office of the future will likely transform *word processing* into *information processing*. The rapid merging of the word processing and data processing concepts makes this transformation not only inevitable but also logical.

Equipment manufacturers and technological organizations are spending millions of dollars each year for research on the office of the future. While most of the research is devoted to product development, the design of systems in the office of the future is also being researched. Several of the equipment components found in today's offices will also be found in tomorrow's offices. However, because of advanced technology, the equipment functions will be considerably different.

Characteristics of the office of the future

One relevant characteristic of the office of the future is the merging of the word processing and data processing concepts. Several factors make this merger not only desirable but also crucial. Much of the data presently processed originates in the office sector of the organization. By merging the technologies of the two concepts, more efficient, economical operations will result. Too, in many instances, the information and data generated by each component are shared. In the final analysis, the merging of data processing and word processing and the sharing of data, equipment, and personnel will result in advantages not possible in today's offices.

Another important characteristic that will be found in the office of the future is the interfacing of equipment, which means that the various equipment components will be electronically connected with one another. This will be an especially important aspect of the word processing concept of the office of the future. For example, the text-editing typewriters will be interfaced with copiers, which will enable the user to make one or more copies of a typed document, simply by pressing a button. In addition, text-editing typewriters will most likely be interfaced with facsimile devices, which, too, will involve no more physical effort on the part of the employee than the pressing of a button. The absence of equipment interfacement, common in today's office, results in reduced productivity.

The office will also make extensive use of integrated systems. Word processing (or information processing) will be an important subsystem of the total integrated system. Already, many organizations extensively utilize integrated systems comprised of such subsystems as accounting, finance, sales, marketing, and so forth. Because these integrated systems utilize computer technology, the data and information put into the system by the various subsystems are accessible to each of the subsystems. Because of the merging of word processing and data processing, it is logical for information processing to become an important subsystem in the office of the future.

Another characteristic that has definite implications for word processing is the predicted paperless nature of the office. There is some disagreement as to when the office of the future will become paperless—some say it will be mostly paperless in the 1990s, while others say this will occur after the turn of the century. There is also disagreement as to the extent to which the office of the future will be paperless—some say it will be total; others maintain tomorrow's offices will be only partially paperless. At this point it is fairly safe to say that the electronic advances in the equipment technology will decrease the amount of paper used in tomorrow's offices.

Another important characteristic is the electronic nature of the equipment. Not only will the equipment be able to function with less human involvement, but also it will be able to function more rapidly and do many more things. The electronic nature of the equipment will no longer require individuals to be physically present to carry out their jobs. For example, it is quite possible that those employees who operate the information processing equipment may be able to work out of their homes. Information will be electronically transmitted over telephone lines. Thus, the information to be processed will come to the employee's home via telephone lines, and the processed information will be transmitted back to the organization through telephone lines. Not having to be physically present in the organization will have a positive impact on energy conservation by reducing fuel consumption in commuting to and from work.

A final characteristic of the office of the future is the one-time keyboarding of information. The storage capability of the present-day word processing equipment makes it possible to capture keystrokes. Once captured, the keystrokes can be held in storage indefinitely. At the time the stored material is needed, it can be easily accessed, which eliminates its having to be manually keyboarded a second time. With the equipment and technology of the office of the future, most, if not all, information will be keyboarded only one time. The net result of this feature of the office of the future is increased efficiency and greater productivity, and with considerably less effort.

Equipment in the office of the future

A discussion of the office of the future would not be complete without taking a look at the equipment that will be used in tomorrow's offices. In comparison with today's office equipment, the equipment of the office of the future will be multifunctional, more compatible with other pieces of equipment, and more intelligent.

Some of the equipment of the office of the future presently exists. The difference is that today's form of this equipment is less functional, less advanced, and less versatile, and requires greater amounts of human effort than will be needed with the equipment in tomorrow's offices. A considerable amount of the equipment developed for the future will utilize microprocessor technology. A microprocessor, which is essentially a computer, is about the size of a fingernail, but has the capability of a room-size computer. As much computer power presently exists on a miniature twenty-dollar silicon chip as existed in a million-dollar computer thirty years ago. Microprocessors will be built into equipment components in order to achieve a level of intelligence not possible in much of today's office equipment.

In the office of the future, it is quite possible that voice data-entry technology will become a primary method of information/data input into the organization's information system. Instead of inputting material into the system by means of manual keyboarding, employees will orally input material. The inputting process will convert spoken words to elecronic codes. Small-scale versions of these devices capable of responding to approximately one thousand different words stored in their memories already exist. It is doubtful that this technique will be sufficiently well developed by the turn of the century to have a very significant impact on the office of that time. When this technology is sufficiently developed, it promises to have as revolutionary an impact on office procedures as data processing and word processing have had.

The design of the text-editing equipment in the office of the future will be significantly determined by the functions the equipment performs. Until the office moves toward becoming paperless, the text-editing devices will resemble those presently on the market. As time passes, the various features of the text-editing devices will enable them to operate more automatically and at faster rates. One significant change that will occur in text-editing devices will be their ability to interface with other devices. For example, text editors will be capable of interfacing with both copy machines and facsimile machines. By interfacing the devices, the equipment operator will no longer have to carry a paper document from the text editor to either the copy machine or the facsimile device. Rather, the equipment operator will be able to activate both copiers and facsimile devices simply by depressing a button on a console at the work station. Communications interfaces will be very prominent in the office of the future, enabling the interfaced devices to communicate with one another.

As word processing and data processing continue to merge, text editors will become more intelligent. The devices will utilize increasing amounts of the technology presently found in data processing equipment. Thus, word processing equipment will be capable of extensively manipulating information and data, a characteristic found on today's data processing equipment but not on today's word processing equipment. A common feature on all text-editing equipment in the future will be automatic hyphenation, made possible primarily because of the utilization of computer technology in word processing equipment. In time, the distinction between data processing equipment and word processing equipment will become less clear.

As the office of the future moves toward a paperless concept, the functions of the text-editing devices will change. When the offices become totally paperless, the printing component of text editors will no longer be needed. Instead of storing paper copies of documents, the office will be able to store data/information in computer memory or on a variety of magnetic media. In addition, micrographics will be extensively used for the storage of data/information. It is already possible —on a rather limited scale, however—to convert the magnetic media recorded by the text editors to computer output microfilm (COM) as a means of storing the finished product. Bypassing the paper stage results in several advantages. To view the microfilm image, special terminals will be used to automatically retrieve and display the desired material.

The copiers in the office of the future will be intelligent, as compared with those found in today's offices. In fact, by the time this text appears in print, intelligent copiers may already be on the market. The intelligent copiers found twenty years hence will be much different from those that are about to be introduced. Intelligent copiers are capable of performing several functions, including copying, generating charts and graphs, printing letters from original input, and transmitting facsimile messages. The intelligent copiers of the future will also integrate micrographics into the system. Just as a clear distinction between word processing and data processing will probably fade in the office of the future, the clear distinction between copier equipment and facsimile equipment will also become more hazy.

The office of the future will make extensive use of electronic document distribution, which is already used to a limited extent in many organizations. Presently, text-editor typewriters are capable of communicating with other geographically remote text-editing type-writers. Facsimile is also used to transmit information between two points. In the future, most, if not all, information will be electronically transmitted. As the paperless office emerges, electronic transmission of data/information will make obsolete the movement of paper documents through conventional distribution channels.

Between now and the time the paperless office emerges, OCR (optical character recognition) will be used increasingly in information processing operations. OCR equipment is used to input data/information onto a magnetic medium, which is then processed on either computer equipment or text-editing equipment. OCR eliminates the need to rekeyboard the material. Because of the efficiency created by OCR, in time all type/print styles will most likely be compatible with OCR equipment. Thus, virtually any paper document can be entered into the system without being rekeyboarded.

In all probability, the equipment in the office of the future will combine into one unit all the features presently found on copiers, facsimile, and OCR devices.

Each of the equipment components discussed up to this point is more likely to be used by those employees presently known as word processing specialists than by those known as administrative secretaries. The administrative secretarial positions, too, will change as a result of technological changes. Administrative secretaries (it is doubtful this title will still be found in the office of the future) will make extensive use of desk-top terminals. These terminals will be used to input material into the organization's information system as well as access information held in the information system. Specific operating procedures pertaining to the use of this equipment are discussed in the following section.

Figure 10–1 presents a schematic drawing of the information processing system in the office of the future. An examination of the illustration reveals that various equipment components are extensively interfaced with one another. The computer is the focal point of the entire system.

Procedures of the office of the future

The nature of the equipment used in the office of the future will have a significant impact on the nature of the work procedures that will be found in tomorrow's offices. Understandably, the procedures will be determined by the functions the equipment is able to perform.

Figure 10-1 SCHEMATIC DRAWING OF THE OFFICE OF THE FUTURE

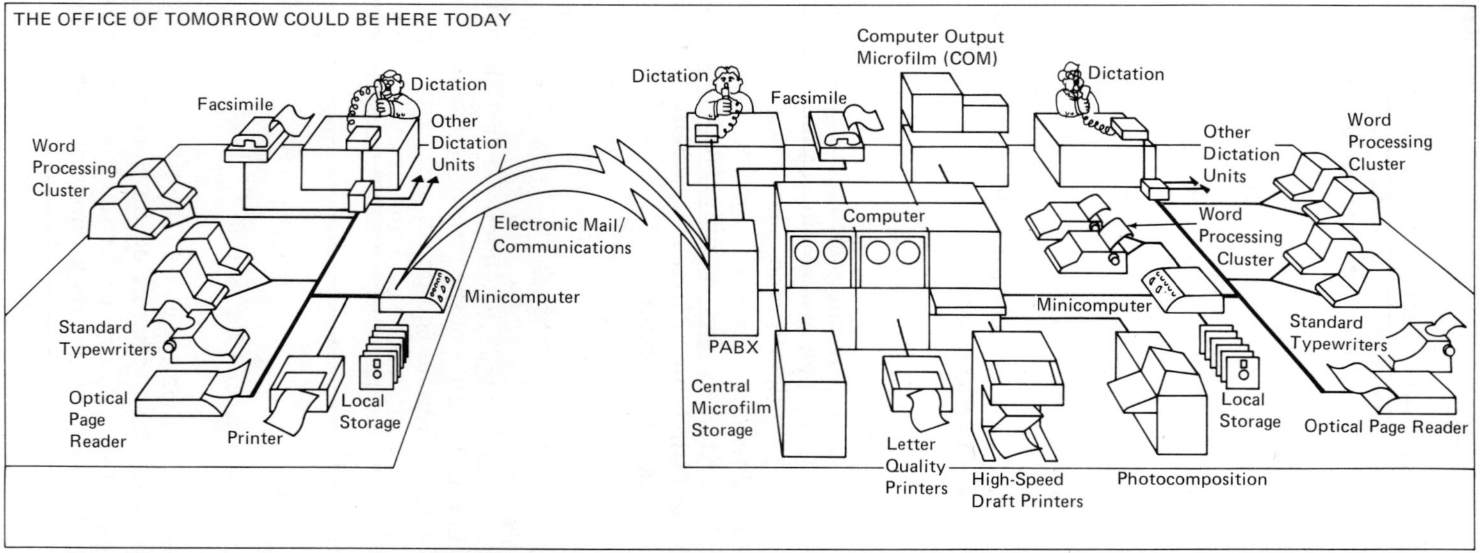

THE OFFICE OF TOMORROW COULD BE HERE TODAY

Source: October 1977, *Fortune*/International Data Corporation special advertising section; reprinted by permission.

252

Many of the procedures will be more automated than those presently found. The amount of human effort involved in the work processes, consequently, will be significantly reduced. The number of routine, monotonous tasks, abundant in many of today's offices, will be significantly reduced.

The storage and retrieval of information in tomorrow's offices will be drastically different. Much of the storage of information will involve some medium other than paper, even before the paperless office is a reality. In most cases, the storage will probably use magnetic media and micrographics. To retrieve material stored on a magnetic medium the proper search code is entered into the system. In a very short period of time, the information will appear on a display screen. If a hard (paper) copy is needed, copier devices will be available.

Because the office of the future will make extensive use of electronic mail, the procedures by which mail is transmitted will change. Increasingly, the mail will be transmitted in electronic code format. But in the near future facsimile transmission, which produces an identical paper copy of the document, will also be extensively used. As the paperless office begins to emerge, facsimile will become less important.

The procedures by which the mail will be received will also change. In the "mailroom," incoming mail will be routed to the appropriate recipient simply by using a keyboard terminal. The mail will be stored electronically until the recipient is ready to receive it.

Each executive will have a desk-top terminal with an attached keyboard and display screen. To access the mail, the terminal will be used to input the appropriate codes into the system. A coded list of the various pieces of mail appears on the screen. To display each piece of mail, the appropriate code is entered into the system. The terminal keyboard is also used to electronically file material that is to be stored, or if a paper copy of the material is desired, a special copier can be used. To discard "mail," the recipient simply enters the appropriate code into the system.

The same desk-top screen will be used by executives to review material they have originated. To make minor changes in the material, the originator can use the desk-top terminal to keyboard the changes. When extensive changes are made, a longhand copy of the changes will be transmittted to the employee who originally keyboarded the material. This employee will also keyboard the changes. Entire paragraphs can be deleted simply by depressing appropriate keys, and paragraphs can be reordered in the same way.

Executives will also use their desk-top terminals for maintaining their appointments schedule, which will be stored in computer memory. To check on their appointments of the day, executives can use the terminal to retrieve the information. When executives are out of the office, their return-call phone messages will also be computerized. Upon returning to the office, the executive may use the terminal to obtain the list of return-call phone messages.

Secretaries will find the computerized executive appointments schedules very helpful when scheduling a meeting or conference. Since each executive's appointments calendar is computerized, the computer determines what times each executive is available for the meeting. This saves a considerable amount of human effort.

The electronic nature of the office of the future may also make it possible for executives not to have to be physically present to carry out their jobs, except when face-to-face contact is necessary. Two alternatives will be available. One alternative is for the executive to work at home, using the electronic devices that will be available. Another alternative is for the executive to go to a satellite work center located in the community. Here, the executive will have access to the electronic equipment necessary to carry out his/her job. The work centers would be available to any firm's employees who need to use the equipment that will be found in the centers.

Because of the extensive amount of equipment interfacing in the office of the future, a communications center will most likely need to be utilized. The center will serve as an information receiving and distribution command post. The centers may resemble scaled-down versions of the space program command centers.

Advantages of the office of the future

When compared with today's offices, the office of the future presents several advantages. One distinct advantage is that executives and others whose jobs consist of considerable amounts of decision making will have access to crucial information when needed. Information will arrive on time and will be of sufficient quality to improve the level of decision making.

Secondly, the equipment and procedures of tomorrow's offices will enable offices to keep pace with other areas of the organization in terms of productivity. In the amount of time that industrial productivity has increased by 90 percent, office productivity has increased a mere 5 percent. The office of the future will enable office productivity and industrial productivity to approximate one another more closely.

Thirdly, the future office will eliminate many of the routine, monotonous tasks found in many of today's offices. Such tasks will be performed by equipment in the office of the future.

Lastly, the office of the future will help control rapidly increasing office costs. The equipment found in tomorrow's offices will help make possible the use of efficient, economical procedures.

Review questions

1. Explain the meaning of equipment interface and how it will be used in the office of the future.
2. Explain the concept of integrated systems in the office of the future.
3. What is voice data-entry technology and how will it be used in the office of the future?
4. Identify the features that will likely be found on the text-editing equipment used in the office of the future.
5. Explain how the storage and retrieval of information will be handled in the office of the future.
6. Identify the functions of the executive desk-top terminals that will be used in the office of the future.
7. What are the advantages that will likely emerge from the office of the future?

Cases

You are the president of the firm Perry and Associates, consultants in word processing. You have been invited to present the keynote address to a group of educators from the fields of computer science, data processing, and word processing. The topic on which you've been asked to speak is "Implications of Technological Progress for You, the Educator." In preparing for your thirty-minute presentation, survey current issues of such periodicals as *Infosystems, Administrative Management, The Office, Modern Office Procedures, Data Processing, Word Processing Reports,* and other references that will contribute to your knowledge of technological advances. Your presentation will be focused upon the interfacing of word processing, data processing, computer systems, telecommunications, and other communication systems you may wish to include. (Your instructor may assign a shorter report to be presented in class.)

• • •

You are employed as director, word processing/administrative services, Farmers and Merchants Bank, located in the midwest. Top management is engaged in the development of a five-year forecast. You have been asked to prepare that part of the forecast which relates to office automation.

You've heard a great deal about the office of the future, but you are not convinced that changes in office automation will continue to take place at the rate business has experienced during the past five years.

On the basis of library research, prepare a three-page report for consideration as part of the forecast for your bank. Include these areas of interest and the implications that these topics may have for banking as a major category of business in the United States:

1. Word processing systems and organization.
2. Word processing installations in the employee's home (where bank communications are processed by employees).
3. Computers for home use.
4. Private automatic branch exchange systems.
5. Confidential document processing.
6. Personnel requirements.
7. Employee performance.
8. Equipment advances.

APPENDIX 1

Word processing user's guide

Purpose of the word processing center

The Word Processing Center exists to serve you. The Word Processing Center is designed to serve the attorneys, secretaries and administrative support people of the firm of Nelson & Harding. The Center offers a wide variety of high-quality secretarial and typesetting services. It is staffed by skilled specialists who use the most advanced equipment available in print-media technology. It is designed to efficiently serve you both in your routine work and in special projects.

Your cooperation is vital. Proper use of the Word Processing Center will enable you to process large amounts of paperwork and complicated reports in a fast, efficient and professional manner. Your cooperation is needed, however, for the Word Processing Team members to insure print media of superior quality and appearance.

This manual is a guide. This manual is designed to provide you with a concise, reliable guide. It describes Word Processing services and outlines basic procedures which will help you receive rapid, smooth service.

Center operations

NOTE

In order for the Word Processing Center to provide fast, accurate, and efficient service, the cooperation of the departments which use the center is essential. Your cooperation will be greatly appreciated and will help avoid misunderstandings.

Source: Nelson & Harding, Lincoln, NE. Sherri Toohey, Word Processing Supervisor. Reprinted by permission.

NORMAL WORKDAY

The Word Processing Center's normal workday is 8:00 A.M. to 9:00 P.M., Monday through Friday. If you have material to be submitted after 5:00 that needs to be done in the evening, prior arrangements should be made with the Word Processing Supervisor; otherwise it will be considered part of the *next* day's work.

SUBMITTING WORK

All work to the Word Processing Center should have an orange Word Processing Routing Slip attached to it. These slips should be completely filled out with all appropriate information concerning the project to which they are attached. Work can be submitted as dictation, handwritten copy (if legible), or typed copy. Large Word Processing envelopes are also available so that tapes and documents can be kept together to avoid loss. These are available in the Center.

PRIORITIES

All work done in the Center is done on completion time priority. We ask that you give us a preferred completion time and an absolute completion time. If at all possible your work will be returned by the preferred completion time. Your work will always be returned by the absolute completion time unless the Word Processing Supervisor makes prior arrangements with you or your secretary to change that time. Please be as reasonable as possible with your completion times. If it is not needed that day, request it for the next day.

TURNAROUND TIME

The average turnaround time for work done in the Center is 2½ hours. Most projects are finished by the absolute time given on the routing slips. The majority of the time it should be possible for you to give the Center *at least* 2½ hours on your project. Emergencies do occur and will be handled as such.

PICK-UP & DELIVERY

Word Processing materials may be placed in the in-out boxes located throughout the firm. Within the firm, mail is picked up and delivered at 9:00 and 11:00 A.M. and at 2:00 and 4:00 P.M.. The Word Processing people will return work when done if needed before these times.

PRERECORDED MATERIAL

Whenever you notice any sort of repetitive or commonly needed written material, please consider the possibility of having it stored in the Word Processing Center for extra-fast processing. Letters, memos, standard-format reply forms are examples.

CONFIDENTIAL MATERIAL

Procedures have been established to handle quantities of confidential material on request within the Center. The processing of confidential information should in every case be discussed with the Word Processing Supervisor to insure proper handling.

PROOFREADING

Proofreading is the joint responsibility of all people involved in the preparation of a document. Word Processing Center personnel proofread all material being prepared as a final document. It is anticipated that material specifically asked for in rough-draft will be read by Word Processing personnel if there is time. If there is not time the rough draft will be marked "Not Proofed." The final on that document will then be proofread. It is essential, however, that user-departments and *particularly originators* proofread material *for content* since personnel in the Center are not specialists in all subject matters. It is also advisable for user-department personnel to proofread for typography as well as a double check. Errors found by user-departments will be quickly corrected by the Center.

ABNORMAL WORKLOADS

The Center is able and willing to handle larger-than-normal jobs. However, if you plan to dictate an unusually high volume of work, please notify the Word Processing Supervisor in advance. The Supervisor will then be able to make the necessary arrangements to insure the quick processing of your work. This is also true of large quantities of work on a rush basis. Arrangements can be made if the Supervisor is notified in advance.

COMMUNICATION CAPABILITIES

The Lincoln Word Processing Center is able to communicate cards to any of our other offices. The best means of using the communication feature of the Center is to have the Center type the document initially and when you have the document ready to send, let them know to which office(s). The receiving office will need time to play back the cards, so we must allow enough time for them to do this. The Lincoln Center can also receive cards from our other offices. If you have any questions on communications, please contact the Word Processing Supervisor.

NIGHT & WEEKEND DICTATION

Night and weekend dictation is welcome. While you're away from your office, you might wish to check out one of the portable dictation units available for short-term use from your department, or use the call-in dictation device located directly in the Word Processing Center. The number to it is 475-1613. Instructions for its use can be obtained in the Center.

RETENTION

All routine work will automatically be stored on magnetic cards or diskettes. Approximately every two weeks, first page logs of all documents typed will be sent to you to mark whether they are to be destroyed or retained. Please mark directly on the log itself and return these to the Center as soon as possible after receipt. If a document is to be used over and over, inform the Word Processing Supervisor so that it can be maintained as a permanent document and set up as such. Do not keep documents on card or diskette if they are not going to be used or revised again.

RESEARCH WORK

The Word Processing Center cannot function efficiently if it must serve as a research bureau. Names, dates, prices, file numbers, addresses and other details needed in a document are the responsibility of the user-department. If you wish, send the file to the Center that contains all information needed for the particular project.

DICTATING HINTS

When using dictation devices, please remember to speak as clearly as possible. Do not rush to "cram more on the tape." Please use *only* side 1 of the 30-minute cassettes. Give all instructions at the beginning of the tape if possible. Tell what the document is going to be. Please spell names and give addresses. If you are dictating a lot of material that is going to have to be underscored, please tell us in advance and let us know when to stop underscoring. On indented quotes dictate when they *begin* and when they *end*. When the machine signals you that you are coming to the end of the tape (beeping), please stop at this point and insert a new tape. Often dictation cannot be heard over this beeping noise. At the end of the tape, please say "End of Tape." If using more than one tape, begin each successive tape with that appropriate tape number (i.e., Tape 2 of the Walker Agreement). If a long document is recorded on more than one cassette and is needed in a rush, it can be split up between operators and sent back to you more quickly than if you record it on one longer tape.

REVISION

When revising a rough copy before it is finaled, you can make any changes you feel necessary. We ask only that you use red pen in making these revisions. Corrections made in pencil or with black ink may be accidentally overlooked by the word processing specialist. Another way to assure we find all the revisions is to circle punctuation changes or make a mark in the right hand margin across from the revision. If extensive revision is necessary, it may take you less time to dictate the revisions rather than write them all out. Any of these means is acceptable. Please do not cut and paste any documents that have been recorded in the Center. If you have extensively changed a document and may make more revisions, you should request a rerough from the Word Center.

If at all possible, send a sample with a document that the Center has not done before. This will save time on both ends with unneeded questions concerning proper format, etc.

OVERTIME

If needed, the operators in the Center can work overtime. If a project can be done by the night person, none of the day personnel will stay overtime. If you need an operator to work on a weekend, please make arrangements with the Word Processing Supervisor on Friday by 4:00 P.M. *Prior arrangements must be made.* When one of the operators is working on a weekend for a particular attorney, she is not required to do work for any other attorney. All overtime does have to be authorized. Law clerks and secretaries cannot authorize overtime.

Processing of documents

Documents to be processed in the Center are defined below.

- Any document that is over three (3) pages in length, any document that is going to be revised, documents that are repetitive, or are going to be communicated to one of our other offices. These documents can be dictated, handwritten (if legible), or typed copy.
- Prerecorded material. Any written information that is stored on diskette or card for automatic playback. The Center is capable of storing both entire documents and individual paragraphs. A finished draft of a stored document can be automatically typed on request and can include variables which can be "plugged-in." Stored paragraphs containing standardized information can be combined with original dictation to form completed documents.
- Special Requests. A special-request document is normally one which is complicated or unusual enough to warrant discussion. It is often wise to bring this material to the Center in person and visit with the Word Processing Supervisor about it. Special-request material should be accompanied by necessary special instructions and/or a standard format.
- Periodic Reports. Periodic reports can be stored in the Center on request. Updates can then be created by simply marking changes on the latest previous version and sending it to the Center.

Documents to be processed in your own department. Routine, low-volume clerical typing can usually be handled most efficiently and economically *within* the department that originates it. In order for Word Processing Team members to devote their full attention to the efficient handling of high-volume materials, the Center will *not*, under normal circumstances, process the following types of documents:

- Mailing labels (unless repetitive addresses).
- Forms (except to design new forms).
- Routine correspondence.
- One-time documents (will not be revised).
- Billings.
- Work sheets (statistical work that cannot be recorded).

If the Center has a low volume of work, the Word Processing Supervisor will contact the other supervisors and inform them of such. In this event the above types of work can be done in the Center. There may be instances when you will want the Center to do something of this sort; if you have a question as to whether it should be done in the Center, contact the Word Processing Supervisor. Arrangements can usually be made to accommodate you.

A final word

We hope that this manual is useful to you in obtaining the best possible service from our Word Processing Center. Center personnel make every effort to treat each "client" with respect and to make sure his or her work is completed promptly and accurately. If at any time you have questions, suggestions, or complaints, please contact us so that improvements can be made whenever possible.

Sherri Toohey
Word Processing Supervisor
Nelson & Harding
April, 1978

APPENDIX 2

Publications containing information about word processing (newsletters, periodicals, and reports)

Administrative Management (monthly)
Geyer-McAllister Publications, Inc.
51 Madison Ave.
New York, NY 10010

Datamation (monthly)
1801 S. La Cienega Blvd.
Los Angeles, CA 90035

Datapro Reports (monthly)
Datapro Research Corporation
1805 Underwood Blvd.
Delran, NJ 08075

Impact (monthly)
Administrative Management Society
Maryland Road
Willow Grove, PA 19090

Infosystems (monthly)
Hitchcock Publishing Co.
Hitchcock Building
Wheaton, IL 60187

Management World (monthly)
Administrative Management Society
Maryland Road
Willow Grove, PA 19090

Modern Office Procedures (monthly)
Industrial Publishing Company
614 Superior Ave.
West Cleveland, OH 44113

The Office (monthly)
Office Publications, Inc.
1200 Summer Street
Stamford, CT 06905

Office of the Future (twice monthly)
   Word Processing and the American Office
   37 West 72 Street
   New York, NY 10023

Office Products (monthly)
   Hitchcock Publishing Co.
   Hitchcock Building
   Wheaton, IL 60187

Office Product News (published ten times each year)
   United Technical Publications, Inc.
   645 Stewart Ave.
   Garden City, NJ 11530

The Secretary (monthly)
   The National Secretaries Association
   2440 Pershing Road
   Kansas City, MO 64108

Viewpoint (monthly)
   International Word Processing Association
   Willow Grove, PA 19090

The Word (monthly)
   Word Processing Society, Inc.
   P.O. Box 92553
   Milwaukee, WI 53202

Word Processing and the American Office (semimonthly)
   Office Management Systems Corporations
   37 West Seventy-second Street
   New York, NY 10023

Word Processing Report (twice monthly)
   Geyer-McAllister Publications, Inc.
   51 Madison Ave.
   New York, NY 10010

Word Processing Systems (monthly)
   Geyer-McAllister Publications, Inc.
   51 Madison Ave.
   New York, NY 10010

Words (quarterly)
   International Word Processing Association
   Willow Grove, PA 19090

Glossary

AM Administrative Management; administrative manager.

AMS Administrative Management Society.

APS Alphanumeric Photocomposer System.

ATS Administrative Terminal System, IBM's term for a software package that programs a computer for word processing work, with text being entered and retrieved through interactive typewriter terminals.

Access time Time required to "get" and "move" recorded material stored in a data processing or word processing system to a point where it is available for transfer, playout, or new storage.

Action paper Carbonless copying paper frequently used in surveys of typing activity. It provides a copy of everything typed during the survey period for the purpose of determining line count, errors, restarts, and formats.

Action officer Army term for "word originator," "principal."

Active document Document requiring original thought. Research, organization, proofreading, and revision are generally required. Error-free copy is often needed.

Activity oriented Term used to define an administrative support operation in which aides are specialized by task, as distinct from one in which aides are "principal oriented" and do many tasks for specific executives.

Administrative center A secretarial group performing secretarial activities other than typing, such as mail handling, filing, telephones, and special projects.

Administrative support One of the two broad areas of specialization under word processing (the other being typing). In general, it comprises all the nontyping tasks associated with traditional secretarial work carried out under administrative supervision.

Allowances Time which is computed into a work standard for fatigue, rest time, activity reporting, and other normal delays.

Attendant phone In a central dictation system, a phone that allows the word originator to communicate with an aide in the word processing center or other remote recorder location.

Availability The percentage of time in a certain period during which a piece of equipment functions properly.

Average letter According to IWPA, a letter in the range of ninety-two to one hundred fifteen words with eighteen to twenty-three lines of twelve-pitch typing. As the standards are difficult to define, this method of measurement is generally unsuitable.

Backlog A reserve of unprocessed work.

Batch A collection of similar work that can be processed at one operation.

Black box Slang term for a central processor unit.

Boiler plate Construction of a document using parts of many other documents or a list of paragraphs.

Breakage The difference between equivalent manpower and actual manpower.

CPS Certified Professional Secretary.

CPU Central Processing Unit, containing the necessary circuits to interpret and execute instructions for multiple input-output devices.

Calendar of conversion A schedule prepared for the implementation of a word processing system.

Career path Line of progression from one position to another, established by management to provide opportunity for advancement to higher level jobs.

Cold type Text, usually intended for offset reproduction, produced by a direct-impression typewriter mechanism or through photocomposition.

Control A warning system that forecasts potential bottlenecks and affords sufficient clues for correcting any problems, errors, or fall-downs (logs, numerical controls, etc.).

Correspondence center 1. A word processing center. 2. A secretarial group performing typing activities.

Critical path method A procedure for planning and scheduling each part of a complex project so that successive steps can be accomplished on time.

Cross training The switching of personnel among various work stations so that they may learn more than one job.

DE Dictation Equipment.

Data analysis The evaluation and analysis of the data collected in the data collection tools.

Data collection The gathering of data used to measure both administrative and correspondence activities within an organization.

Data collection tools Tools used in the study to gather information about the present and proposed word processing system, both administrative and correspondence.

Dedicated recorder Recorder devoted exclusively to one type of dictation or specific individual(s).

Discrete media Term applied to recording media that are individually distinct; that can be filed, mailed, moved, and otherwise separately handled. In dictation equipment, for example, belt, disk, cartridge, and cassette are "discrete media"; endless loop media are not.

Endless loop Term applied to a family of dictation equipment systems that employ sealed, continuous loops of magnetic tape as recording media. The tapes are kept in containers called "tanks."

Feasibility study A study made to determine whether conversion to a word processing system can improve office operations.

Flexible staffing Use of temporary/casual/part-time employees to meet peak workloads.

Flowchart A graphic representation of the flow of work from origin to completion in which symbols are used to represent operations and equipment.

Galley proof A preliminary printout of type in columnar form, for checking purposes.

Glide time A timekeeping principle where, within limits, an employee can set his/her own starting and stopping times.

Global change The ability of a word processing system to change a word or other text element everywhere it appears in a document with one instruction. (Also called "global search and replace.")

Hard copy Typewritten copy of any description.

IWPA Abbreviation for International Word Processing Association, a word processing user group headquartered in Willow Grove, Pennsylvania.

Implementation The phase following management approval of a word processing system, during which the details of the system are developed and carried out.

Job description A definition of what a worker should do. A written statement of the duties, responsibilities, and requirements of a specific job.

Job enrichment The opportunity for an employee to exercise more independence in his/her work through task assignments or delegation of authority.

Leading Amount of space between lines of type, usually referred to in terms of "points." The notation "10/12" or "10 on 12" means 10-point type in a 12-point space, or, expressed another way, 10-point type with 2 points of "leading" (pronounced ledding) between lines.

Learning curve A theory by which the learning process of an operator can be estimated.

Line Transcribing work is most commonly measured by number of lines, a standard line being a six-inch line of elite type (twelve characters to the inch) or seventy-two typewritten strokes. Because lines could include rough drafts, etc., such statistics would be meaningless. Therefore, only "net" lines (those lines of finished typing ready for dispatch) are usually counted. Allowances are made for headings, endings, carbon copies, and envelope addressing.

Log sheet A document prepared and maintained by supervisors or word processing operators to keep track of incoming and outgoing work, turnaround times, and the like.

Logging A method of recording incoming and outgoing work to assist in monitoring it and controlling its flow.

MTM Methods Time Measurement. A work measurement technique that recognizes that certain motions, or combinations of motions, occur repeatedly in work and assigns time standards to these operations for purposes of evaluating performance.

PERT Project Evaluation and Review Technique. A method for planning and controlling complex projects efficiently. Sometimes called the "critical path" method.

Power typing An application of magnetic media typewriters that increases productivity by allowing a typist to type at maximum or "rough-draft" speed without concern for errors. This was heavily used in the late 1960s as a prime selling technique for the MT/ST.

Photocomposition A form of "cold type" text production in which each character is exposed photographically on light-sensitive paper, which is then developed to become a reproduction-quality proof.

Principal An individual within an organization who originates paperwork and requires secretarial support; an executive; a word originator.

Procedure The step-by-step process for completing a particular job.

Random access In data processing and word processing a storage technique in which the time required to obtain information in memory is relatively independent of the location of the information most recently obtained. Disks are generally regarded as randomly accessible media, in contrast to tape, which is "serial."

Reactive document A routine document that is rarely revised and infrequently proofread.

Revision cycle Path of a typed document from initial keyboarding to final output.

Satellite A station, terminal, or other unit of equipment connected to, but at some distance from, a centralized data processing or word processing system.

Secretary, administrative A specialist who supports principals with activities other than typing, such as mail handling, filing, phoning, and special projects.

Secretary, correspondence An individual primarily responsible for transcribing dictation and producing documents on a word processing typewriter; a word processing operator.

Shared logic Term applied to a type of text-editing system in which several keyboard terminals simultaneously use the memory and processing powers of a single central processing unit.

Short interval scheduling The assignment of a predetermined increment of work and systematic follow-up for a completion on a planned, predictable basis.

Slave An output unit, such as a printer, operating in parallel with, and controlled by, a master unit.

Software All materials needed to control and operate the "hardware" of an automated system, such as flowcharts, manuals, programs, and the like. Support personnel are often referred to as the software of a vendor.

Split keyboarding A production technique in which material is keyboarded and edited on one word processing unit and played out on another. Assemblyline approach to work. Was considered most productive method in early 1970s, until it was discovered that it causes an enormous drop in morale and high turnover, consequently lower production over the long haul.

Standard data A predetermined time standard obtained and accepted for a particular activity as reliable and representative of the work performed.

Stat typing Priority typing.

Study team Group that surveys the needs and working conditions in an organization as a basis for deciding on the feasibility of converting to word processing.

System 1. An assembly of components united by some form of regulated interaction to form an organized whole. 2. A network of procedures designed to carry out an overall major activity. 3. The operations, procedures, personnel, and equipment through which a business activity is carried on.

Systems approach The examination of an overall situation or problem with the aim of devising a total solution, as opposed to dealing with the separate functions that constitute the whole.

System survey The study, analysis, and improvement of the systems that service, control, and coordinate all the operations of an enterprise.

Task data sheet A record of jobs by time period during a single work day.

Task list A detailed record of each type of work performed by each worker and the average number of hours spent to do it per week.

Text processing A term generally synonymous with word processing though often applied specifically to applications dealing with lengthy documents, such as articles for publication, which go through several editing cycles.

Throughput The complicated cycle from the origination of a thought until it is typed and ready for distribution.

Turnaround time The total elapsed time between the beginning and the completion of a task. Should include "wait for processing" time and delivery time.

User's manual A book of instructions issued to word originators outlining procedures for proper dictation and setting forth other documents, style, and word processing standards used in the organization.

Utility typing Short, out-of-the-ordinary typing tasks not sent to the word processing center, but handled more or less informally by administrative support personnel.

Word originator A principal; an executive who dictates "copy" for transcription into final documents.

Word processing The transformation of ideas and information into a readable form of communication through the management of procedures, equipment, and personnel (Word Processing Standards Committee definition).

Word processing center The room or area with equipment and personnel for systematically processing written communications.

Word processing system The combination of specific procedures, methods, equipment, and people designed to accomplish the transition of a written, verbal, or recorded word and distribution to its ultimate use.

Work distribution chart A consolidation of task lists and activity lists to show what a department's activities are.

Work group Separate functions with two or more full-time staff members who engage in doing tasks which make the function operate. A work group may be an entire establishment, a department, or a section within a department, but it is always an entity in itself.

Work measurement A process of determining how much time is required to do a given amount of work.

Work sampling A work measurement technique that determines the amount of time spent performing various activities by random sampling.

Work simplification A planned way of modifying a job through the combination or elimination of its parts to increase production per employee hour.

Work standard The time fixed as reasonable for completion of a task, as determined by work measurement studies.

Work station An identifiable work area for one person.

Index